Bill Coulter

EMYR HUMPHREYS

Conversations and Reflections

Edited by M. Wynn Thomas

University of Wales Press • Cardiff • 2002

First published 2002.
Reprinted 2004.

British Library Cataloguing-in-Publication Data.
A catalogue record for this book is available from the British Library.

ISBN 0–7083–1735–9

First edition published with the financial support of the Arts Council of Wales.
Reprint published with the financial support of the Welsh Books Council.

Typeset at University of Wales Press
Printed in Great Britain by Dinefwr Press, Llandybïe

I
Richard Dinefwr,
ysgogydd cyntaf y gyfrol hon

Contents

Editor's Preface

This volume of conversations and essays has been constructed to reflect the subtle interconnectedness of a creative writer's reflections on his life, his work, the work of others, the politics of culture and the culture of politics. While most of the essays are the product of the last twenty years of the twentieth century, earlier work is also included, so that the collection more or less spans the half century and more of Emyr Humphreys's work as novelist, poet and dramatist. The material is not, however, arranged in chronological order. Rather, the essays are grouped around conversations that explore related preoccupations. A novelist, in particular, emerges from a given time and a given place, and Emyr Humphreys grew up in an Age of Anxious Uncertainties and Isms. Much of the material in this volume shows how he needed to work out for himself a viable view of the world that would accommodate his precarious sense of vocation. The interweaving of conversation and essay offers the reader an interesting contrast between the spontaneous and the considered; between material composed some time ago and conversation in a continuous present. The format is intended to allow the two modes to touch on and to illuminate each other.

In being addressed to issues of particular pressing concern at the time when they were written, many of the essays stand as a valuable record of twentieth-century Welsh cultural history and convey the tension and drama of their occasion. No closeted writer, Emyr Humphreys engaged throughout this period in political activism on behalf of the Welsh language even while producing a remarkable body of creative work – poems, historical overviews, literary criticism, plays (for radio and television) and of course an entire world of fiction. But the elegant trenchancy of the writing endows it with the power to long outlive the occasion that called it into being and to speak to readers of another century. The material is impressive in its breadth of vision, as Emyr Humphreys's intelligence ranges far and wide, from sixth-century Wales to later twentieth-century 'media studies' (his is a shrewd portrait of the Monitor mogul, Sir Huw Wheldon). There is always a sharp political edge to his discussion of Welsh cultural issues, and his analysis of the ideology underpinning Matthew Arnold's passion for the 'Celtic' is a small masterpiece of post-colonial criticism. In many ways, Emyr Humphreys is an intellectual in the Continental tradition – one who believes it is a writer's duty to bring intelligence to bear on any issue that concerns the preservation of a civilized social order. The social order that has specifically concerned him throughout his long and distinguished career is, of course, that of Wales, and this collection represents an important extension of what he has memorably called 'The Taliesin Tradition', the spinal contribution made by writers (particularly poets) from the sixth century onwards to the preservation and transmission of a distinctively Welsh cultural identity. This, Humphreys has written, 'has contrived to be a major factor in the maintenance, stability, and continuity of the Welsh identity and the fragile concept of Welsh nationhood . . . which has persisted stubbornly down to the present day . . . without the exercise of military or political power and without any indigenous control of the economic base' (*The Taliesin Tradition*, 2–3).

In addition to being valuable cultural documents, the essays are also illuminating of their author's creative work, whether they address the various cultural commitments from which his writing derives its force and takes its bearings ('The Third Difficulty'), the vexed issue of readership ('The Empty Space'), or issues of genre and technique ('Notes on the Novel'). What is on offer is a map of the historical and cultural hinterland of his powerful creative work, and the conversations seek to add further detail to that map by exploring some of the intellectual concerns and motifs that have regularly recurred throughout all his published writings. But there is also an intriguing sense in which several of these essays are miniature narratives or character sketches; unexpected instances of a novelist's art.

A reader may, of course, dip into this collection at any point at will, but an attempt has also been made to fashion a volume that may be read in a more consecutive, sustained fashion. Each group of essays is roughly keyed to the conversation that precedes it. Echoes of Emyr Humphreys's comments on the significance of place and time in the first conversation are to be heard in the essays that follow; the political and cultural values to which the lives and actions, as well as the writings, of authors may bear witness is a theme of the second conversation amplified in the next group of essays that includes a classic imaginative portrait of his intellectual master, Saunders Lewis; 'A Lost Leader' and

'Television and Us' include reflections on modern mass media, an aspect of the process of globalization that is of pressing and intimate concern to Emyr Humphreys in the third conversation; and as the discussion of the late novella, *Ghosts and Strangers*, leads the novelist on, in the fourth conversation, to consider wider issues of fictional form, so does the final group of essays bring together his writings about the forms that fiction might take in present culture and the inflexible respect for the unique genius of a language that characterizes the 'born' writer.

But the interrelationships between the different elements are not as one-dimensional as the foregoing would suggest, nor is the flow of thought in one direction only. Writings anticipate discussions to come as well as echoing those that have gone, illuminating remarks in conversations radiate meaning backwards as well as forwards, and juxtaposed essays strike up an interesting conversation with each other. The overall impression is of a creative intelligence whose constant integrity of purpose nevertheless allows of sallies of daring thought in new, unexpected directions at the promptings of an irrepressible intellectual curiosity.

Many of the essays in this collection have previously appeared in print elsewhere and Emyr Humphreys and I are very grateful for permission to reprint them here. This volume, a companion volume in some ways to *Dal Pen Rheswm* (University of Wales Press, 1999), is based on a suggestion made by Richard Dynevor and it is accordingly dedicated to him, with sincere thanks for his longstanding commitment to the work of Emyr Humphreys. As ever, the staff of the University of Wales Press have been meticulous in their care and attention, and in thanking them we should like particularly to mention Ceinwen Jones and Liz Powell.

M. Wynn Thomas
Centre for Research into the
English Literature and Language of Wales,
University of Wales Swansea

Conversation 1

MWT: In 'The Crucible of Myth' you say: 'The inhabitants of hilly or mountainous territories invariably entertain a profound attachment to the physical characteristics of the land of their birth.' Now, I know that landscape has meant a great deal to you as a Welshman and as a writer, but if I take you back to your native landscape of Trelawnyd, what is striking is that when you looked east what you saw was the English peninsula of the Wirral.

EH: For a country child of my time, the real fascination was the city. From Clip y Gop, the huge man-made mound on top of the limestone hill above our schoolhouse, you could see clearly the tower of the Anglican cathedral in Liverpool – more a citadel of power than a religious symbol. Around it were the famous football teams, Everton and Liverpool. We bought 'transfers' of football jerseys to stick on the backs of our hands – red for Liverpool, blue for Everton – and footballers were folk heroes with euphonious names like Dixie Dean. My father had been a keen footballer before he was wounded in the Great War. He was an Everton supporter. As an interest it came second only to his male-voice choir.

The Gop and the whole of our valley was our playground. Our life was an uncompetitive game in which we were all perpetual winners, equal kings in our own country, and the landscape belonged to us. The kind of freedom we enjoyed would be unimaginable in this day and age. There were rules, of course, laid down by our parents. My father had a whistle, and no matter how far we wandered, when we heard it blow we had to run straight back home.

MWT: Yet, you could also see from your 'mound' the distant silhouette of Snowdonia. So when did the Gop first seem to you to point you in that direction?

EH: It was all nothing but a wonderful playground until adolescence. And then there was a sudden upheaval, a kind of earthquake in the mind. I turned to look not west but south in the first place. I remember I stumbled across the poems of Gerard Manley Hopkins in the library in

Rhyl, and I was fascinated to see that he had lived in Tremeirchion, to the south of where we lived. The incantations of 'The Leaden Echo and the Golden Echo' were all about St Winifred's Well in Holywell, where so many of my mother's brothers went to market. And what about the 'cordial air' of the Vale of the Elwy? It could have been my relatives he was writing about. The inmates! It was difficult to know if he was being complimentary or critical. It is safe now to reveal a deep secret of my youth. Due to this and other influences – reading Saunders Lewis, I suspect, and *GK's Weekly* – I made secret journeys on my brother's bike to a priest in St Asaph to learn more about how to become a Catholic. My parents would have been so horrified that I have suppressed this piece of information for most of my life.

MWT: Was it, then, by degrees such as this that you came to understand that you were living in 'one of the four corners of Wales', as Michael was to put it years later in the opening sentence of *A Toy Epic*?

EH: When you live in the shadow of the Gop, points of the compass tend to dominate your thinking. Matthew Arnold has a celebrated passage about standing on top of the Great Orme above Llandudno and making out the difference between east and west in terms of the difference between Saxon and Celt. I didn't know the passage at the time, but I realize now that we lived much further east and what we saw from the top of the Gop was more literally the difference between England and Wales. It was in a sense the view from the border, so the romantic attraction of Snowdonia in the distance was deeply ingrained in my consciousness and was part of growing up.

MWT: So it's perhaps useful for us to remember that you grew up in border country. Offa's Dyke ran more or less directly through your territory, didn't it?

EH: We were just east of Offa's Dyke, which ran through the next parish. Most of the Flintshire of my youth lay to the east of the Dyke, which reaches the coast at Prestatyn where I was born. Flintshire lies behind us, and the connections of my mother's large family – she had nine brothers – all extended deep into Flintshire as far as Queensferry. You might say to the gates of Chester. There was another divide between the English-speaking members of the family and the Welsh language of the others. This tended to follow religious affiliations: the Methodists were Welsh-speaking and the Anglicans spoke English. My father's school was a Church school and virtually by going to church we became an English-speaking family. My brother and I spoke only English.

MWT: The Welsh-language poet Bryan Martin Davies, long settled in Wrexham, once memorably wrote of all those who now live in Wales, 'Ynom mae y ffin' (Offa's Dyke now runs through all of us). Did this apply directly to your family, with the language divide coinciding with the 'fault line' of religious affiliation?

EH: There were elementary facts as well as elemental factors that I must have been aware of as a child. Church and chapel make it sound black and white, but in reality it was much more grey. My mother's sister played the organ in a chapel that no longer stands, in Gwespyr, and I never heard her speak Welsh, but she took part in the services and her whole attachment was to 'Yr Hen Gorff', the Welsh Methodist church. I have comical memories of her entertaining the preacher – part of her family inheritance; there was a bedroom reserved for the visiting minister. I would hear her saying something introductory in Welsh and she would go straight back into English, and out of politeness the poor minister would abide by her way of speaking. Socially, it was a complex situation. Just a generation earlier and she would have been obliged to conform to his choice of language.

MWT: If we go back to the issue of landscape and the sense in which the geographical reorientation of looking westward in adolescence was also a part of a cultural reorientation in your life, it's interesting that you should mention Hopkins as being instrumental in your change of outlook. This is presumably a sign that, since you yourself at that stage had no Welsh, you naturally shared with him as an English-speaker a view of Snowdonia in the west as a romantic, otherworldly land?

EH: There were other things that I was perfectly aware of. My father came from that very part of the world, the Snowdonia region. He was an immigrant into Flintshire from Blaenau Ffestiniog, and he and his family were clearly and entirely of that place, and couldn't be anything else. I have a vague recollection of his father, my grandfather, coming to stay with us, and I don't think he had much English. I remember him vividly, but I don't remember being able to talk to him. He lived to be older than I am now. He'd been a blacksmith working in one of the big quarries in Manod (the kind of social setting of which I later became aware in Kate Roberts's fiction). This was another big mysterious world I was aware of, but I only became really anxious to know about it after adolescence.

MWT: How that awakening happened, and what its consequences were for your writing, is an important subject. But first, let's go back to the landscape of Trelawnyd and to that hill known as the Gop.

EH: Local legend had it that it was Boadicea's grave. But of course it wasn't. It is the largest man-made prehistoric mound in Wales, and it has been excavated. It was a fascinating lump on top of the hill, and that was our playground. And lower down there was a prehistoric grave, where bones of human families had been excavated.

MWT: Does that mean that you grew up aware of its being a haunted landscape, wrinkled deep in time?

EH: Not as a child. It was just a playground, and it was a fantastically enchanting playground, which is not available in the same way to children now. Most of the points of entry we had have been closed off, the site enclosed, and there's a lot of afforestation that's gone on the other side of the hill. But in my day, there was a vast space that was ours, and what in particular we had was a sense of freedom. It was later that the sense of deep time developed. Once I'd been told that this was a prehistoric grave, with ten thousand bones inside it, then it took on another colour.

MWT: The landscape 'taking on another colour' when something is revealed to you of its past: that was an important part of your imaginative awakening during adolescence, wasn't it? That looking west, that opening up of Wales, and moving in imagination towards Snowdonia, was presumably dependent on your acquiring that other language, Welsh, that allowed you to read the landscape?

EH: Yes, but only eventually. A number of things collided: the protest burning of the bombing school at Penyberth by three Welsh nationalists who were leading intellectual and artistic figures in Welsh-language culture, and the connection with Mr Moses Jones, the schoolmaster who introduced me to Welsh history and politics, all happened before I began to learn the language. So it would be more accurate to say that I first began to acquire a sense of national identity by being provided with the historical and political understanding that allowed me to review the landscape, and only after that did I begin to acquire the language.

MWT: So through an appetite for reading you learnt this land had a history. Then you realized that history was written mostly in Welsh. Was that the order?

EH: Once you desire to acquire the language, the place-names around you become drenched in history: they take on a significance they never had for you as a child. From being friendly little noises they become something very meaningful, even local finger-posts. As a child you'd be just going to Trelogan, Llanasa or Gwespyr. Now place-names suddenly acquire a strange meaning beyond the mere furniture of childhood. How amazing to discover Gwespyr is the Cymricized form of Westbury. How did that happen?

MWT: Would you say that one important intention in your fiction has been to awaken your anglophone Welsh readers to the historical significance of landscape; and to a realization that the Welsh language is the key with which to unlock this land's past?

EH: I suspect that that's a kind of missionary function that comes much later. For a young person who wants to be a writer, it's just like any other kind of artistic activity, you're looking for raw material, and it seemed to me there was a richness of raw materials lying around me waiting to be used. It's only later you become aware of problems, such as that so much of this material belongs to a language that one doesn't have. So then you have a problem that lives with you for the rest of your life. How can you express the material, and use it to the best advantage, in a language that is, in a sense, hostile to that material?

MWT: And in facing this difficulty of how to translate one culture into the language of another, you also inevitably become highly conscious of your readers.

EH: Yes, you have the problem of bringing your audience along with you, since you find readers need to share more than a fiction, they need to have some knowledge of the historical circumstances in which that fiction is embedded. But in Wales by and large they don't, since they have only limited access to their own past. You then need to have a sort of potted history that runs alongside the fiction. It's a necessity, because it's needed to explain what you're trying to do. I think that's a continuing problem, and in its widest aspects – as a problem resulting from a lack of shared cultural knowledge between writer and reader – it's true not just for the Welsh writer who becomes bilingual, but for almost every writer in the twenty-first century. There's the fundamental problem of cultural coherence, and common points of reference, so that the author has to find ways of reconciling his vision with the experiences of the wider world. There's also the related problem of how different cultures can relate to each other without subordinating one to another. This can be seen at the political level as the European Union faces the challenge of giving due recognition to all its component parts. It's a matter of avoiding the melting pot of America on the one hand, and of avoiding political and cultural atomization and disintegration on the other.

In my case, I'm acutely aware of the problem of making my individual vision available to my readers, many of whom are culturally situated very differently from me. There's therefore a sense in which every artist has to create his own audience. And because of the lack of social cohesion and coherence this is now particularly difficult. When you have a social order, or civilization, where there is more or less an equilibrium between artist and audience you have a degree of unanimity. And if I may plunge on in that direction, the greater the unanimity the more frequent the occurrence of artistic anonymity. So the big watershed in European experience is that between the medieval and the modern. During the medieval period, when our Welsh literature possibly flourished at its best, anonymity was the norm, individuality was unusual. It's very unusual to come across somebody like Giraldus Cambrensis, because much more typical was the author of the *Mabinogion* – completely unknown, although far superior in every respect. Similarly, the great cathedrals are the product of a unanimity between the artist and the body of society, which breaks down at the Renaissance, and proceeds to deteriorate further until, by the time you reach the twentieth century, the whole emphasis is on the exceptionality of the individual vision and not on the commonality.

MWT: So, in the end, your concern with Wales opened out to these great issues which, for you, are key issues of the modern world. But initially your interest in Wales was as a resource – the landscape as a storehouse of materials. Is that because, as you became aware of the history of Wales and its language, the compactness of Wales made this material not only rich but manageable?

EH: Either subconsciously or consciously that was absolutely the case. It is an advantage to have a crucible in which you conduct your experiments.

MWT: So the crucible image that recurs in your writing when dealing with these matters partly means a container, which also functions as a cooking-pot for the imagination?

EH: Also, among the basic ingredients of the novel as a form throughout the nineteenth century are two outstanding features. First, a strange kind of democracy, in which you're interested in people not because they're important but because they have some special appeal to you in their own right. Secondly, the structures of the fiction very much reflect the structures of the family, so that being orphaned, or lost, or exiled from the family is a major theme. The family is one of the major structures of fiction. Now in our time, as we've seen the family to some extent disintegrating, you have the rise of socialism and the centralized state, and the relationship between the ancient shapes of the family and the newer forms of technology; these are the battlegrounds of people's lives, and this is where fiction finds its source. So if you have a container, a shape, a society which is fairly small and comfortable to exist in, there is a limit to the size of the battleground which makes it more possible for the novelist to bring it to book, so to speak. And the landscape is basic to this process.

MWT: So now, in retrospect, as you look back to the time when you began to turn westward and to penetrate that bowl of hills, you can see that you were also discovering a crucible of imagination that was to continue to be important to you throughout your life as a writer. Such an experience of mountainous Wales would seem to be the very opposite of that of the Romantic movement, when it could be argued that great English Romantics, such as Wordsworth and Shelley, reduced Wales to mere landscape, evacuating it of its language, history, culture

and its distinctive people. They came here not for the people but for
the mountains. It would seem that your own collection of poems,
Landscapes, is an attempt to reverse that process – to reclaim the Welsh
landscape for Wales. You try to read the landscape and show how it
embodies a culture and is haunted by the past of its people.

EH: Yes, but there's also an interesting contrast within the Romantic
period between the responses of writers such as Wordsworth and Shelley
and that of Walter Scott. So perhaps the novelist cannot help but
be interested in people. It's partly due to the nature of the form as
well as the individual. Scott, whose son was educated by the principal
of Lampeter, had contemplated writing a historical novel about Owain
Glyndŵr, so he was automatically drawn to the people, whereas a
Romantic poet concentrates on the relationship between self and landscape, as, for instance, is magnificently exemplified in 'Tintern Abbey'.
So for someone like myself, who is more a novelist than a poet, the
automatic interest must be in people, so that you move from the people
into the landscape.

MWT: It's also said of the Romantic poets that in their treatment of
Welsh landscape they perfectly exemplify the colonial mentality. They
come to a place and fail to see the culture because they see the landscape
only as a natural resource of which they're free to make whatever they
like. And your collection, *Landscapes*, can be read as being intended for,
or addressed to, a colonized people who have been deprived of the
ability to see how the record of their pre-colonial history lies all around
them in the now mute language of the landscape. So your poetry is an
attempt to remind them of what has happened here to make it the place
it is.

EH: Well, I suppose everything I write in English does that. It is a
Kulturkampf, between the imperial language and the defeated native
language, and what I've been doing in both poetry and in fiction
in English, whether I like it or not, is using the language of cultural
supremacy to try to express something that comes directly from the
suppressed native culture.

MWT: So that meeting between yourself and the Welsh landscape
is an instance of the ground or territory where that meeting, that
Kulturkampf, happens.

EH: And it's something that haunts the condition of someone like myself, born into the minority community, or the subordinate community. It's a classic situation – you can trace it in black cultures as well.

MWT: It's what post-colonial theory calls the subaltern imagination.

EH: Yes, but on the other hand these theoretical considerations come later. When you're actually writing, the impulse that comes to make you do it is 80 per cent unconscious. When it's exploded, when it's grown, when it's come, when it's around, you mould it, but analysis comes later. The kind of intuitive writer I am starts with intuition, not with rational processes, or purposes. You find it's something that's been delivered. A writer ploughs a lonely furrow at the best of times. A Welsh storyteller writing in English has to struggle most of the time in competition with himself. As they used to say on school reports, 'must try harder'.

MWT: The relationship of the Welsh to their landscape is, then, for you an aspect of their relationship to their history, their past. And clearly in your writing there is a recurrent feeling that the Welsh need to reconnect with their landscape, and so with their past, because it is a source of energy, direction and so on, which they're in danger of losing. But there are also instances in your writing, for example in *The Gift of a Daughter*, where it would seem that that connection has got its dangerous aspects, and that the landscape is so strongly imbued with a sense of the Welsh past that it's in danger of overwhelming the Welsh present. Is this a conscious concern of yours, that the Welsh might come to be swallowed up by their own history, and therefore be unable to live in the present in appropriate, constructive terms?

EH: I'd put it rather differently. It is the actual writer who is absorbed in these matters who is himself in such danger, rather than the Welsh people. In the case of Aled Morgan, in *The Gift of a Daughter*, it is his escape from the less pleasant aspects of his existence. It's a retreat to the study, and through that to aspects of the landscape that allow him to live in the past. So it's a selective response, a selective view of history that provides him as an individual with a refuge. But in the case of the Welsh people in general, they know far too little of their past. I remember going on a journey with a friend, and, as usual, getting on my companion's nerves by talking endlessly, as did my father-in-law, about the history of the places we were passing. We were going through

Talgarth, and I was explaining that over there, in that churchyard, was the very spot where Howell Harris was standing on top of a tomb to preach when his words riveted the attention of the young William Williams, Pantycelyn, who was passing by just as we ourselves were passing by . . . I was in the middle of this dramatic exposition when my friend suddenly said, 'Oh, look, there's a rabbit!'

MWT: So a character like Aled Morgan is closer to you, the writer, than he is to the Welsh reader of today.

EH: Yes, and again this is a figure that recurs in my writing. In my poem 'Roman Dream', there is a poet figure who is escaping from Caesar's Praetorian Guard who are searching for him, and there's also the character of Boethius in *The Gift of a Daughter*. Such a figure emblematizes a great dilemma: how does a rational being come to terms with a world that is violent, aggressive and wicked in its operations? What influence can such a person ever bring to bear on human affairs?

MWT: The other recurring figure of this type in your writing is that figure from ancient Welsh legend and literature, Myrddin Wyllt, who was reputedly driven mad at the battle of Arfderydd and thereafter chose to live in the woods as a wild, unkempt hermit. So he, like Aled Morgan, finds the world altogether too much for him, and seeks refuge in the landscape and in the past.

EH: And even if you did go over to the cohorts of power, thereby becoming a violent figure in yourself, then in my fictional world you would be stricken with the guilt of what you're doing. There is a kind of moral equation that then requires you to identify with the victim, so whatever the victim suffers, you would be absolutely certain to suffer yourself. There's a human equilibrium which makes us very conscious of this particular aspect of, in a sense, original sin.

MWT: The form which, in your writing, the past takes, the way in which it informs the landscape, is not infrequently the form of myth. For instance, in *National Winner*, there is that important scene where the young man, Peredur, takes his English girlfriend, Maxine, to the very spot where, according to the great story of Blodeuwedd, Lleu Llawgyffes is 'killed' by Gronw Pebr. In what respects, then, does the past speak to the present for you through myth?

EH: The wonderful thing about landscape is that it calms the relationship, and it immortalizes experience, so as the stream of life flows on, and we are carried with it, the residue that it leaves in landscape is myth. This is what human beings of the past left behind them; and what they left behind them is now part of our present. So it's a deposit, a vital deposit, a raw material in the literal sense. Just as you dig down for gold, or coal, you dig down for myth as well. It is a raw material vital for your well-being.

MWT: And it is the deposit of history, the significant residue of history, in the sense that it is what is abidingly significant about the past. That which is merely transient and of its period has been washed away by time.

EH: Yes, that puts it very well. It is the past made available for reuse, and it has both a geological and a seasonal reference. The rocks and stones and trees – everything that is rolled round in earth's diurnal course – are deeply mythological, and if you miss this you miss an enormous amount. And for anybody who writes, it is a vital part of the whole process.

MWT: So you would accept the David Jones sense that the earth is a sleeping lord, a great outstretched sleeping Arthur?

EH: Absolutely. And similarly Geoffrey Hill's *Mercian Hymns*, and for that matter Philip Larkin's 'Whitsun Weddings'. It's all myth, in the widest possible sense – all the ways in which we adjust ourselves to the passage of time.

The Crucible of Myth

First delivered as the W. D. Thomas Memorial Lecture,
University College of Swansea, 21 May 1990.

A map is in itself a form of metaphor. When Offa put up his dyke it was hardly a Great Wall of China (as it happens, it passes to the west of my native parish), but it served to transform our mountainous peninsula into a cultural fortress that became both a crucible of myth and a cauldron of rebirth. The more thoughtful of those ninth-century Britons must have realized that the fabled lost kingdoms were now lost for ever. A demographic swing had solidified into an accomplished fact and become part of the landscape. The once powerful and extensive kingdom of Powys had been cut in two. The old capital Pengwern was reduced in the Cymric imagination to a smoking ruin somewhere east of Shrewsbury and the Hall of Cynddylan permanently haunted with the despairing cry of his sister Heledd.

> Stafell Gynddylan ys tywyll heno,
> Heb dân, heb wely;
> Wylaf wers: tawaf wedy.

These ninth-century lines remain part of the Welsh cultural consciousness as familiar as any first line of a Shakespeare sonnet to an English ear.

Under siege conditions the Welsh psyche developed early an intense awareness of its own identity. Since the poetry of the Old North, the traditions (and pedigrees) of the Lost Kingdoms and the last traces of *Romanitas* were in their special care, this haphazard collection of little principalities would leave off the pleasurable indulgence of warfare among themselves long enough to ward off the threats that surrounded them by sea and by land. For five centuries the Cymry were at full stretch defending more than any ordnance survey could reveal. The function of the bards and the storytellers with their repertoire enriched by the accumulation of mythological cycles from the wider Celtic world was to strengthen the general resolve to hold out: to keep a warrior aristocracy buoyant and confident with versions of a more glorious past that also promised, against the evidence of mounting casualties, an even more glorious future.

Although this Cymru was a confined and restricted area riven with dynastic quarrelling like an endemic disease, it resembled more closely a world than a nation state. This was the great stage on which providence had arranged they, the Cymry – the same name for the place and the people, the landscape and the inhabitants – should play leading roles as lords and princes. The constant military and naval pressure on every side did nothing to curtail equal opportunities for the acquisition of renown and glory. Actors often tell us that a small acting area can provide occasions for more thrilling performances. It would not be difficult to devise an urbane Peacockian caricature of some petty Welsh princely house, cheered on by its bards and storytellers, giving a sustained display of the old Celtic panache and individuality on the unmown turf of some medieval Arms Park, but this should not be allowed to belittle their achievement.

Between the eighth and the thirteenth centuries both the land of Wales and the imagination of its beleaguered inhabitants assumed the dimension of a cauldron kept constantly on the boil by fires kindled by Saxons, by Danes, by Vikings, by Normans, all in turn. It was into this cauldron that a steady sequence of triumphs and disasters, splendours and miseries were tossed to be mixed with more ancient material from a pre-Christian past, from the Old North, from Ireland, from the Celtic areas of emerging England, from all the Lost Kingdoms, to produce an entire dramatis personae, a new race of heroes and magicians capable of capturing the imagination of the medieval world. An equally potent, if less obvious, product of this prolonged process was, and to some extent is, the Welsh character itself.

The inhabitants of hilly or mountainous territories invariably entertain a profound attachment to the physical characteristics of the land of their birth. This can occur in spite of the barren nature of the terrain. While it is perfectly true that no one can subsist for very long on a view, it is remarkable how closely human beings can identify with geographical features and attribute to them qualities that must, in fact, have originated in their own deepest feelings and inward aspirations. *Bro* in Welsh is a wide-ranging, evocative word. It means a particular region, a native haunt which is also a neighbourhood and a country of the mind. *Bro* can refer to the limits of land, to invisible frontiers, to the 'march' where one country meets another before it contracts to denote a fertile and tranquil vale where the native can return to take his ease secure in the knowledge that the land belongs to him just as he belongs to the land.

When space is limited and well defined, there are more occasions upon which the past can impinge and press in on the present existence of a people. In such a defined area their daily lives force them into a close relationship with the place where they live. This need not mean that they are dwarfed or deprived or condemned to a narrower existence. If that were so, this world itself would become an inadequate home for the human race. We are not here for ever, but in our time and in our season a familiar landscape is capable of supplying us with all the significant features our inner natures need to see. A cliff or a headland can become a magic platform where anyone who stands on it can be transformed into a poet: wherever the sea winds blow they besiege the lungs with a persistence of divine breath demanding an entrance. We may not be older than the rocks among which we sit, but our tenancy has lasted long enough to award us a glimpse of our predecessors assembling in this landscape to appreciate the art of their appointed storyteller. Even a society organized for defence as well as subsistence and retribution is entitled to relax on a summer evening and submit itself to the reflective magic of language as it contemplates the ebb and flow of the western sea. In the sophisticated written version left to us in *Llyfr Gwyn Rhydderch* we may sense the ageless power of renewal that the story shares with the element in which it moves.

> Bendigeidfran and the host of which we spoke set sail for Ireland, but the sea then was lower: he went by foot. There were no more than two rivers then. Lli and Archan they were called. For it was after that time that the waters multiplied and rose above the drowned kingdoms. And so he walked there with such string musicians as he needed on his back and made his way to the Irish shore.

We inherit a landscape which preserves trace elements of the wonders that walked through the imagination of our remote ancestors. The stories still reach out to touch us. Robert Williams Parry looks out from his home in the slate-quarrying village of Nantlle and sees the magical cattle of Pebin emerge from the lake to graze their ancient meadow, and Gwenallt, overlooking Cardigan Bay, hears the birds of Rhiannon whose song can break the sleep of the dead and give sleep to the living. At the end of his poetic drama on Blodeuwedd, Saunders Lewis takes a melodic line from the original Fourth Branch of the Mabinogi and creates a symphonic variation so that the woman conjured up from the landscape of Ardudwy can be understood as a comment on our twentieth-century experience of science intervening like magic in the processes of sexual love. John Cowper Powys, at the age of sixty-four, returns to what he believes is the land of his ancestors and looks across the river from the little house he has bought, to the ruins of Dinas Bran, 'whose fallen walls make a massive stone coronet . . . to initiates of Welsh mythology it is of Brân the Blessed rather than of the flocks of black-winged birds – since Brân means a crow – that still hover about it, that this wild fortress must speak'.

A struggling smallholder has left an iron boiler to rust in a corner of a field near Powys's house. It could have had many uses: storing chicken-feed, scalding pigs, watering cattle in the dry season. Now it fills a hole in the hedge. Powys stares at it through his cottage window, and even as he stares it become 'an enormous iron cauldron, bronze-red from rust, and resting – ever since I visited it with awe and reverence – upside down upon the slope'. There is a sense in which we may say that he continued to stare at it until the *Bro* of Edeyrnion was transformed into a vast cauldron of literary rebirth. He became so well-versed and so absorbed in the mythological origins of the landscape and history of Wales that he was able to use them as keys to a cosmogeny of his own. The strength of his understanding allowed him a control over dynamic forces reminiscent of those possessed by the family of Don in the Mabinogi. The restraint inherent in the landscape in both cases kept in check powers that might otherwise have been unacceptably destructive.

> 'Moreover, I shall complete your restitution more handsomely still,' said Bendigeidfran. 'I shall give you a cauldron and the peculiar nature of the cauldron is, should one of your men be killed, throw his corpse in the cauldron and by tomorrow he will be as sound as ever he was and fight as well, except for a loss of speech.'

The King of Ireland was greatly cheered by this gift, as well he might be. The following night, as they sat together, the two kings were extremely amiable as only statesmen can be when both sides feel they have obtained rather more than they were prepared to settle for. Matholwch of Ireland expressed a keen desire to learn how Bendigeidfran had come by the cauldron. He probably knew the story well enough already, in one version or another. But it is a part of the politeness of kings – and academics – to listen to stories they have heard before. They console themselves inwardly by making an ongoing criticism of the style of re-telling. Irish and Welsh heroes, including the great Arthur himself, had led raids to the Otherworld in order to carry off magic cauldrons that could supply every lord with the food of his choice and could always hold sufficient, no matter how great the number waiting to be served from it. In the case of this gift, it reappears in grim form towards the end of the story, which resonates in our own experience of the agonies inherent in our Celtic inclination towards internecine warfare.

> And while they all reached for their weapons, Bendigeidfran held Branwen between his shield and his shoulder . . . and then the Irish began to kindle a fire under the cauldron of rebirth. And then they threw the corpses into the cauldron until it was full, and they rose up the following morning as efficient fighting men as before, except that they could not speak. And when Efnisien saw that there was no room for the rebirth of any one of the fallen of the Island of the Mighty, he spoke in his mind, 'Oh God, I blame myself. I am the cause of this heap of corpses of my fellow-countrymen. Let me be cursed, if I do not find a way to make amends.' And he thrust himself among the Irish corpses so that when two bare-bottomed kerns reached him, they flung him in in his Irish guise. And when he was in, he stretched himself until the cauldron broke in four pieces, and until his heart also broke.

We see another cauldron, with more creative virtues, play a vital role in the tricky task of relocating a mythic figure from the Old North into a more immediate landscape inside the Cymric cultural fortress. This cauldron was never allowed to rust. It belonged to a feverishly studious witch who lived in Bala (always an appropriate site for the feverishly studious) on the fringe of John Cowper Powys's adopted *bro* of Edeyrnion. In that 'History of Taliesin' which managed to insinuate itself with characteristic agility into Lady Charlotte Guest's *Mabinogion* we learn that Cyrrid-Fan (the crook'd-back'd woman) – whose ancient name is transmuted into Ceridwen (the fair one) – in order to increase her store of wisdom and pass it on to her phenomenally ugly son, Afagddu, is prepared to boil every known type of virtuous herb in her cauldron in order to produce those three shining drops that would give knowledge of those three things that govern the politics of human destiny – Past, Present and Future.

Her not so humble servant, Gwion Bach of Llanfair Caereinion, gives a demonstration of opportunistic quick-thinking which must have amused native audiences for a variety of reasons. He substitutes himself for the witch's well-born but hideous offspring at the crucial moment. When this particular cauldron shatters it utters a cry and the three scorching drops that are the essence of universal wisdom land on Gwion Bach's finger. He sucks it and immediately becomes the best informed man on earth and takes to his heels with the infuriated witch in hot pursuit. The processes of reincarnation weave themselves through the Welsh landscape until the wonder-child, with the shining brow, Taliesin, is washed up on his appointed wave of time on the appropriate Welsh shore.

In the version of the story recorded by Elis Gruffydd, the Soldier of Calais – born in our parish of Llanasa – when the boy Taliesin is required by King Maelgwn Gwynedd to explain his presence and reveal his true identity, he gives a tantalizing reference to the fact that he had once been known as Myrddin: 'Iohannes Ddewin a'm gelwis i Merddin.' In a narrative so dominated by the theme of shape-shifting as this one, it is as well to keep as firm a hold as possible on locality. At least until the advent of late twentieth-century physics, time and space have been the most reliable instruments by which a modern mind can make its way through the bewildering metamorphoses available to the semi-divine poets and prophets of the remote Celtic past. Maelgwn's court was in Degannwy. Maelgwn himself is an authentic and important historical figure of the sixth century. You will recall how he incurred Gildas's displeasure by paying too much attention to the fulsome flattery of his Brythonic bards. It is these same bards at the same court that the wunderkind Taliesin reduces to incoherent stuttering in the Elis Gruffydd version – written down, I suppose, one thousand years later.

Earlier still in proto-British history the excesses of praise-poets are brought to heel by the wisdom of a boy-wonder. It happens at the temporary headquarters of Vortigern, that classic villain of Cambro-British historiography who first opened the door to the Anglo-Saxon invaders. This wonder-boy had been sought for. Vortigern had proved to be as bad at architecture as at everything else he touched. His sycophantic magicians had advised him to build an impregnable citadel in the heart of Eryri (Snowdonia). Vortigern could not make his tower stand up, surely the most apalling shortcoming of all in a Celtic king. Once again he consulted his poetic soothsayers and the advice they gave reverberates with a race-memory of a distant Indo-European pagan past: 'Unless you discover a child without a father and he be put to death, and this citadel be sprinkled with his blood, it will never stand.' The king's messengers travel the length and breadth of Britain in search of a boy without a father. According to the earliest written account of their search, which we find in the early ninth-century *Historia Brittonum* (History of the Britons) by Nennius, they came across the child by chance, playing ball in a field on the outskirts of Llanilltud Fawr (Llantwit Major, in its less illustrious English form). They travel between the mountain stronghold of Eryri in the north-west and the south-east of Wales where *Romanitas* lingered longest, and bring us within sight of the very walls of the monastic school of St Illtyd, which played such a pivotal role in the preservation and expansion of Celtic Christianity.

The marvellous boy confounds the false prophets at Vortigern's court, in a manner reminiscent of the twelve-year-old Jesus astonishing the doctors in the Temple. At this point the abiding force of Celtic myth and a vigorous Cambro-British patriotism obliges Nennius to supply the lad with a practical political pedigree. 'And the king said to the boy, "By what name art thou called?" The boy answered, "I am called Ambrosius." And he was seen to be Emrys Wledig. And the king said, "From what stock art thou sprung?" And he answered, "One of the Emperors of the Romans is my father."' This is a not so subtle adaptation of the time-honoured inclination of Celtic storytellers to attribute some measure of divine origin to their human heroes. As a pupil of Bishop Elfoddw (Elvodigus), the learned and long-lived archbishop of Gwynedd who had persuaded a reluctant Welsh Church to submit to the full authority of Rome in 768 (the last of the Celtic churches to join that earlier European community), Nennius, writing in his patchwork Cymric Latin, clearly deemed that sufficient divinity still clung to the glamorized notion of a Roman emperor as a father.

Nennius made no claims to scholarship or literary elegance. In his disarming preface he wrote: 'I beg that every reader . . . will pardon me who have dared after so many others to write down so many things as these as if I were a garrulous bird or some sort of weak witness.' With the passage of time his odd compilation, or 'heap' as he himself calls it, increases in value. The fragments he has left behind are vital clues to so many aspects of a fascinating story that would otherwise be completely lost. I know that there are scholarly uncertainties about the author of the *Historia Brittonum*. On the basis of the sympathetic character sketch teased out of the evidence by Sir Ifor Williams half a century ago, I still cherish the image of a modest monk from the border country – the threatened frontier on either side of Offa's Dyke – struggling to assemble the bits and pieces of neglected tradition in order to establish that the besieged minority to which he owed allegiance was, in fact, the true and legitimate heir of a dramatic British past which reached back before the Foundation of Rome to the Fall of Troy.

It is in this compilation we find the first prose references to a leader called Arthur. It occurs a few paragraphs after the story of Vortigern and the boy Ambrosius (Emrys Wledig), and is presented as authentic history. Here was the *dux bellorum* who had actually succeeded in turning back the Anglo-Saxon tide. It all has the ring of simple truth until we come to the twelfth battle: 'On Mount Badon, in which there fell together in one day nine hundred and sixty men in one onset of Arthur, and no one laid them low save himself alone . . . And in all the battles he remained victor.' It is possible to detect here three distinct strands in the mind of the man who wrote that sentence. In the first place, as befits a cleric, there is an echo of the martial prowess of an Old Testament King David. This merges easily into the Celtic hero of divine origin who is capable of supernatural degrees of slaughter. The phrase *dux bellorum* has an imperial ring about it. This is also a general defending classical civilization from the savage attacks of swarms of barbarians threatening the peace and prosperity and ordered life of the Empire.

More than three hundred years after Nennius's day, a native of that same productive corner of the Cymric world, Erging, completed his *Historia Regum Britanniae* (History of the Kings of Britain). Geoffrey of Monmouth was a far more wordly-wise cleric, indeed an accomplished courtier, whose purpose was to glorify the Plantagenet royal house in such a way as to gain for himself political and/or ecclesiastical preferment. In his dedication to Robert of Gloucester, the illegitimate son of Henry I, Geoffrey makes fulsome reference to the brilliant books written by Gildas and the Venerable Bede. He also claims to have been given a 'certain very ancient book written in the British language'. But he makes no mention of Nennius's *Historia Brittonum*, which is in fact the obvious source of a borrowed concept of former British glory and a prophesied future greatness. It summarizes the consolation of *darogan* vaticination, prediction essential to the spirit of a whole society under centuries of siege. It is from Nennius, too, that Geoffrey derives two of the most remarkable characters in his majestic sweep of 1,900 years of the history of the Britons from the mythical Brutus down to the last British king, Cadwaladr: out of Ambrosius, Emrys Wledig, with a wave of the fiction-writer's wand, he manufactures Merlin, and he converts the Welsh Arthur, the *dux bellorum*, into the role model of the ideal emperor that would provide a more than sufficient precedent for the imperial ambitions of the Norman kings.

In the twelfth century the political situation in Britain had changed, but as far as the native Welsh were concerned, the more it changed, the more it was the same painful thing. Invasions were fated to continue with triadic regularity. Since the basic plot was unchanged the amount of adaptation needed in the more popular storylines was minimal. Heroes were called upon to be even more heroic and magicians to be even more ingenious and resourceful. Whether Geoffrey was Welsh or Breton, it seems most likely that he had first-hand knowledge, for example, of Arthur's Table. He had probably visited Gamber Head, like Nennius before him, on the road from Monmouth to Hereford to stare at the tumulus reputed to be the grave of Arthur's son; and the well nearby, as Nennius had recorded early in the ninth century, was known as Ffynnon Llygaid Amir (the well of Amir's eyes).

Cymric Arthur displayed in abundance those qualities Geoffrey of Monmouth and his Plantagenet masters would consider essential for a royal hero: dauntless courage, public charisma and an authenticated curriculum vitae as a battle leader with an insatiable appetite for cutting his enemies to pieces. Welsh legend also tended to present him as an un-killable killer. In this respect he was a refinement on the dumb products of Bendigeidfran's cauldron. At the end of any campaign the worst that could be expected was that Arthur would take a prolonged rest in some mountain cave or other and be ready to leap to the defence of his country whenever the necessity arose.

To a pragmatic Norman cleric like Geoffrey, the Celtic exuberance of heroic qualities attached to Arthur presented a number of obstacles that had to be cleared from the path towards what contemporary journalists would term 'international status'. In the first place, in spite of those loyal protestations at coronations encouraging the new monarch to scatter his enemies and live for ever, the Christian church took the common-sense view that for ordinary mortals any forms of immortality had to be restricted to the world to come. Quite apart from the recorded defects in his character, it would have been blasphemous to present Arthur as a royal hero armed with the secret weapon of arising from the dead. Celtic legend had already worked out a solution to this predicament: the unconquerable hero could only be conquered, that is to say killed, by treachery or by magic or by a combination of both. For example, the end of Pryderi, the putative hero of *Pedair Cainc y Mabinogi* (The Four Branches of the Mabinogi) is described: 'and by power and by strength and fierce force and by magic and enchantment Gwydion was victorious and Pryderi was slain and in Maentwrog, above Y Felenrhyd, he was buried and there you will find his grave'. With such disarming simplicity the elusive forces of magic are given a local habitation and a name.

We can assume that Geoffrey's first-hand knowledge of the behaviour patterns of princes and politicians, quite apart from his wordly-wise view of the Wheel of Fortune and his suppressed fiction-writer's taste for melodrama, inspired him to elaborate in Arthur's case an end brought about by treachery. He took up the reference in the *Annales Cambriae* to a battle of Camlann 'In which Arthur and Medraut fell', and elaborated an account of that battle to such effect that later Welsh chroniclers revised their records to make them conform more closely to the commanding vision of the ultimate political treachery conjured up by Geoffrey. That accounted for the death of the hero. The matter of his conception, the sexual act that would give the birth of the hero an imperial legitimacy, was not so simple.

The name of Arthur, so crucial to the record of British resistance and so potent in popular Celtic legend, did not appear in any of the more exalted British pedigrees with which Geoffrey had made himself familiar. This would mean that a piece of vital evidence in any claim the British could make to a lineage as ancient and exalted as that of any Roman emperor, was missing. Again it was to Nennius's humble work that Geoffrey turned to extract the raw material his imagination needed to solve this problem. A mere sleight of hand and change of name transformed the boy-wonder, Ambrosius, into the prophetic figure of that Myrddin whose name was so closely associated with the poet and shape-shifter Taliesin. To give the transformation authenticity, he sent Vortigern's messengers to Caer-Fyrddin instead of Llanilltud Fawr and had the boy without a father play outside the town gate of Carmarthen. According to that urbane scholar Gaston Paris, Geoffrey changed the boy's name from Merddin to Merlin in order not to offend French ears. Certainly Geoffrey embellished and extended the prophecies the boy made to King Vortigern in order to affirm a British imperial future under the leadership of a Norman royal house. This reconstituted Merlin would arrange for the Treachery of the Long Knives to be for ever commemorated by the transportation of the Giant's Circle from Ireland to Stonehenge. (This could be read as a symbolic representation of the transfer of the furniture of Celtic myth into an Anglo-Norman domain, neatly foreshadowing the removal of Arthur from tenebrous Welsh caves to the bright light of the playing fields of Eton.)

The stones in their circle and Merlin's prowess were there to remind Geoffrey's readers that however powerful and privileged they felt themselves to be, they were dwarfed by a mightier race that had once ruled the land that they now ruled. Did this modest author not have access to documents of great age in the oldest language of the island recording the great deeds of heroes, saviours and defenders of such great stature as to put Caesar and Charlemagne in the shade? As a more acceptable substitute for shape-shifting or miraculous conception, Geoffrey provided Merlin with a drug and had him administer it to Uthr Pendragon. In this way a Romanized consul-king could take on the shape of the Duke of Cornwall in order to sleep with his wife, the most beautiful and well-born woman in Britain and the essential receptacle: 'that night she conceived Arthur, the most famous of men who sub- sequently won great renown by his outstanding bravery.'

In journalism and propaganda there is little to be gained by being too sensitive or too subtle. Geoffrey's design may have been inspired by Virgil's epic poem *The Aeneid*, but in his prose we often hear the undertone of knowing triumph with which the well-educated investig- ative journalists of our day publish the details of yet another 'scoop'. Scoops and intimate revelations are fashioned for the widest possible circulation. We are often told that Geoffrey's book became what could be called the first European best-seller. It is fair to deduce from his style alone that he wrote with the most influential possible circulation in mind. However, his absorption in the contents of our crucible of myth was real enough. Before the end of his life he returned to the source of his inspiration and composed a poem in hexameters of 1,500 lines that gives the life story of the original Myrddin of Welsh tradition. In many ways this is a more interesting work. In stark contrast to the *Historia Regum Britanniae* the *Vita Merlini* (Life of Merlin) was not well known and survived in only one manuscript.

Geoffrey, of course, wrote in Latin, a 'derived tongue' kept alive as an educational lingua franca, well developed for the dissemination of information and the processes of philosophic discourse. If we turn to literature in the vernacular inside the Cymric cultural fortress, we can identify literary qualities that were well outside the range of Geoffrey's Latin. *Pedair Cainc y Mabinogi* demonstrates how far Welsh prose had developed by the twelfth century. In sophistication and in elegance and wisdom this work probably could be claimed to exceed anything then being composed in any European vernacular. This could be briefly tested by a close textual comparison of Geoffrey's account of the origins of Arthur with the effects of Pwyll's sojourn in the Underworld (and the birth of Pryderi) in the First Branch of the Mabinogi.

Ac y cerddodd Arawn rhagddo parth a'i lys i Annwfn . . .

Arawn the King of Annwn returned to his court in the Underworld, and it was a secret joy to him to be reunited with a retinue he had not seen for a year. Everything was as before; the same courtesies, and merriment and conversation. And when it was time to quit the feast, the King made ready for bed and his wife came to him. He spoke to her with great affection and gave himself to the pleasure of love. This was something she had not been used to for a whole year and the thought passed through her mind, 'Lord God, why should it be different this night from what it has been this past year?' The thought troubled her. He awoke and addressed her, a second time and a third, but no answer did he get from her.

'Why will you not speak to me?' he said.

'I shall tell you,' she said. 'I have not spoken this much in this bed for a whole year.'

He said 'How can you say that and we being so lovingly intimate this night?'

'Let it be my shame if it must,' she said. 'For a whole year since, from the moment the bed-clothes covered our bodies, there has been neither pleasure nor talk between us, nor have you even turned your face towards me.'

And then it was his turn to think.

'O Lord God, such a steadfast prince, and such an unswerving friendship have I found in that man who took my place.'

And he told her the story. And she testified before God that her husband had found an incomparable comrade, able to keep faith and strong in the face of continuing temptation of the flesh.

Here we have a texture of easy discourse which anticipates modern developments of prose fiction at several points. The sentences may appear naive but they possess a tensile quality that gives them the capacity to produce character in the round with remarkable economy. The unnamed queen of the Underworld, for instance, in the passage I have just translated: every word she utters, and these can include her thoughts, every move she makes create a memorable personality, a unique individual in a way that seems to anticipate the technique of the best twentieth-century short stories. In fact, we would be hard put to it to recall any nameless woman from modern fiction capable of making so deep an impression on the reader in so few words. And behind the story lies the coded message for aristocratic listeners or readers: he who would rule others must first discipline himself.

It has been remarked more than once that Geoffrey of Monmouth, like so many medieval authors – including such an important figure as Chrétien de Troyes – was a poor hand at portraying women or attempting to understand their psychology. Perhaps women counted for so little except as objects of desire in their view of the world that they could not be bothered with them, at least until they lost their youth and beauty. Hags and crones were so much easier to animate or caricature. The anonymous author of *Pedair Cainc y Mabinogi* is once again a brilliant exception to the rule. Can there be in medieval fiction a more memorable assembly of female characters? Rhiannon retains the aura of her mythological descent and yet behaves like a woman of flesh and blood who knows her own mind, chooses her own mate and confronts the painful vicissitudes of her destiny with unfailing dignity and spontaneous wit. She radiates that mysterious capacity reserved for great literary creations to flower anew each time we encounter her on a page. In the tragic story of Branwen ferch Llŷr, which can be read as a shrewd and biting commentary on the burden of dynastic responsibilities for the female of the line, Branwen never loses her long-suffering nobility: also in the minds of mothers the clash of swords resounds and inflicts incurable wounds. In the Third Branch we are given as it were in passing a small but well-lit portrait of a snob, the fastidious and class-conscious Cigfa. In the Fourth Branch we encounter three meticulously observed specimens of the *Ewig-Weibliche* ('eternal female'): Goewin, the king's virgin foot-holder; Arianrhod, the wilful offspring of a family of magicians; and the celebrated Blodeuwedd, a creation of untamed emotions and appetites, literally the child of nature with the face of a flower, a lawless heart and no conscience to speak of.

Few things in literature are more difficult to convey than the magic inherent in one language through the well-established aesthetic channels of another. In the case of Welsh and English there are historical difficulties – I almost said hostilities – to overcome. No English translation that I know of begins to reproduce the unique music of *Y Pedair Cainc*. Maloryesque pastiche or the *faux naïf* inevitably obscure rather than reveal the succinct power and clarity of the original. Part of the particular difficulty is to do with the odd nature of the text itself. In a very real sense it is poetry masquerading as prose and, as we are so often told, poetry is the thing that gets left out in translation. This poetry may be inherent in the state of the language as the author finds it in the eleventh and twelfth centuries: it is also inherent in his vision and his literary intention. He is a creative writer who has removed himself with deliberate intent outside the orbit of praise poetry in order to bring into being a new and more critical form of celebration. I cannot for one moment accept the much quoted opinion of Matthew Arnold that this author

> is pillaging an antiquity of which he does not fully possess the secret . . .
> like a peasant building his hut on the site of Halicarnassus or Ephesus . . .
> full of materials of which he knows not the history, . . . stones not of this
> building but of an older architecture, greater, cunninger, more majestical.

Sustained works of art are never put together by accident. This author knew exactly what he was doing. Every line of his narrative demonstrates a genius for restraint coupled with depth of understanding. He possesses that rare capacity for making the delicate transition from the tragic to the comic that brings to my mind the art of Anton Chekhov. If this comparison may seem too distant and far-fetched it is as well to remember that great art reserves an anachronistic residue as part of its capacity for becoming an experience, a memorable experience, in the life-cycle of any given reader.

The oral and written traditions of a given people, their laws, their praise poetry, their annals, their pedigrees, their sagas, their wonder-tales and their residual mythology are all legitimate raw material for the use of the artist. With the wisdom which we may wish to attribute to historical hindsight, we must accept that. If I may persist with the image of the Welsh peninsula as a crucible of myth bubbling away between the eighth and the thirteenth centuries, these are all elements that the long process struggles to coalesce. We should judge the merits of the artist using these elements by the finished product rather than by laboratory analyses of vestigial remnants of more ancient material made in order to trace their previous characteristics. A work of art is a living thing and not dead matter.

Geoffrey of Monmouth, I would argue, motivated by a perfectly respectable urge to get on in the world and to bring pressure to bear on the course of events to his own legitimate advantage, plundered the cauldrons and the crucibles of the peninsula with the enthusiasm of Dr Frankenstein; and by dint of effort and persistence more than by magic and enchantment (if I might echo that sentence in the Fourth Branch recording the defeat and death of the hero Pryderi) managed to produce two prototypes, two powerful political engines, Merlin and Arthur, with sufficient dynamism to march across the centuries and down the corridors of power at Westminster and the White House, the Reichkanzlei and the Kremlin. (This is not the appropriate occasion to draw unseemly parallels between the Round Table and the Politburo.) Politics and popular entertainment have always been closely linked – never more closely than in our own time with electronic devices transforming senates and parliaments into playhouses. For Arthur and Merlin it is but a short step from the stages of the West End and Broadway to sessions of shape-shifting in the political arena.

The anonymous author of *Pedair Cainc y Mabinogi* makes no such attempt to force myth and wonder-tale into the straitjacket of history and politics. He chose to write in Welsh rather than Latin. I suspect that he was as familiar with Virgil and Boethius as Rhygyfarch the son of Sulien, the author of the *Vita Davidis* (Life of David) who composed creditable Latin verse, or indeed Geoffrey himself. The text itself provides enough evidence of the author's understanding of the mythic origin of his material. He was aware of the classic Celtic view of the human condition that linked the well-being and material prosperity of a society to the abiding wisdom of Divine Providence through rulers elevated from the ranks of a warrior-aristocracy by tests of character and exemplary courage. With deliberate art he detaches his narrative both from its mythological matrix and from the earth-bound inexorable treadmill of history in order to present his audience and his readers with an intimate commentary on the human condition, or, if one may borrow another of Matthew Arnold's well-known phrases, 'a criticism of life'.

A criticism of life cannot be conducted *in vacuo*. It has to be directed at an audience in a receptive mood waiting to hear the old songs in the language they are accustomed to enjoy. While they are in the mood the skill of the author presents them with illuminating variations on those themes which touch their lives most closely. Underlying the narrative surface of the *Pedair Cainc* there is a symphonic structure equipped with figures and melodic phrases and almost Wagnerian leitmotif. These make fresh music from the hazards and splendours of marriage, whether medieval or modern, from the delicate relationship between honour and friendship, from the dire consequences of irresponsible quarrelling and internecine warfare, from the dangerous side-effects of heroic age ideals, from the absolute necessity of organic law and the habits of self-discipline. We have no means of measuring the extent to which his contemporary audience appreciated his artistry or took in his message. The evidence suggests that in the twelfth century the Welsh ruling class opted for Arthur. There are more than sixty translations and adaptations of Geoffrey's book in Welsh and it sometimes seems as if there are always more liable to turn up. Among his own people our anonymous author suffered almost catastrophic neglect. You will know that it is nothing less than a miracle that the bits and pieces of manuscript survived the ravages of almost seven centuries before surfacing to be taken seriously by the Romantic Revival. The original text was not edited seriously until Sir Ifor Williams took it in hand only sixty years ago. (In terms of English literature it is as if Shakespeare was still hidden away in one manuscript due to be rediscovered in about the year 2200.)

In our day there is little value attached to anonymity either in the saleroom, or the media or, dare I say it, in the groves of academe. Publicity and presentation need names to hang on to and embellish. The scrappiest sketch can acquire the monetary equivalent of a holy relic once the right artist's name is attached to it. It was not always thus. There are many medieval masterpieces by anonymous authors. Living as we do on the Celtic fringe of a newly unified Europe, we should turn more often to the Middle Ages in order to anticipate important aspects of the kind of world that lies ahead of us.

These legendary territories in which we live and work are haunted by the ghosts of gods and goddesses as well as men and women. Pwyll and Rhiannon, Arawn the king of Annwn, Pryderi and Manawydan, moved in this landscape when it was as resplendent in its own way as that garden Satan discovered in the Fourth Book of *Paradise Lost*. They understood just as clearly as we do that the living earth and all its creatures when left alone are more likely to retain the mysterious gifts first given them. When the human urge to dominate and exploit is restrained and replaced by an even more powerful urge to celebrate and worship, this Dyfed author is telling us, we have a better chance of satisfactory survival. Like the cromlechs and the sculpture of stone circles these stories enrich the landscape with ancient secrets in order to ensure that we and the land we inhabit will flourish better with them rather than without them. In such a case, anonymity, like Shakespeare's 'ripeness', is all.

Taliesin's Children

First published in Sam Adams (ed.), *Seeing Wales Whole: Essays on the Literature of Wales* (Cardiff: University of Wales Press, 1998), 14–24.

The edges of Wales could have been designed for the specific purpose of converting people into poets. It is true that from one end to the other of the western seaboard of the British Isles there are bays, cliffs, golden sands and rocky shores and islands in abundance, and over all, unrepeatable sunsets infusing the waters with an illumination that beggars description. But poetry feeds off the specific. I do not know the exact spot where Robert Williams Parry stood when the exultant final couplet sprang into his mind: 'Digymar yw fy mro trwy'r cread crwn,/ Ac ni bu dwthwn fel y dwthwn hwn', which amounts to saying, in loose and unsuccinct translation, that he had discovered, with that force of revelation which is the essence of poetry, that his native heath in all its resplendent poverty, the truth that lies in the heather and the grudging acres, was incomparable through all creation and that the present moment was life's most elusive miracle.

A poet has to take pride in his place and in his people. This is an elementary truth to be taken into account by every generation as it grows up to confront its own hunger for abiding certainties. There are of course other nagging questions to be answered and these are shaped by the prevailing concerns of the society on whose shores the bewildered would-be bard finds himself washed up by the tide of time. An education system provides him with the reading and writing he will eventually need to pursue his calling: also an intimidating mountain of information. At the end of the twentieth century, he will be told that he shares 98.4 per cent of his genetic material with chimpanzees. By courtesy of television film he will see that apes are more capable than human beings of demonstrating the poetry of motion. He will be squeezed into 1.6 per cent of his being in order to demonstrate any qualitative difference. It is true that he has speech and the facility of written language, but this precious gift he is obliged to share with the global manipulators of opinion who operate ever more sophisticated networks for power and profit – two goals that have always been low on a poet's list of priorities. There was a classic confrontation in Wales between these two unequal forces not so very long ago. In 1979 some two dozen poets and concerned writers signed a letter to the press in support of the benefits of devolution. The tabloids snorted their contempt; but it was the editor of the *South Wales Echo* who delivered the *coup de grâce*. He printed the names and then asked his readers in bolder print, 'ever heard of them?' These were not film stars or royalty or politicians or famous footballers: not even authors of airport novels. They were a gaggle of obscure poets worrying the tatters of an old song and about as relevant to contemporary issues as a bin full of discarded newsprint.

Was it ever thus? Taliesin's forebears, we know, were obliged to contend with the vituperative disapproval of Gildas. We know this from his *De Excidio Britanniae* and that oft-quoted description of the praise poets of those early centuries, 'a pack of scoundrels bawling out like drunken revellers their lies and foaming phlegm spattering everyone within reach'. We still need to ask ourselves what they thought they were up to, the bards on the one hand and the querulous monk on the other. The monk has the advantage of writing in Latin and his words still lie before us on the printed page. He is quite specific in his motives.

> I gazed on these things and many others in the Old Testament as though in a mirror reflecting our own time: and then I turned to the New Testament also and read there more clearly what had previously been dark to me . . . I read that the Lord had said, 'I have not come except to the lost sheep of the House of Israel.'

Gildas could boast an impeccable intellectual pedigree. He had sat at the feet of Illtud, at Llanilltud Fawr, the most illustrious seat of learning in Britain. This Illtud, 'the most learned of all Britons', had been a disciple of Germanus of Auxerre, whose business we know, along with St Martin of Tours, was to preserve the remnants of Roman civilization in Europe by converting the barbarian hordes rather than killing them. (It is worth noting that these stalwarts of the faith had been high-ranking military and civil officials of the Empire before this basic change of approach took place.) Germanus visited Britain in 429 to combat the Pelagian heresy, and he is also given the credit for leading the embattled Christian Britons to victory by bidding them shout 'Alleluia!'.

These links with his immediate past help us to understand more fully Gildas's attitude to unruly princes and poets. Apostasy and heresy were more offensive than the pristine innocence of pagans, however fierce.

They could at least be saved if they could be persuaded to put down their weapons long enough to take in the message and the means of salvation. The praise poets and their Brythonic princes were lapsing into all sorts of reprehensible habits under the relentless pressure put on them by the land-hungry Anglo-Saxon barbarian invaders. Like Jeremiah before him, Gildas is unsparing in his condemnation of the errant Children of Israel. His chosen people and their disreputable bards were putting their trust in what he considered revived heathen practices, glorifying their ancestry instead of glorifying God.

At the inauspicious start of what some scholars call 'The British Heroic Age' – which we can take to be the two or three hundred years which followed the withdrawal of the Roman legions – there appears to have been a propaganda battle in progress between the Church and a revived order of poets for the hearts and minds of the beleaguered British. The bards were committed to a revival of praise poetry that would glorify the courage and generosity of a military aristocracy that was all that stood between their people and slaughter, dispossession and serfdom. 'Then Talhaearn Tad Awen gained renown in poetry and Aneirin and Taliesin . . .' Out of a highland zone that stretched from Edinburgh to south-west England there emerged a resurgence of interest in the Celtic past where there was a wealth of myth and legend to console the British as well as tantalizing glimpses of lost religions that held out promise of earthly paradise and immortality. What could have been more alluring to a minority at the mercy of massive demographic swings than the idea of a 'Cauldron of Rebirth'? The use of this miraculous utensil is vividly demonstrated in the second branch of *Pedair Cainc y Mabinogi*: 'Should one of your men be killed, throw his corpse in the cauldron and by tomorrow he shall be as sound as ever he was and fight as well, except for the loss of speech.' This device for the recycling of soldiers must have had a special appeal for a minority suffering from a manpower shortage.

This was not the only cauldron available. There was the Irish 'Cauldron of Plenty', an invaluable asset that both Culhwch and Arthur were willing to fight to possess. Furthermore, and perhaps most challenging of all, there was the 'Cauldron of Inspiration and Knowledge' which was of vital importance to poets in particular. In the folk-tale preserved in *Hanes Taliesin* a country boy is put in charge of the cooking process, and by accident as much as by design acquires the three drops of the magic potion that transform him from a yokel into the most knowledgeable man in the world. His knowledge as it were supervises his metamorphosis and in the end Gwion Bach is reborn as that prince of magic and poetry, the second Taliesin.

Between Gildas and the bards we catch glimpses of a culture struggle in progress. Gildas wrote in Latin and he saw himself as the standard-bearer of Romano-British culture as well as an anointed prophet. His influence ranged from Clydeside to Brittany. He was an important agent of the monastic movement that was to preserve so much of classical Christian values throughout two centuries of turmoil. During this same period so often described as the Dark Ages, certain features of this culture struggle took root in the Cymric psyche. The contrast between the ease of movement to the west and the growing constrictions and barriers across the land frontiers to the east become a graphic physical expression of a 'Welsh Situation' even before 'Cymru' emerges as a recognizable entity. We need only look at the 'Lives of the Saints' to catch an early reflection of this contrast burgeoning in the Welsh character. Westward all is openness, warmth, generosity, an altruistic enthusiasm to embrace the whole world and share with it the joys of revelation. It is fair to say that the spirit of St David was a vital part of the initial impetus of a movement which flourished around the western sea routes, and in due course sent missionaries ever further afield. Even the praise poets begin to share in the enthusiasm and suffuse their myths and legends with Christian significance.

Facing east all is changed. The Cymric face seems to darken with apprehension and suspicion. There is a palpable withdrawal of the spirit. How could divine Providence allow a heathen invader to triumph and cast down the Christian defending his own country? Should he withdraw to the hills to commune with himself and shrink like a snail into what he hopes is the protective covering of his own saintly shell? The general condition of the British Church in the eighth century is nowhere more vividly illustrated than in Bede's *Historia Ecclesiastica Gentis Anglorum*. Bede relies heavily on Gildas for his outline of the history of Britain before and during the Saxon invasions. As a public-relations expert for the Latin-reading public he makes skilful use of the material to demonstrate how the Saxons became the Chosen People, a new Israel advancing to occupy the Promised Land of Britain. His English nation was predestined to merge the British Isles into God's plan for a universal Roman Church. It is Bede's pleasure to push the unworthy Britons out of a nest that was far too good for them in the first place. In his eyes this was more than one ruling class replacing another or a mere demographic shift. A new nation was being born, and he outlines the choosing of the English in scriptural terms. In those dark centuries a new agreement had been forged and this new testament took precedence over the old.

The pivotal character in Bede's drama is Augustine, the apostle of England. He tells us how this imperious and high-minded ecclesiastic called a meeting in AD 603 somewhere in the English Midlands, in a place which was still known in Bede's day as 'Augustine's Oak', between himself, sponsored by King Ethelbert, and certain Cambro-British bishops. Augustine made three demands. He wished the British to accept his authority as the representative of the pope; he wished them to bring themselves into line with all the customs and practices of the Roman Church; and he demanded their active assistance in the great business of converting the heathen Saxons. None of these proposals was acceptable to the British. Less than twenty years had gone by since the bloody and fateful battle of Deorham when the Saxon invaders had ruthlessly destroyed churches in the valley of the Severn, cutting off the British of south Wales from the British of the south-west. It is doubtful whether Augustine had any true understanding of the struggle that was going on.

Bede tells us that there were two meetings. At the first his hero Augustine – in a ploy that must have been calculated to remind his readers both of Elijah on Mount Carmel and of St Germanus on his celebrated trip to Britain to combat the Pelagian heresy – arranges a test of miraculous prowess: a blind Englishman is prayed over by the British bishops with negative results. Then Augustine, the missionary from Pope Gregory who wants to make angels out of Angles, restores the blind man's sight. Bede gracefully allows the reader to draw the appropriate conclusion. The uneasy Britons decide to return home for consultations. They could not make changes in their ancient customs without the consent and authority of their people. This could have been an exercise in primitive democracy. Certainly the British would claim that they had a strong line of their own in saints and miracle-workers. It was no part of Bede's brief to mention these. It was only necessary for the sake of the elegant symmetry of his storytelling to inform the reader that the delegation went off to consult a hermit before returning to confront the formidable Augustine. This in itself indicates that in the Celtic order of these things, anchorites took a guru-like precedence over bishops and doctors of the Church. How was the delegation to know whether or not this autocratic missionary to the heathen Saxon was truly a man sent from God? In Bede's narrative, the hermit answers by quoting a verse from St Matthew's gospel: 'Take my yoke upon you and learn of me; for I am meek and lowly in heart.' This must have seemed on the face of it sound scriptural advice. But the British bishops pressed the hermit further. It was a critical turning-point in history, and they felt the need for a sign. The hermit gave it them. And Bede makes certain that his readers understand that the advice they get is so misguided as to make the source whence it came suspect for all time.

> Do you contrive that he with his followers be first to arrive at the place of meeting, and if as you approach, he rises up to meet you, with the knowledge that he is a servant of Christ, hear him willingly; but if he despise you, and does not choose to rise up before you, since you are greater in number, let him also be despised by you.

Of course Augustine does not rise to greet them, and the conference, as we would say, gets off to a disastrous start. There was no common ground. Augustine, strengthened by the prerogative of Rome, expected submission to authority. The British, among whom bishops seem to have been two-a-penny, looked in vain for signs of what they would consider spiritual fitness. To the venerable Bede, however, the whole occasion represented a great deal more than the inability of two forms of Christianity to understand each other. The Britons were in deadly error and they would deserve any punishment the Lord might see fit to visit upon them. He cannot conceal his satisfaction when he records that ten years later a cheerful pagan king from Northumbria put a large assembly of the monks of Bangor Is-coed to the sword. In the pen-ultimate chapter of his book 'On the present state of the English nation and the rest of Britain (AD 725–31)', he has some quite nice things to say about the Irish. And even the Picts have a treaty of peace with the English and 'are glad to be united in Catholic peace and truth to the universal church of Rome'. Only the Cambro-Britons are still singled out for condemnation. They have 'a national hatred for the English and uphold their own bad customs against the true Easter of the Catholic Church'. The underlying thesis of his History is to demonstrate that the English are God's chosen people. In order to please God, the dispossessed were called upon not only to respect their oppressors but also to find them particularly lovable.

Gildas and Bede between them have reverberated down the centuries and played havoc with the Cymric imagination. Their writings made the Cambro-Britons mourn a lost paradise which in fact had never been theirs. Generations of clerics seized on the pseudo-history, and a tendency set in to equate the loss of Britain with the Fall of Man. This process laid the foundation of what can only be described as a highly developed national sense of inadequacy and sin.

The theme of dispossession took over any account of Welsh history whether by clerics or by poets. By the ninth century this was coupled with the belief that the Welsh were of Trojan origin, their descent being traced from Brutus, the grandson of Aeneas, the Trojan refugee who founded Rome. This Brutus had been fated to slay his father and mother by accident. For this primeval sin he was driven from Italy and eventually arrived in this island, which took its name from his. These origin myths, recorded in Latin, complemented each other and allowed for much subtle variation and development: just as the fallen man could be saved so the fallen nation could be restored to its former glory. In the weaving of the myth there was a place for political prophecy, bright hope and endless expectation as well as punishment.

The age of the lost kingdoms coincides with the age of the saints. This is hardly surprising. Saints tend to establish kingdoms in the next world rather than in this one. Scholars have shown how important the western sea routes were to the movement of those pioneers of Celtic Christianity who were also responsible for capturing so much of the essence of oral Celtic culture in writing. But the presence of a land corridor from Dumbarton in the north to the Severn estuary through to the south coast of Devon was of equal importance as long as it remained open. Just as the saints could preach and teach, the poets could sing. It could have been possible for an early Welsh-speaking minstrel from the Old North to move south through Rheged and Elmet into Lancashire and the counties of the Welsh border, to Devon and Cornwall and even across the sea, singing and reciting stories in early Welsh without ever entering the present borders of Wales. It is in this sense that Welsh tradition is correct in postulating a lost greater Britain, and it is out of this British experience and perhaps a desire to reoccupy a lost world that so much of the strength and power of medieval storytelling in Wales arises.

In the poetry of Aneirin and Taliesin we glimpse something of the vitality and virility of *Gwŷr y Gogledd* (Men of the Old North): and it is no accident that the names of so many of the knights of King Arthur's court, and indeed the name of Arthur himself, can be traced back to these sources. In the beginning Arthur belonged to the bards. In stanza 102 of the *Gododdin*, a warrior named Gwawrddyd is praised for his impetuous ferocity: 'On the castle wall crows feasted on their flesh. He saw to it they had their fill although he was no Arthur.' The poem seems to celebrate a belated attempt to copy Arthurian strategy at a time when Saxon numbers have multiplied to such an extent that his vaunted victories could never be repeated.

As a policy for rearmament, cauldrons of rebirth could never provide a practical solution. As crucibles of myth, however, there can be no question of their efficacy. Cauldrons of inspiration transformed Taliesin into a prophet. He and Myrddin (Merlin) became the dynamic duo of a Cymric resistance that lasted through the centuries until the figure of Arthur was elevated to the position of ideal emperor in most of the literatures of western Europe. In a violent world he was the figure who could show the way to an effective balance between strength and legitimacy. Blessed by the Church, the hero-king could demonstrate on all occasions that might was right. When Henry Tudor snatched the Crown of England, the Welsh bards heaved a sigh of relief and reassurance when he named his eldest son Arthur.

History has no claim to be an exact science, but it is always capable of being the most effective propaganda. At no time is this more evident than during the Tudor period. There would appear to be a cultural *droit de seigneur* that belongs to the victor: so much he will annex, so much ignore, and so much obliterate. Having extracted the vital elements that he needs to preserve and enhance his power and prestige, he has few qualms in proceeding to exterminate the language that was their source and origin: 'and also that from henceforth no person or persons that use the Welsh speech or language shall have or enjoy any manner office or fees within this realm of England, Wales, or other the King's Dominion.'

The saving grace for our language in that time of crisis was the word 'British'. 'Brytyshe' was a magic formula. As that enthusiastic Protestant William Salesbury put it, 'the Brytyshe language that by continuall misnomer, the recorder of the aunciente hostilitie, is called Welshe.' The earliest name for Protestantism in Wales was *Crefydd y Saeson* – the religion of the English. With a combination of scholarship and casuistry men like William Salesbury and Bishop Richard Davies were able to use the writings of Gildas and Bede to turn the propaganda weapon right round and equate *Crefydd y Saeson* with detestable Roman Catholicism. As Davies argues in his 'Epistle to the Cymry':

> That Christianity which Augustine brought to the Saxons did fall short of the purity of the Gospel and the definitions of the primitive church . . . The Britons were distressed to observe such a mixing of this pollution of Christ's religion. Wherefore, when the English took so impure a

Christianity unto themselves, the Britons could see no worthy way to communicate with any of them.

At any time in history it seems misconceptions and antipathies have a strange power to fertilize each other. Even as I write, London newspapers are working up an enthusiasm for celebrations afoot in Canterbury to mark the arrival of Christianity. Whatever went on in the Celtic fringe at that time is dismissed as remote and irrelevant. The long arm of the Venerable Bede reaches out once again to inject his version of history into the innocent minds of the category described by the advertising industry as serious readers.

We are, of course, all of us impressionable creatures. It is possible to imagine that when the figure of Arthur was hijacked by English authority a permanent distortion or at least reorientation occurred in the Welsh mind. For centuries previously, even as far back as the age of the megaliths, the territory of Wales occupied a pivotal position in the cultures and civilizations that flourished along the western edge of Europe. It was the centre of a Celtic sea province and of a provenance of the imagination. When the Tudors occupied the English throne with an heir called Arthur, Welsh eyes were turned with fatal ease to London. The wildest prophecies had been fulfilled. Out of the cauldron of myth that had been kept bubbling by generations of bards down the centuries had sprung a recycled hero. At last the dream had become a reality. The ancient Brytyshe were back at the top of the heap. The power and the glory were there for the taking.

There was, as we all know, a rude awakening: for snorting sleepers there always is. In spite of an increasingly pathetic desire to please, once the Tudors were replaced by the Stuarts, the value of Welshness slid down on the stock exchange index of reputation to bottom out just above the level of derision and contempt. The peaceable pretensions of the Welsh were only acceptable when exercised in the service of an expanding English empire. This attitude of amused superiority remains the hallmark of cultural imperialism. Not so very long ago Jeremy Hooker quoted a metropolitan critic as saying: 'the difficulty of the Welsh language may be hiding from non-Welsh readers the best poetry being written in Wales, but one rather doubts it.' There was a further implication that Welsh poets writing in English, unlike their rebellious Irish counterparts, needed to be mad or bad but not dangerous to know to be worthy of a footnote in the more substantial literary journals.

The fact is that we all owe a debt of honour to our senior language. By being more or less irrelevant to power, profit and prestige, it has gone a long way to stockpile a spiritual inheritance to sustain us through a struggle that is far from ended. The vital core remains untranslatable and that is how it should be. Stimulating pilgrimages aim at inaccessible shrines. We may be in many ways double in ourselves, but it will be the poets in the end who will make it possible for us to continue to enjoy the best of both worlds without becoming permanently two-faced. The true source of our being is in a language and a tradition so old that it shapes the landscape in which we live and move. It is this landscape that sustains and inspires us. In relation to the depth of our past we are in the best sense peripheral, and for this reason we need our chronicles and companions. Succeeding generations will have good reason to be grateful to the recipient of this Festschrift (Meic Stephens). To determine where they are going, at the very least they will need to discover for themselves a clear idea of the nature of their inheritance: a spiritual capital hidden in that mysterious 1.6 per cent.

Arnold in Wonderland

First published in *The Powys Review* (Summer 1978).

On a Saturday in August in the year 1864, Mr Matthew Arnold, Professor of Poetry at the University of Oxford and Her Majesty's Inspector of Schools, sat in number 10, St George's Crescent, Llandudno, writing holiday letters to relatives and friends. The date, as always, is very relevant. In the dim caves of Mount Helicon where history is being constantly rewritten, dates are like glow-worms that provide the weavers with the only source of light. But so is the address. Middle-class and robustly anglophile. St George's Crescent. An architectural scimitar lying across the dragon's throat.

The distinguished letter-writer is forty-two and in a state of pleasurable excitement: in Llandudno, on the Welsh coast, there was a distinct possibility that his poetic career, that seemed so ominously complete, could be resumed – the visionary gleam could be returning. The Inspector of Schools, braced and refreshed by the Celtic breeze, would turn once more to the 'grand business of modern poetry, that moral interpretation, from an independent point of view, of man and the world'.

'The poetry of the Celtic race', he wrote to his mother, 'and its names of places quite overpowers me and it will be long before Tom forgets the line, "Hear from thy grave, great Taliesin, hear", from Gray's Bard, since I have repeated it a hundred times a day on our excursions.'

After all his mother was Cornish. Her maiden name was Penrose, a word surely cognate with that Penrhos through which he walked with his brother Tom on several of his excursions. Being half Celtic had become a stimulating concept. Perhaps it brought relief to the intensity of moral earnestness, labelled Teutonic by his father and headmaster, deeply instilled in childhood and youth and then reinforced by a mature sense of mission. 'Then also', he writes to Lady de Rothschild, 'I have a great penchant for the Celtic races, with their melancholy and unprogressiveness.'

It is never difficult to trace the sources of Matthew Arnold's ideas and enthusiasms. He made little attempt to conceal them. His stance as an advocate of high culture and arbiter of literary taste in England did not depend on originality. The driving force of his message lay in its concern with, and application to, the English situation. His business was with the refinement of the condition of middle-class success. History was clearly in the process of delivering the wide world into the hands of the English. England was the new Rome. A new form of Empire had come into being apparently as much by accident as by design. Such rude vigour and crude success had to be provided with a higher purpose. By some divine accident which a more superstitious age would have called a miracle, the imperiousness of the Norman, the honesty of the Saxon, the thoroughness of the Teuton and the Titanism of the Celt had been combined to create the potential of a new race of supermen. The Church of England, his father had already pointed out, needed to be made more flexible, to accommodate wider concepts. A place had to be made for the drive and dedication of Dissent, for the reorganization of Education, for the fruits of Science and the power that came with extended Trade and Knowledge. Dr Arnold of Rugby was an opponent of Disestablishment for his own reasons.

> The Church, never disestablished but dedicated to England . . . of all human ties that to our country is the highest and most sacred: and England to a true Englishman ought to be dearer than the peculiar forms of the Church of England.

In that mild way which in the end merely reinforces the fact of apostolic succession, Matthew Arnold had rebelled against his father. For him, C of E meant the Culture of England. An improved breed of English poets and men of letters would eventually replace the old ministry. An elevated culture would be capable not only of providing a 'criticism of Life': it would also replace dogma to become the true source of righteousness and personal morality. But there was a great deal of hard work to be done. Wordsworth, Keats, Shelley, Byron, Tennyson, Browning, talented as they were, had not succeeded in lifting English verse up to the Olympian levels of the work of his hero Goethe. Until the whole body of modern English writing could be seen to combine the virtues and excel the output of German and French, the language could not take off and provide the best parts of the nations of the earth with the appropriate cultural extension of universal practical Christianity.

A man with a mission has earned his rest and he has a right to relax on his holidays. Reading *La Poésie des races celtiques* by Renan, Arnold had learned that this obscure body of poetry was characterized by spirituality, melancholy and a heightened awareness of nature. Arnold had no knowledge of Welsh or of any Celtic language. But the poet in him quickly overpowered the educator. As he stood barefooted and bareheaded *ar ben y Gogarth*, that most conspicuous of headlands, did he not feel within himself the exquisite sensations of spirituality, sweet melancholy and a heightened awareness of nature? True his feet were bare for mundane Teutonic reasons. He had a blister on his big toe as a result of too much excited tramping about on Wordsworthian 'excursions'. The place is now the Great Orme's Head and the site of cafés, overhead railways, litter bins and funfairs, but in 1864 the coastline of Wales could still provide a poet in any language with the feeling that he could be treading on sacred ground. Bays, inlets, rocky shores, promontories and deserted beaches combined with the generous sea to provide an infinite variety of symphonic sunsets.

> At last one turns around and looks westward. Everything is changed. Over the mouth of the Conway and its sands is the eternal softness and mild light of the west; the low line of mystic Anglesey, the precipitous Penmaenmawr, and the group of Carnedd Llewelyn and Carnedd David, and their brethren fading away, hill behind hill, in an aerial haze, make the horizon; between the fort of Penmaenmawr and the bending coast of Anglesey, the sea, a silver stream, disappears one knows not whither. On this side, Wales – Wales, where the past still lives, where every place has its tradition, every name its poetry, and where the people, the genuine people, still knows this past, this tradition, this poetry, and lives with it and clings to it; while, alas, the prosperous Saxon on the other side, the invader from Liverpool and Birkenhead, has long ago forgotten his.

The prose style is still beguiling. In an easy urbane fashion, it exercises its own authority. It is an active world of assertion from which all coarseness and vulgarity has been excluded. It has the strength of concern and the delicacy of a cultivated aesthetic sense. And it has more. For the purpose of these four lectures on *The Study of Celtic Literature*, Professor Arnold has donned druidical robes. The Order of his own making. As befits a poet who is attempting to synthesize a modern mythology, his utterance is reaching out towards incantation. To achieve his effects he is prepared to pay the price of over-simplification. The levy is not onerous. In dealing with such an obscure subject, accuracy is not important: the effect is all. Somehow or other, the haughty Philistines of England must be made aware of the Celtic species expiring on the westward perimeter of the world's most advanced and prosperous state. Here was the son of Arnold of Rugby,

'That Teuton of Teutons, the Celt-hating Dr Arnold', telling the world that the despised and dejected Celts still had something valuable to offer.

> When I was young, I was taught to think of Celt as separated by an impassable gulf from Teuton: my father in particular was never weary of contrasting them: he insisted much oftener on the separation between us and them than on the separation between us and any other race in the world.

The central argument of Arnold's message of reconciliation between conquered Celt and all-conquering Saxon was something he declared to be scientific.

> The Celt's claims towards having his genius and its works fairly treated as objects of scientific investigation, the Saxon can hardly reject, when these claims are urged simply on their own merits, and are not mixed up with extraneous pretentions which jeopardise them.

An adroit manipulation of syntax conjures up the illusion of an atmosphere of scientific detachment. At the same time, the impersonal calm, the judicial manner, the authoritative concern for the English commonwealth, underline the fact that the Celts, in the manner of tramps, gypsies, poachers, disrespectful labourers and other elements from the unstable sediment of an otherwise well-ordered society, are up before the bench. In the end, sentence will have to be passed. The most pressing question at issue is which set of laws should be applied in this case. From his chosen stance as judge-advocate, there is no doubt in Arnold's mind.

> What the French call the *science des origines* – the science of origins, – a science which is at the bottom of all real knowledge of the actual world, and which is every day growing in interest and importance – is very incomplete without a thorough critical account of the Celts and their genius, language and literature.

In order that no one should doubt his good intentions, in his introduction to the lectures, Arnold gallantly defends the hapless Welsh and their Eisteddfod from the following blunt, blistering and blustering verdict of *The Times* newspaper:

The Welsh language is the curse of Wales . . . An Eisteddfod is one of the most mischievous and selfish pieces of sentimentalism which could possibly be perpetrated. It is simply a foolish interference with the natural progress of civilisation and prosperity . . . Not only the energy and power, but the intelligence and music of Europe have come mainly from Teutonic sources, and this glorification of everything Celtic, if it were not pedantry, would be sheer ignorance. The sooner all Welsh specialities disappear from the face of the earth the better.

Arnold is opposed to the harshness and the brutal frankness: the unacceptable face of Anglican uniformity and Teutonic intolerance. What he offers is a softer approach to the first of the final solutions based on the science of origins which so deeply stirred the imagination and even the 'imaginative reason' of the men of the nineteenth century and provided the twentieth with its most terrifying popular myth. He cannot help being sorry for the Celts, particularly 'the quiet, peaceable Welsh'.

his land is a province and his history petty, and his Saxon subduers scout his speech as an obstacle to civilisation, and the echo of all its kindred in other lands is growing every day fainter and more feeble: gone in Cornwall, going in Brittany and the Scotch Highlands, going too in Ireland and there above all, the badge of the beaten race, the property of the vanquished.

That summer of 1864, the Eisteddfod pitched its tent in Llandudno. Professor Arnold's little boys were disappointed when they discovered it was not a circus. The professor himself, expecting too much from a Bardic Congress conducted in a language he could not understand, was disappointed to discover that it was. The Gorsedd was held in the open air. The weather was bad. The speeches were long. The presiding bard was got up in some absurd costume. Inside the tent things were no better. The back seats where the Welsh should have been seated were nearly empty. The front seats were occupied by Saxons who came there from curiosity, not enthusiasm. And when a speech was made in English, powerful as it was, by a Nonconformist divine, he inevitably spoilt his case by overstating it. His eloquence was given a stony Teutonic response: 'The whole performance on that particular morning, was incurably lifeless.'

The Arnold family's diversions during their Llandudno stay were not confined to romantic 'excursions' or attending eisteddfodau. As he wrote to his sister when he mentioned spending three and a half hours on the Great Orme in bare feet, 'There are one or two people here.' By this he means not the Saxon hordes he saw swarming in from Liverpool, or the natives, those obscure descendants of the myth-making Celts, selling vegetables and hiring donkeys to the prosperous invaders. He means the social life of his own kind: the privileged members of the middle class connected with the aristocracy, with the Church of England, with Oxford colleges, with government circles and less openly perhaps with commerce. 'There are one or two people here: the Liddells, with whom we dined; the Scudmore Stanhopes, him I slightly knew at Oxford; the dean of Chichester, a clergyman or two, who have called.'

The Liddells, of course, were the family of the Dean of Christ Church, Liddell of Liddell and Scott, the Greek lexicon that was as much a pillar of English public school education as Dr Arnold's Rugby reformations. Among 'the clergymen or two' was the Revd Charles Lutwidge Dodgson, lecturer and tutor in mathematics at Christ Church. It is not unreasonable to conjecture that he may have deserted the West Shore to look in with clear-eyed curiosity at the proceedings of the Eisteddfod. And the three little girls could have accompanied him: Lorinda Charlotte, Edith and Alice. As far as I know there is no record of their reactions. The language barrier was insurmountable. They must have returned to the West Shore to continue listening to the Walrus and the Carpenter. Alas, the pre-adolescent wonderland was not available to the Welsh. Like the oysters in the poem they were scheduled for polite but firm extinction.

The Eisteddfod existed to celebrate the antiquity and honour of the Welsh language, in what could only appear the most harmless manner. It is not easy to discover Matthew Arnold's deepest objections to the Eisteddfod. He states that he found the proceedings at Llandudno 'incurably lifeless', yet in a letter to Hugh Owen he becomes quite fulsome:

> When I see the enthusiasm these Eisteddfods can awaken in your whole people, and then think of the tastes, the literature, the amusements, of our own lower middle class, I am filled with admiration for you. It is a consoling thought and one which history allows us to entertain, that nations disinherited of political success may yet leave their mark on the world's progress, and contribute powerfully to the civilisation of mankind.

This would appear to be a remarkable insight on the part of an intelligent foreigner into the true nature of the institution and its origin. Iolo Morganwg, like Lewis Carroll, had a passion for literary anonymity. Carroll wished to forge a world of innocence out of his obsessive observation of little girls between the ages of eight and twelve. Iolo's forgeries were more ambitious. He wanted nothing less than to restore the supremacy of the Cambro-British. The Gorsedd and the revived and enlarged Eisteddfod were the creation of a private patriotism of demented proportions. This Welsh Jacobin and Unitarian created a necessary institution for the unprecedented expansion of Welsh consciousness that occurred in the first half of the nineteenth century. The Welsh were as hungry for identity as they were for religion. But Arnold writes of the Celt that his speech 'is growing every day fainter and more feeble: gone in Cornwall, going in Brittany, and the Scotch Highlands, going too in Ireland . . .'

Going. Going. Gone. This is the language of the auctioneer, rather than that of the literary critic. A sale of remnants is afoot and the auctioneer from Oxford is anxious to persuade his Saxon clientele that there is something among the job-lot that is worth buying as well as burying. We cannot tell whether it is wishful thinking or a love of masterful generalization that plays Arnold false. As far as the Welsh language was concerned, he could not have been more wrong. Unlike Cornish, Gaelic or Breton, Welsh in the mid-nineteenth century was expanding more rapidly than ever before in history. The Eisteddfod with all its trappings was only one external manifestation of this expansion. It was to be encountered in Chicago, Philadelphia, Cape Town, London, Sydney as well as in Llandudno. The Welsh, rather like the Jews, sober and relatively prosperous, full of pretensions and those hated 'particularities', were irritatingly everywhere, carrying their language and their institutions with them.

There was a sound economic basis for this growth. Unlike Ireland and the Scottish Highlands, Wales in the nineteenth century was not ravaged by famine or depopulation. The industrial valleys of the south and industry in the north (and that extension of Wales into Merseyside and Lancashire which gave us David Lloyd George and Saunders Lewis and gave them Selwyn Lloyd and Enoch Powell) were well able to absorb the population explosion. With the Welsh, religious and political motives remained as powerful as the drive for economic improvement. If Matthew Arnold had stayed long enough on the Great Orme's Head, with or without his boots on, he would have seen the first ship of yet another Welsh exodus – no Chosen People is worthy of the title without this chapter in its story – the converted tea-clipper *Mimosa*, just avoiding the rocks off 'mystic Anglesey' on her way to an exclusively Welsh wonderland in South America. *The Mimosa* was their *Mayflower*.

Perhaps Arnold was not so unaware of the rising tide of Welshness after all. The trouble with the language was not that it was going, but that it was stubbornly refusing to go. On either side of the Atlantic the congregations of the dissenting chapels were growing larger from one revival to another. The princes of the pulpit who had once governed this worldwide Welsh commonwealth with as firm a hand as Dr Arnold's at Rugby had been obliged to bow to the popular desire for a wider culture and declare the Eisteddfod at least as respectable as the *Cornhill Magazine*. The occasional touch of royal patronage made it easy to conceal the republican and radical origin of Iolo's fancies under the eisteddfodic robes.

But Professor Arnold was not easily deceived by such superficial symptoms. He recognized a dangerous disease and prescribed a remedy. While he waited in bare feet on the Great Orme's Head, the inevitable spark from heaven fell. 'I must say I quite share the opinion of my brother Saxons as to the practical inconvenience of perpetuating the speaking of Welsh.' 'Practical inconvenience' still has a contemporary ring about it. The language of government does not easily change. (It sounds equally well in the accent of Oxford or Tonypandy.) 'Perpetuating the speaking of Welsh' is more characteristically nineteenth-century; it smacks clearly of the 'Welsh Not': 'the change must come and its accomplishment is a mere affair of time. The sooner the Welsh language disappears . . . the better; the better for England, the better for Wales itself.'

At last the nature of the sacrifice has been indicated, together with its true purpose. 'The moral interpretation', 'the independent point of view', has been transformed into an irrevocable judgement and the romantic practitioner of the grand business of modern poetry is suddenly transformed on that windy afternoon in Llandudno, somewhat in the manner of a Hollywood Dr Jekyll, into a relentless Benthamite. Welsh was a totally unsatisfactory appliance of communication because it had never been used by Mr Jeremy Bentham or learnt by Mr Matthew Arnold. It had made and was making an inadequate contribution to those utilitarian twin ideals of Progress and Success. It was no good for England, and therefore no good for Wales. It was insufficiently useful. If it was not useful, it could never be virtuous.

If it was not virtuous, much merit could be gained by discarding it. Ministers of Education (as it turns out Mr Arnold's brother-in-law is the Minister of Education in 1870) must use the elementary schools to hammer Welsh out and English in, and 'hammer it harder and harder'. Arnold's phrase evokes the celluloid image of Mr Hyde with his top hat on and his cloak flying, hammering away with his walking cane at the unconscious body of the faded prostitute lying on the pavement. Between punctuation marks he rushes back to the laboratory and swallows a draught of the restoring fluid before continuing in the more measured tones of the literary critic ready once more to do battle on behalf of culture and high art against the ranks of Philistia. The restoring fluid, we may guess, is by Taliesin. Three drops. Those oft-repeated invocations have not been made in vain. 'Hear from thy grave, great Taliesin, hear!' Since the Reverend Dodgson was in the vicinity he may have found a bottle with the words DRINK ME beautifully printed on it in large English letters. There should be no mistake in signs of this sort. It was not marked poison and it was perfectly safe to drink it. And that was how our hero first tasted 'Celtic Magic'.

Those of us who wonder how our grandparents came so easily to abandon their native language, and our natural heritage, at a time when it seemed to be prospering as never before, should consider the correspondence between Matthew Arnold and that ubiquitous Benthamite busybody, Hugh Owen. In the 1860s Welsh dissent, Welsh-speaking dissent, was poised to become an independent political force. Arnold with his lifelong fear of Irish Fenianism could not have been unaware of this. And the Welsh at that time were organized in a way that was still beyond the capability of the Irish. Throughout the first half of the nineteenth century chapels had been going up at the rate of one a fortnight. At first Welsh dissenters had been content to confine themselves to theology. Unlike the science of origins that so took Arnold's fancy, theology was an exacting discipline. In their own language this people possessed on a popular level an extraordinary ideological network and a language which supported such a variety of newspapers, magazines, encyclopedias, pamphlets and books could hardly be described as dying. Every chapel and every meeting-house was a potential political cell. Arnold understood this. As an Inspector of Schools it was part of his duty to be aware of any hidden threat to the uniformity of the state. He was as much devoted as his father had been to the concept of the state as a God-ordained, mystical and sacred entity. From Hegel they derived that notable Teutonic ideal that states and the laws of states were nothing less than religion manifesting itself in the relations of the actual world. 'The fusion of all the inhabitants of these islands into one homogeneous, English-speaking whole . . . the swallowing up of separate provincial nationalities, is a consummation towards which the natural course of things irresistibly tends.'

Arnold's elevation of the concept of culture can be interpreted as an attempt to extend a Hegelian reverence for the state. This would account for his implacable hostility to the Welsh language on the one hand and his eagerness, on the other, to make Celtic magic easily accessible for the enrichment of English civilization. The Welsh language was an unreliable and volatile spirit which could give too much life to Welsh dissent and encourage an endless succession of disruptive and even seditious movements. Working-class movements, trade unionism, manifestations of rural and industrial discontent, all had their origins among chapel people. Disestablishment of the Church of England in England which had caused his father so much concern was hardly more than an academic issue: in Ireland and in Wales, provincial nationalisms tainted religious controversy. A separate language was an ever present threat of separatist intentions.

But Arnold need not have worried. There was absolutely no cause for alarm. In the Wales of the 1860s the leadership of the denominations, which still exerted what could almost be described as a spiritual dictatorship over the lives of the majority of the Welsh people, was securely in the hands of men dedicated to many of the ideals of Thomas Arnold of Rugby. (There is indeed an interesting parallel between the father–son relationship of Lewis Edwards, the Pope of Bala, and Thomas Charles Edwards, who became the first principal of the University of Wales, and the relationship between Thomas and Matthew Arnold.) Nationalistic sentiments and separatist aspirations were safely channelled into such unrealistic ventures as a Welsh state in Wisconsin or Patagonia. Already the Welsh were faced with an embarrassment of choice. They could be assimilated in one way in North America, in another way in South America and in a variety of ways within the Empire. The one option that seemed not available was to go on being themselves.

The institutions of Wales, such as they were, presented no threat to the integrity of anybody except the Welsh. The Eisteddfod, which Sir John Rhŷs was able to describe at the end of the century as 'a thoroughly popular assembly representing the rank and file of the Welsh people . . . and a rallying point of Welshmen who live apart from one another, whether in Wales or other parts of the United Kingdom', was already securely under the control of respectable bourgeois anglophile social engineers like Hugh Owen. To quote Sir John Rhŷs again:

> about the middle of the present century, it struck some of the leading Welshmen of the time that the Eisteddfod was to a considerable extent a neglected force that might be utilised for the benefit of Wales. So Sir Hugh Owen and his friends undertook the attempt to regulate it and to add to its meetings opportunities for discussing social and economic questions connected with the future of Wales.

The key verbs in this passage are 'utilise' and 'regulate'. They reveal the motives behind Hugh Owen's tireless activities. Schools, colleges, societies, eisteddfodau, the Cymmrodorion and the network of denominational interest were all 'appliances', active agencies for the dissemination of a comprehensive concept of social progress that he and his kind were adapting to suit the Welsh Nonconformist temperament. The chapel, that key institution which had been brought into existence for the salvation of Welsh souls and therefore for the unspoken affirmation of Welsh identity, could now be utilized to introduce a system whereby the children of the most respectable and the most hard-working could be set on the road to an improved material position in an ever improving material world. This was the moment when 'getting on' became part of the Welsh way of life. In that eisteddfodic hierarchy of morals debased into mottoes, 'eled ymlaen' and 'dyrchafiad arall i Gymro' superseded 'y gwir yn erbyn y byd' and 'oes y byd i'r iaith Gymraeg'. The eisteddfod was also 'useful' to foster the competitive spirit. As theological passions waned, social progress quietly overtook the progress of the soul.

Arnold, in his first lecture, pokes mild fun at Hugh Owen's eisteddfod: 'The recitation of the prize compositions began: pieces of verse and prose in the Welsh language, an essay on punctuality being, if I remember right, one of them; a poem on the march of Havelock, another. This went on for some time.'

The subjects are of course characteristic of the twin passions of the mid-nineteenth century in Britain – utilitarianism and imperial expansion. No doubt the subjects were set, as I believe they still are, to please the committees and gain the approval of the men in charge. It would not be unfair therefore to attribute to men like Hugh Owen the noticeable coarsening of sensibility that overtook so much of Welsh literature in the second half of the nineteenth century. There is something peculiarly sad in the spectacle of the greatest poet of the time, Islwyn, being a consistent eisteddfodic failure. And it is ironic too that his greatest work, *Y Storm*, would have been the one composition of that time in the Welsh language that would have gained Matthew Arnold's enthusiastic approval. His youthful admiration for *Sturm und Drang* and the great Goethe would have helped him to recognize an affinity that escaped Welsh critics until Mr Saunders Lewis drew attention to it in the 1950s. Alas! as far as contemporary Welsh literature was concerned, Arnold, in spite of his perceptive appreciation of Lady Charlotte Guest's translation of *Pedair Cainc y Mabinogi*, was as insensitive as any Benthamite philistine:

> if an Eisteddfod author has anything to say about punctuality or about the march of Havelock, he had much better say it in English; or rather, perhaps what he has to say on these subjects may as well be said in Welsh, but the moment he has anything of real importance to say, anything the world will the least care to hear, he must speak English.

When Arnold's lectures on Celtic literature were first published in the *Cornhill Magazine,* Hugh Owen, apparently overwhelmed with admiration, and with a servility that still nauseates the reader, hastened to invite the great man to use the Chester Eisteddfod as a platform on which to read a paper on some fresh aspect of the Celtic genius. One cannot believe that such a thorough-going utilitarian was so much taken with the idea of Celtic magic. 'Celtic' as a category that bundled the Welsh Calvinistic Methodists into the same bag as the Catholic Irish or Bretons or even the Wesleyan Cornish would not automatically commend itself: neither was 'magic' a word commonly used in the administration of the Poor Law or the deliberations of any of Hugh Owen's innumerable committees. What clearly delighted Owen and his friends was the prospect of doors of acceptance opening. A little more effort and a little more regulation and fresh paths of promotion and preferment would become available. Knighthoods were in sight – even OBEs for all. The Welsh-speaking Welsh were ideal material for the appliances of Benthamite brainwashing: a proud and ancient people not actually in chains but with all their natural ambition still repressed, rendered docile by the even more effective fetters of an exacting and puritanical religion. If the price of the earthly paradise was no more than curtailing the growth of the native language this was a negligible price to pay.

It should therefore come as no surprise that when Hugh Owen's University of Wales eventually opens its doors in 1872, the national language should be overlooked. Hegel was in comfortable residence some time before Taliesin came knocking at the door. In this kind of university, lip-service was the last thing the language could expect. The first principal, Thomas Charles Edwards, was a noted preacher among the Welsh Calvinistic Methodists. He was in American political parlance 'their favourite son'. Possibly to placate some diehards of this powerful religious constituency, and to improve the collection of quarrymen's pence, a place was found for Welsh literally in a cupboard under the stairs. (Long before Arnold's prestigious lectures, Lewis Edwards of Bala was writing to his son Thomas Charles, urging him to avoid preaching in Welsh in order to improve his English style – this in spite of the fact that he himself was a Welsh writer of some distinction and editor of the best quarterly of the time, *Y Traethodydd,* a magazine which I am happy to say still flourishes in spite of the forecasts of Matthew Arnold and the steady gnashing of the teeth of Hugh Owen's appliances.)

In the Welsh wonderland, this unlikely brew, 'Celtic Magic', became the elixir of Assimilation. In less than a generation the University of Wales could take a Welsh Calvinistic Methodist or a Welsh Baptist and transform him with an efficiency bordering on the Japanese into an extraordinarily lifelike imitation of one of Matthew Arnold's new Englishmen, 'more intelligent, more gracious and more humane'. Being Welsh, which for their forefathers was compulsory, became optional for the educated, less essential than going to chapel. (This was the age of the *Inglis Côs.*) When the new Welshman stared at the Tree of Knowledge he saw two instead of one. The most dangerous thing about 'Celtic Magic' was not that it made people larger or smaller, but that it introduced a permanent state of double vision.

It must be added that 'Celtic Magic' also filled a vacuum in that vital process of myth-making whereby the tribes and the nations reaffirm their faith in their own continuing existence. History like everything else is written from a point of view. In the nation-making process it is a vital industry. In the Welsh context the historian inherits the function of the bards and the poetic tradition. The breakdown of the bardic tradition may well be interpreted as the dissolution of a nation. When it was replaced eventually by an education system which is an amalgam of utilitarianism and cultural imperialism, strange results were bound to occur. And indeed they did. And still do.

But it was in the political rather than in the poetical arena that 'Celtic

Magic' really made itself felt. Historical truth obliges us to record that without the help of any imported brew or magic bottle, for three centuries Welsh Utopias rose and fell with monotonous regularity: the Quaker Welsh Tract in the Peaceable Kingdom; Morgan John Rhys's Beulah; Robert Owen's New Harmony; Richard Lloyd-Jones's Valley of the God Almighty Jones; S.R.'s crazy Tennessee experiment (only nine miles from Thomas Hughes's Anglican Fool's Paradise, Rugby Tennessee); William Bebb's Venedotia; and last but not least Michael D. Jones's Patagonia. Michael D. Jones may have failed in Patagonia, but Emrys ap Iwan was surely right to describe him as the Welshman most worthy of honour. Certainly his national spirit and spirited nationalism gave two young politicians that confidence in themselves and in a vision of their own kind that seems essential for the completion of a successful enterprise. Thomas E. Ellis of Cynlas Farm, Bala, became a successful Liberal politician. On the way he also went to University College of Wales, Aberystwyth and took his first taste of 'Celtic Magic'. In a grandiose essay entitled 'The Influence of the Celt in the Making of Britain', he begins:

> I desire at the outset to express my gratitude as a student and as a Celt to Mr Matthew Arnold and the band of literary and scientific men who determined to see things as they really are, have endeavoured to understand the Celtic peoples and appreciate the Celtic genius.

The essay continues as a bare-faced takeover bid of all the virtues ever displayed by the peoples of Britain. Arnold's magic brew has touched off a more ancient intoxicant. Whose voice are we listening to? Taliesin's Urien Rheged or this product of Aberystwyth and Oxford? 'Is it not this very Celticism which gives to Britain that special power and genius, that distinctive gift which differentiates Britain from Germany and which gives it the pre-eminence?'

Michael D. Jones's other disciple was the first Welshman to invite a Fenian to address a Welsh radical meeting. Michael Davitt and David Lloyd George appeared on the same platform at Ffestiniog in 1886. Could Arnold have been right after all to suspect that a radical and Fenian spirit was lurking in the remoter recesses of the native language? Lloyd George was aggressively Welsh and he was not encumbered with a University of Wales education. His cultural interests may have been sporadic but there was no doubt that he had Style in abundance, and enough Titanism to set any British audience jumping off their seats. But again Matthew Arnold's ghost can rest in peace. The most demonic personal nationalism since Iolo Morganwg's was soon harnessed to the imperial cause. In the Great War the cloak of Arthur and the white hair of Merlin were visible attributes of the Celtic Magic that led the steadfast patriotism of the English and the imperial fantasies of the peripheral Celts to victory.

It is not too crude a simplification to maintain that the institutions of Wales, old and new, were prepared to abandon the mother tongue in exchange for a mess of pottage with Celtic Magic. But Wonderland is a country provided with a variety of antidotes. As in any other children's story, a rescue can arrive at any moment and from the most unexpected quarter. Thanks to Arnold's barefooted sojourn on the sacred earth of Penygogarth, a chair of Celtic was created at Oxford. From this dizzy cultural elevation, it was inevitable in the course of time that scholarly privilege would percolate to the provincial extremities. Even at Aberystwyth, Welsh (if not *Cymraeg*) could come out of the cupboard under the stairs. The disciples of Sir John Rhŷs arrived like missionaries in the bush, burning to spread the new light of philology among their unenlightened kith and kin. But the language of instruction remained English, as Matthew Arnold would have maintained, the only appropriate medium for scientific investigation and all modern purposes.

Wonderlands are unstable. They are always liable to disappear. Someone has to sit on with closed eyes and re-create the dream, otherwise it will dissolve and be forgotten for ever. Out of Hugh Owen's Aberystwyth and into Arnold's Oxford, Owen M. Edwards came. He reoccupied that cave on Mount Helicon that had been left vacant far too long.

> Mae'r oll yn gysegredig. It is all sacred. Every hill and every valley. Our land is a living thing, not a grave of forgetfulness under our feet. Every hill has its history, every locality its own romance, every part of the landscape wears its own particular glory. And to a Welshman, no other country can be like this. A Welshman feels that the struggles of his forefathers have sanctified every field, and the genius of his people has transformed every mountain into hallowed ground. And it is feeling like this that will make him a true citizen.

Owen M. Edwards laid the foundation for a brilliant literary revival because he re-established the links between the Welsh people and their own past and made a new beginning possible. Like Matthew Arnold he made his appeal to a landscape. The difference was that he belonged to it.

MWT: Looking back over a period of over fifty years as a fiction-writer, does it seem to you that your career divides into phases at all? Is there any pattern to it?

EH: Only in the sense that one can be wise after the event. One's work responds, and corresponds, to one's life. In a curious way, my writing is quite autobiographical, much more so than I thought at the time. My kind of writer does tend to find an objective correlative for whatever is disturbing him at a given time of his life. It's like finding a receptacle and pouring one's concerns into it. At the time, it appears that it's the receptacle that is important, but in retrospect the contents become more clearly apparent. It's a very strange, irrational process – some kind of intuition of connection which excites the writer sufficiently to make him want to choose a particular narrative as a kind of receptacle. Sometimes in responding blindly like this and scrabbling around a writer can make a false start. But in the end he hits on something that is working and then in distant retrospect it becomes apparent that it worked because it was a suitable vehicle for his concerns at that time.

MWT: So, looking back, do you feel that some of your novels were, in the terms you've described, better than others? Or do you feel that in their time each was answerable to its period?

EH: A writer is always hoping not only that he is maturing as a human being but that he is also perfecting his craft as a craftsman. So there would be some early novels that I would consider immature now, and yet there are qualities in them that are peculiar to the time when they were written. They have a validity, and a kind of quality of persistence, of living, which is of its own. It's like all forms of creating – creativity being a part of our nature as human beings – it satisfies when it is an effective piece of work in itself, on its own terms. So something like *A Toy Epic*, for example, has the freshness that characterizes that early period in a person's life: the actual form managed to capture this freshness in an effective artistic way. When that happens, the book pleases me more. Whereas *The Italian Wife*, for instance, is a novel that has too much un-digested material in it, and relies too much on the attempt to follow the myth, the myth of Phaedra, and to drag it into the modern period. In this case, the devices are not adequate for what I was attempting; nor is the characterization. It seems to me an interesting, reasonably readable failure.

MWT: When, then, would you say you entered into a degree of maturity as a writer? Some critics would suggest that it happened around the time of *A Man's Estate* or *A Toy Epic*, and that it was due to your discovery of a subject, namely the Welsh experience, that thereafter you developed and explored to very great effect. Is that the way you see it?

EH: I think you get taken over by your material. The autobiographical element gets to be better objectivized when you have more effective control over your material. It's not for me to say when exactly that happens, and which of my novels are the best. Looking back over my career what strikes me is that we as a family have always lived a very busy life. There is a part of the brain which is reserved for creative writing, and there have been times when I've had jobs – for example, at the BBC (1955–65) when I was absorbed in doing other people's work. And it's the same energy that goes into doing that kind of creative work as is drawn upon when writing a novel. So there was a period before I went to the BBC, when for instance I received the Somerset Maugham Award, when I had the time to produce a work like *A Man's Estate*. Then even when I was working for the BBC there were two periods when I took unpaid leave, and I wrote *The Gift* in one and *Outside the House of Baal* in the other. So during my period with the BBC my actual fiction output was quite small. Then I took up a university post at Bangor, which again consumed a lot of time and energy, so that I achieved little in the way of writing. On leaving that post I was able to concentrate on fiction again, but that was so uncommercial, and also my sense of what I was fated to write made me committed to Welsh-language work, and so I turned to television, which enabled me to support my family financially by writing in Welsh. Therefore the pace of writing my own fiction slowed down. Then in the 1980s, when I was in my sixties, I had a very fruitful period when I could concentrate entirely on my own work, and that is when I completed the series called 'The Land of the Living', published *The Taliesin Tradition*, and produced short novels like *Jones* and *The Anchor Tree*. There's been that kind of rhythm to my career, and it's one I've actually welcomed. I'm not sure that I'm one of those writers who could live in extreme poverty and concentrate entirely on my vision. Also I have a kind of back-burner in the brain, which allows my ideas to simmer for long periods of time, whereas for some other writers that would have been an unbearable way of working. But it suited my family and other sorts of obligations. So in a strict sense I have been a part-time writer. And one of the fundamental differences between a fiction writer and, let's say, painters or musicians is that the writer needs to have deep tap-roots in everyday life, because his raw material is the life that is going on around him. But the painter – think of an abstract painter – can concentrate entirely on his medium and his technique, and the same is true of a musician. The fiction writer always needs to get a life, to use the idiom of today, and the more integrated he is into a community the better it is for him.

MWT: Integration into a society you say, and this has been a constant theme of yours in talking about yourself as fiction writer. And yet, back in the late 1940s, following the period when, at the end of the Second World War, you had been working in the refugee camps and based in Italy, you note in your journal: 'In Florence I developed the balcony attitude to life.' Do you now therefore feel that you could not have become a fiction writer without abandoning the balcony attitude to life?

EH: I would have been a very different kind of fiction writer, because the balcony attitude involves a certain detachment which is fine for a writer like Alberto Moravia, for example, who looks on the low life of Rome from the secure, upper-class position of one who is watching the antics in the forum below. That's one way of doing it. But the element of emotional commitment that I find is important means that you have to come down into the street and to be part of the whole scheme of things. There are certain elements that I think are central to my kind of writing. One is palpability, by which I mean that when you're creating a scene it is there, vividly sensuously present. Another is an emotional charge which extracts some kind of poetry from the situation. The poetic element in the fiction is very important to me, although I don't know why. There are analytical writers whose abilities are beyond me. I can only write what I feel, in a sub-rational kind of way.

MWT: And yet presumably that comment of yours in the journal suggests that you were at one time attracted to the balcony attitude?

EH: Oh, very much. It's part of my make-up as a human being. Because I have an excessively emotional nature, I don't like revealing my emotions, and you're safer if you're sitting on the balcony. I like to control myself, and I like to control my writing in the same way.

MWT: So your writing is a kind of compromise between detachment and aloofness and committing yourself to a deep direct involvement?

EH: Yes, absolutely. It's like the thesis and the antithesis producing the synthesis. What you write reconciles the two extremes, you are deeply concerned and yet you have the detachment to perceive it accurately; just as the painter's hand must not tremble when drawing a line. The very disciplines and necessities of the craft help you to control your emotional intelligence.

MWT: So that translates into style and technique in your writing. It would help explain the short sentences that are pregnant with further implication and meaning. And why you also like a narrative technique that allows a great deal to be unsaid, left implicit in the writing.

EH: Yes, I think it must do. And from the point of view of taste, you must write in the way you yourself approve of and like, which makes writers very often poor critics, because what they're looking for is what suits them. They're also ready to pinch whatever it is they see!

MWT: That reminds me of what W. H. Auden wrote in his essay on 'Reading': 'The critical opinions of a writer should always be taken with a large grain of salt. For the most part they are manifestations of his debate with himself, as to what he should do next and what he should avoid.' So what, then, are we to make of your own writing about writers? Take, for example, 'Under the Yoke', the essay on Kate Roberts's great novel *Traed Mewn Cyffion* (Feet in Chains). I've always felt that to be a very interesting essay not just about her but about yourself. It is so in two ways, it seems to me. On the one hand, it unconsciously identifies for us a similarity between her writing and yours, as when, for instance you write: 'Time itself, Welsh time, is of the essence in her novels.' The phrase 'Welsh time' is a marvellously apt one for the historical world we enter in so many of your own novels.

EH: I am certainly very much drawn to what appears to me to be distinctive about the Welsh past, because it is such a marvellous encapsulation of the human condition. And I think she felt the same. She had the extraordinary gift of being able to funnel an entire way of life into the small compass of a short story.

MWT: Yes, and in 'Under the Yoke' you persuasively suggest that even her novel, *Traed Mewn Cyffion*, could be read as a collection of short stories. But the same could be said, too, about such novels of yours as *Outside the House of Baal*, or the seven works in the 'Land of the Living' sequence. You, too, like to build novels by adding together short pieces of narrative.

EH: Yes, because the more amorphous and ungraspable the overall pattern is, the more important it is to have strength in each individual constituent unit. So that when they're all put together the whole is more than the sum of the parts. In some ways this works in a manner not unlike that of certain kinds of abstract painting, where you have the juxtaposition of different kinds of items producing a multi-perspective design and image.

MWT: So, in these respects we've so far been considering, you could be said, in 'Under the Yoke', to be recognizing yourself in Kate Roberts. But there's also a sense in which you see a mirror image – the very reverse – of yourself as fiction writer in her work. For instance, you say that what you admire about her is that 'she belongs to that select category of artists whose work emerges from a given landscape with the numinous power of a megalith'. Your relationship to your landscape is surely very different from that, even perhaps the opposite of it, because you've always felt uneasily, and ambivalently, related to Welsh Wales, as a writer who is not of it in the sense of having been produced by it, and therefore not organically part of it, and yet still wanting to recognize it and commemorate it.

EH: That is absolutely right. I feel a profound envy that she has this insider knowledge of what she's writing about, and which I can only have to a certain extent. It's not that I haven't got it, perhaps, but that I'm using English to write about a way of life that is inseparable from the Welsh language. English has shapes and constraints within which you have to work, and that is partly why I try to reduce my language to a minimum; by being minimalist I try to minimize the distortion involved in this kind of cultural 'translation'. So I try to turn the weakness into a strength, using this kind of stripped-down English in an effort to capture the quintessence, as opposed to the general texture, of the Welsh life with which I am dealing. So, too, the small scenes are attempts at recording epiphanies, moments of heightened insight into this world which is foreign to English. Again, though, it's not an entirely rational process, since it's intuition that tells you where something essential can be found.

MWT: There's another interesting relationship between Kate Roberts and yourself that occurs to me. There are those who would say that both you and she are, broadly speaking, realist novelists, but that there is a significant difference between you in that you are separated from her by a whole generation. The realist mode, such critics might go on to say, was a viable one for Kate Roberts, since she was born in the late nineteenth century when realism could still seem to be an appropriate style of representation for a society that believed in permanent fundamental realities. Realism is a style of writing that is itself underwritten by a confidence in one's capacity to understand the world and to represent it. But this kind of confidence is not, and cannot be, available to twentieth-century writers, so that your practice of realism would then seem to be belated, inadvisable and inauthentic.

EH: But I'm not sure that I am all that much of a realist. And my novels vary considerably in respect of the techniques I employ. The two basic ways of telling a story, for me, are either the first-person narrative or the third-person narrative; and the way you combine these two ways of proceeding determines the kind of fiction you produce. I'm not interested in fantasy at all – life itself is to me so remarkable that it doesn't need any fantasies. Or so it seems to me. Which may, of course, mean I don't have very much imagination, or rather that the only kind of imagination I've got is quotidian and pedestrian, so that flights of fancy are not an option available to me.

MWT: What, then, is the difference, in your own experience as a writer, between adopting a first-person and a third-person point of view?

EH: It is an absolutely vital difference. When writing in the first person there are clear limitations and parameters. As for writing in the third person, I find it's essential to avoid any appearance of omniscience, so that the structure of the narrative is then as objective as you can make it. In an extreme instance, you would record only what you can see and what you can hear. That is close to my understanding of what realism is.

MWT: So the same self-denying ordinance applies irrespective of whether you're writing 'in character' or not. You deny yourself, and of course your reader, the privilege of omniscience. Why do you do that?

EH: The convention of omniscience came to an end about 1914; it is no longer a viable mode of operating. One of the impulses to story-telling is an awareness of the mystery of human life; and the writer is attempting always to catch and convey a glimpse of that mystery. The convention of omniscience would be far too limiting, because I cannot persuade the reader to believe that I have the kind of complete knowledge and understanding that is implied by it.

MWT: This was already part of your writing creed as early as 1953, when you wrote as follows in 'A Protestant View of the Novel': 'Every situation is not merely an event to be described, or even to be carefully and honestly interpreted: at the heart of each significant situation there is a mystery – like the universe in the grain of sand – which the artist must touch or at least approach: and the mark of his power will be a glow and a flourish about his work that indicates the sureness of his aim.' How important a statement of your practising belief as a novelist does that essay now seem to you to be?

EH: I think it's a very dated document – it is, after all, fifty years since I wrote it. I think on the whole I would stand by a lot of it, but the one thing I would change is the word 'protestant'. I would like to change that to the word 'protesting' – or adopt the much later expression 'a dissident novelist'.

MWT: So in exchanging the one term for the other what exactly are you doing? Is it the case of being unhappy with the specifically religious associations of the word 'protestant'?

EH: Yes. At that time there was much talk of the Catholic novelists, such as Evelyn Waugh and Graham Greene, and there was also a great post-war awareness of the French novelist Mauriac. So I was using the word 'protestant' in contradistinction to them. I wouldn't want that religious connotation any more, because such Catholic writers as Saunders Lewis and David Jones have been possibly more of an influence than any other writers on me. So the phrase 'protestant novelist' is not applicable any more, whereas the term 'dissident novelist' is, because the primary characteristic of serious writers during the twentieth century has been that of dissidence. You can't think of a great writer of that period that wasn't dissident, or an outsider – Brecht, Ezra Pound, even Eliot was an exile from St Louis living in London. Lawrence was a man who loved England so much he couldn't bear to live in it. And in the Welsh-language context these dissident writers are necessarily conservatives – fighting against the threat to the culture to which they belong. In that sense they are both dissidents and insiders, unlike the mainstream of dissident writers who are outsiders.

MWT: I wonder where your concept of the dissident derives from? I'm struck by the extent to which your mind was formed during the 1930s, a period when you had both the totalitarian systems of fascism and communism and also the reaction, here in Wales, by dissident writers like Saunders Lewis, against the centralized powers of an anglophone and anglocentric British state that was antipathetic to Welsh values.

EH: There's truth in that, but dissidence is not limited to the period and circumstances you describe. It has become a permanent condition. I look at the world, and see that the isolation and alienation of the artist is no less than it was in my youth. If anything, it's worse because the globalization of technology and mass communications drives the in-dividual vision to a permanent state of dissent. So it's as if there had been a geological change in the relation between the writer and any audience he might hope to have.

MWT: That's a theme that recurs in your major essays. But what interests me is the apparent paradox that such a radical critique of modern mass media should be produced by one who has worked in the media.

EH: As a storyteller, every fiction writer feels tempted by film, not least because working for film is far more profitable than writing a novel. I can remember at the very beginning of my career, after my second novel had been published, being taken out to dinner by an American film producer whose surname was Davis – the Americanized version of the Welsh Davies. He worked for Metro-Goldwyn-Mayer and he was entertaining young novelists to lunch because he was looking, money no object, for someone capable of providing a young star, by the name of Audrey Hepburn, with the appropriate vehicle for her talents. I was quite hurt by the fact that he wasn't the least bit interested in my fiction, but simply looking for a vehicle for an actress. But that just shows how the film industry works – and how innocent of that world I then was. Such a wooing of the writer continues down to the present time, and it often results in a Faustean bargain being struck between a novelist and the mass media. Hence my emphasis on the need to respect the dissident writer who tries not to enter into any such contract – at least, not on a permanent basis.

MWT: Yet the modern writer's relationship to the media is inescapably an ambivalent one?

EH: Absolutely. And of course I have myself worked for the media with some pleasure, particularly during the 1950s when I was able, as a BBC producer, to bring the work of writers such as Saunders Lewis and John Gwilym Jones into the mass media – if you can call it such, because by today's standards, where the mass media is of global extent, it was a pretty local affair. I also felt at that time, and later, that television could have been used, and could be used, much more effectively to protect Welsh culture. And that was an important aspect of the work I did for the BBC in Wales. I was once asked to move to London, which would have been a more profitable life, and in some ways a more interesting one. But given my family commitments, Wales was a much more suitable field for working in.

MWT: I take it, too, that you had – as perhaps every writer that is serious about his talents must have – a lingering hope that your work might, through its quality, help redeem the media in which you were working, or at least might temper its vulgarity?

EH: Yes, and it is an outlet that is still available. Indeed, the mass media itself depends on a steady infusion of original new talent to keep it going; otherwise it would atrophy, it would sink under its own dull weight. There has to be fresh new vision, and that's why writers like Dennis Potter and Ingmar Bergman and the writer of *Heimat* all made notable contributions to television.

MWT: In the context of your respect for the role of the dissident writer you have remarked more than once in your essays that in Wales there is a constant need for a sacrificial victim, who lives and dies in order to ensure the capacity for independent thinking. And as I understand it, the example *par excellence* for you of that is Saunders Lewis. Would you count yourself as being such a figure?

EH: No. I haven't got the courage that he had. And I haven't got the equipment that he had. His was a very, very rare capacity, because it falls between the ability to lead, which implies the ability to have a vision, and the strength of character to be courageous and to drive on in spite of all obstructions. I don't think that a timid storyteller has any of the qualifications for this kind of role. All he can do is make a celebration of the need for this kind of figure, and in the end – and it's a universal truth – this is why Christianity is such an attractive religion, because the necessity for a saviour is true and is true at all times and in all places.

MWT: So is this implicit in the title of your essay on Saunders Lewis, 'Outline of a Necessary Figure'?

EH: I wasn't quite thinking there of a sacrificial figure, which would be the Christ figure. Rather, a 'necessary figure' is one who has the courage and vision to lead at a certain given, and crucial, time in the life of a certain society. That is a limited, temporal concept, whereas the sacrificial figure is a universal one.

MWT: Yet when this kind of figure occurs in your fiction – I'm thinking of JT in *Outside the House of Baal*, or Val Gwyn in the early novels in 'The Land of the Living' – you hedge it about with reservations of a kind you certainly do not have about Saunders Lewis. For example, it's uncertain whether JT is a charismatic visionary or a narcissistic bigot; whether he's overflowing with redemptive generosity or whether he is, as his wife accuses him of being, deeply selfish. So how is it that in real life you're able to believe in such a figure, without qualification, whereas in your fiction it seems that you're questioning and cross-examining the very concept of such a figure?

EH: It's the difference between fiction and what might be called historical reality. I don't have many reservations about Lewis Valentine, or about D. J. Williams, or about my late father-in law who was one of those Nonconformist ministers who seemed to me to be absolute heroes throughout the twentieth century. But fiction deals with characters who have as many weaknesses as strengths. Moreover, whereas what you're saying about JT is absolutely true, I still find him an enormously sympathetic figure.

MWT: Since you've touched there on the complex matter of the way that fiction relates to historical reality, it seems appropriate here to try to understand the relationship between historical fiction, such as you've written, and history. You've written as follows in one of your essays: 'History, like everything else, is written from a point of view. In the nation-making process it is a vital industry. In the Welsh context, the historian inherits the function of the bards and the poetic tradition.' It is frequently said that the twentieth century was a remarkable century for Welsh historiography. How do you see yourself as a novelist in relation to that tradition?

EH: Well outside it. I am totally idiosyncratic. All I'm concerned with is finding the raw material for creating fiction, really. But I stand by the thesis of *The Taliesin Tradition*, because I can't see anything else that would justify the effort we make to perpetuate and renew our existence as a visible, recognizable, unique society.

MWT: *The Taliesin Tradition* is, I take it, a work that places writing at the centre of Welsh history, and sees Wales itself as being, in important respects, sustained by its writers and its writing over a period of almost 2000 years?

EH: Yes, and I think it's possible to make a good argument for that. You remember the famous story that Gildas has about the poets pouring their praise over the head of Maelgwn Gwynedd. It's a very potent image, because it's a situation that recurs throughout Welsh history – you can think of Gruffydd ap yr Ynad Coch's 'Marwnad Llywelyn', or even of the great translations of the Bible by William Morgan and John Davies Mallwyd. In all these instances, surviving and salvation are both aspects of the same thing, and the same thing happened in the nineteenth and twentieth centuries. The Methodist Revival was all about salvation, and words – poetic words – were central to that whole process. So in William Williams Pantycelyn you have the survivor and the salvationist and the poet all combined in one figure. So this seems part of the reason why there is still a Welsh identity – and in a way 'identity' is a better term than 'nation', because when you get down to what a nation consists of, and what institutions a nation needs, we fall apart. Even now, with the National Assembly, it is not 'national' in any great meaningful sense, because it hasn't got the law-giving powers that belong to a proper National Assembly, as found in Parliament, or Senate, or whatever. And also the sad fact is that now that there is this degree of autonomy and devolution, the poetic tradition has become just a decoration – a cherry on the icing on the cake. It's a masquerade rather than a meaningful transformation.

MWT: In *The Taliesin Tradition* your emphasis is on the way in which Welsh-language writers have perpetuated identity. Would you now recognize that in the twentieth century English-language writers also played their part in doing that?

EH: Only to a very minor degree. The concerns of the very talented 'Glamorgan School' were individualistic, iconoclastic and not really setting out to offer any kind of national expression. And where their writing had any kind of social impulse, it was on the side of communism, socialism and internationalism, which belonged very much to the 1920s and 1930s and which I would have thought are no longer relevant.

MWT: You talk of the 'Glamorgan School' of writers, but you could say there was also a 'Glamorgan School' of historians, with one of whom – Gwyn A. Williams – you enjoyed a friendship. How would you describe your version of history compared with his?

EH: The basic difference is that his is Marxist and mine is Christian – Christian in the sense of taking a Kierkegaardean, existentialist view of the human situation. But I had enormous respect for him, because he had a really penetrating analytical power, and he had an eloquence which, when it was fully disciplined, was brilliant. This oral tradition which he exemplified is, in a way, a feature of one kind of Welsh poetry. You see it manifested, too, in the great preachers of the nineteenth century, and Gwyn was a preacher, because as a university lecturer he had an audience and, like all the figures who belong to this Welsh tradition, he functioned best when he had an audience. But there is also another tradition in Welsh poetry, which is eloquent in quite a different way – it thrives on the minimum use of words, as instanced in the *englyn*. The one style is miles away from the other. I admire both these styles while not fully belonging to either.

MWT: You've mentioned that yours is a Kierkegaardean Christian view of human life, which I take it means that you place the responsibility to choose at the very centre of individual, and indeed social and national, existence. This, of course, was something on which Saunders Lewis insisted, as you note in 'Outline of a Necessary Figure.' You quote him as writing: 'A man is a responsible being, to this end he enjoys the freedom to choose.' That would seem to me to be a fundamental tenet of your writing, and to be at the very heart of your treatment of character and action in your novels.

EH: That is probably so. Saunders Lewis had another parallel statement – he was given to making large pronouncements: he would pause and ruminate, when you were having lunch or whatever, and would then come out with an incisive aphorism. It was the way his mind worked. 'Bod cymdeithasol yw dyn' is what he wrote in *Egwyddorion Cenedlaetholdeb* – man is a social being – and if he's responsible and he's social, then you are dealing with an existential situation that is the basis of all my novel-writing.

MWT: And this configuration recurs. Wherever I look in your fiction I see a binary structure, where a character is faced with a clear choice between two alternatives. Not infrequently, it involves someone choosing between two lovers, as Amy has to choose between Val Gwyn and Pen Lewis, and JT chooses between Kate and Lydia.

EH: That's true, now you mention it. It's a terrifying thing to say, but you go all through your life thinking you've written a variety of things, but in a way you've written the same thing, over and over again, although perhaps in different ways. But you don't realize this, of course; you're spared that knowledge.

MWT: Certainly this seems to me to be a constant pattern in your fiction, from its beginning to its end. It is one of those aspects of the structure of your fiction that I find particularly interesting. Another is encapsulated in one of the most suggestive, but enigmatic, comments you make in your essays: 'The structure of a novel can have an architectonic relationship to the truth.'

EH: Perhaps 'mimetic' might have been better than 'architectonic'. A work of fiction must relate to some truth by virtue not only of its content but also, and principally, of its shape – there must be a meaningful overall design to it, a kind of song running through it that ties it all together. Without that it is nothing. It's like listening to a song of life – you're hearing and playing a tune that awakens a response in the reader.

MWT: Is that why, when you deal with the past in your fiction, you positively advertise the fact that you have no intention of being literally faithful to any place or time? So, for instance, when you're dealing with a place that inference would strongly suggest lies on the coast of Llŷn at a spot similar to that of Cricieth or Pwllheli, you deliberately avoid giving that place the actual name of either of those towns, opting instead for the entirely fictional name of 'Pendraw'. The implication is that this place has a significant relationship to places like Cricieth and Pwllheli but must not be mistaken for them.

EH: It's like a parallel existence. Fiction is a possibility – it could be, but it isn't. The world of fiction always floats a few feet above the actual ground, and enjoys a climate and atmosphere all of its own. I heard someone quote Donne on the radio not long ago: 'what is poetry but the counterfeit of creation.' It's a wonderful phrase, and corresponds exactly to my understanding of what I have been involved with.

MWT: I also get the impression that for you the function of a historical novel is to disclose the past on terms very different from those that are known to, or recognized by, historians as 'history'.

EH: Yes, there's no authorized version. You scoop water at random from the river of time and suddenly find that it's turned solid. As I mention in 'Under the Yoke', this is the gift of Kate Roberts, and it's a terribly important part of the function of fiction.

protesting or overviolent [handwritten annotation]

A Protestant View of the Modern Novel

First published as 'The Protestant Novel', *The Listener* (2 April 1953), 557–9.

It would be as well for me to begin by saying what the title of this talk does not mean. I do not intend to survey the theology of modern novels or the beliefs of modern novelists as such. My concern is the expression of religious and moral problems in terms of technique; or, if this sounds too rarefied, how a novelist's attitude governs the way in which he writes; or, simpler still, how what the novelist has to say influences and conditions the way in which he says it. A useful alternative title would have been 'some problems of technique in the post-Joyce era of English fiction'. But this sounds too specialized and too pompous, since what I have to say should be of some interest to readers in general as well as to students of the contemporary novel.

Problems of form and expression

It is obvious that any distinction between what is said and how it is said, between matter and manner, between content and form, between meaning and style, is largely artificial. Without technique, without talent, an artist cannot be said to exist in the professional sense. However I wish to make use of this hypothetical distinction, but only as a scaffolding which can be knocked away as soon as the structure of my main argument is apparent. My reason for drawing attention to this distinction is, very simply, that the most gifted English novelist of our century chiefly concerned himself with problems of form and expression. Joyce belonged to that great stream of English Romantic writing which gushed forth with the publication of the *Lyrical Ballads* in 1798. In a recent book Sir Herbert Read has written about two aspects of this great literary movement: the cult of sincerity, and the urge to extend the general range of human consciousness, both giving the Romantic writer a sense of mission and an urge towards something resembling prophecy. Joyce was a 'late romantic' writer whose sense of mission derived from his passionate desire to preserve and keep fit for artistic purposes a language that was being rapidly debased by the vulgarizing processes of a blatantly commercial age; from an urge to hew and hammer out of the confusion of his age a work of fiction elevated to the stature of 'giant-art'. Like the great poets who were his contemporaries, T. S. Eliot, Ezra Pound and David Jones, he strove to save the lines of communication, to purify the signs and the signals, so that the honest artist could continue to communicate a valid experience of living to the honest, fastidiously honest, reader.

It is salutary to consider what might have happened to the English novel without *Ulysses* and *Finnegans Wake*: for not only are these gigantic works of art in themselves, but also they have dammed up for ever the yawning gap through which a flood of meretricious literary kitchen waste might easily have poured, to bury the tender communication line that must always bind the present moment to the whole living body of English prose. It is not too soon to say that Joyce saved us from being smothered in the spurious: without Joyce (without Eliot and Pound) the atmosphere of English literature today would be that of the bar of a suburban golf club. Honest, serious, sensitive communication would have become practically impossible. Every novelist of any consequence writing since 1922 has benefited from Joyce, in every aspect of his craft: in language, method, presentation, in the entire scope of novel composition. To novelists learning their craft at any time during the past twenty-five years this figure towered above everyone else – too big, too unique to imitate, too disturbing, too great to ignore.

Before his death, Joyce had already become a thesis industry in the United States; and in Britain, novelists whom Henry James had picked as future winners in 1912 never became anything more than Nissen huts at the gates of the Joycean park. It was also natural in a climate of literary experiment that small talents should disport themselves with gay abandon in rabbit warrens of obscurity. Bloomsbury, too, gave its solemn benediction to a sort of pure mathematics of aesthetical experimentation, which especially blessed the 'fragments of a work in progress' or 'chapters of an unfinished novel'. There was a general conviction that in technique, as in everything else, it was better to travel hopefully than to arrive. While it is true that in our era – the post-Joyce era of the novel's development – every serious novelist is presented with acute problems of form and technique which he must solve in his own way, today it is futile and unhealthy to go on doodling with formal experiment in the hope that if one doodles assiduously enough one will eventually stumble upon something worth saying.

Joyce, then, was as much a writer with a mission as any nineteenth-century giant, but his mission was with language and form, the means of expression. He was a high priest of language, perhaps a prophet *manqué*; never an Englishman, no longer an Irishman, nor even a cosmopolitan, but a voluntary exile, dedicating his entire life to the ritual of a shrine which was his own genius.

If only to free himself from the tyranny of Joyce, the contemporary novelist gropes for the limitations of the benefit it is possible for his generation to derive from this mighty source. The first limitation arises from the fact that Joyce's romanticism was confined to problems of expression; unlike the intense concern that the romantic artist of the nineteenth century displayed for the progress and well-being of the human race, Joyce's attitude to the human situation was in many ways strangely detached. Having torn himself away from Ireland and her troubles, from the Roman Church and her authority, all western Europe became his laboratory. In this sense, his attitude to humanity in general was strictly empirical, or 'scientific' in the popular sense of the word. He divided the human race into two categories, the first consisting of himself, the second everybody else. The first, the artist, the second, the raw material of his masterpieces – that twentieth-century phenomenon, the man in the street, chiefly embodied in the robust and elephantine figures of Leopold Bloom and H. C. Earwicker. Category one, the artist, exists in order to create a work of art; category two, to live as greedily as possible the daily round, the commonplaces of the city-dwelling human race, drawing towards it in its diurnal course, by a kind of gravitational pull, 'the uncreated consciousness of the race'.

Joyce's attitude to life

For Joyce, being the man he was in his time and place in history, this attitude may have been strictly necessary and perfectly suited his purpose. This attitude of Joyce to the human situation was extraordinarily detached: detailed data, carefully accumulated and assembled by the scrupulously impartial sleepless observer. Joyce's attitude to life around him was what some philosophers would call an 'I-it' relationship: cool, unshockable detachment was all. Such an attitude, apart from attaching more significance to moment-by-moment sensation than I am prepared to accept, for reasons perhaps too devious to pursue in detail at this juncture, presupposes for the writer an independence and detachment (a variant of the Ivory Tower) of a kind that is no longer possible, or even altogether desirable.

For although the later works of James Joyce are still too 'modern' for far too many readers – and this is a disturbing and melancholy fact – history has already left James Joyce behind. Before reaching a reasonably wide public, he has become what ex-President Truman (as prototypical a man-in-the-street in some ways as Earwicker or Bloom!) calls a pre-atomic-age man, as remote from us as Dante, or the anonymous cave artists of Altamira and Lascaux. Human existence has complicated and simplified itself many times over since Mr Bloom's eventful twenty-four hours in the Dublin of 1904. Joyce's *petit-bourgeois* heroes have been overwhelmed and the working classes of the world – the white, yellow and black masses – have become a key factor in the technique of political power: monstrously large, frighteningly gullible, defenceless as a jelly fish – the raw material of the dictator's or the advertiser's art.

As for the artist – category one – his predicament was never more uncomfortable. Not only the thorny problems of making a living and getting his work published beset him with unprecedented urgency; the conditions of our time are fiercely inimical to the practice of the arts. Art: the very word invokes derision, contempt, suspicion, impatience. Artistic detachment, of the kind Joyce achieved at no small cost to himself and his family, is no longer possible. The balcony overlooking the Mediterranean is closed, in need of repair; the patrons, like the nymphs, have departed, and the great Romantic illusion, freedom, is shrunk to a place for one in the queue. All around us wars, revolutions, persecutions, famine, witch-hunts, martyrdoms, crises, rumours, nameless fears, burn like bonfires along the hillside on a dark night.

Uncontemporary detachment

Furthermore this detachment, this 'I-it' relationship governing the writer's attitude to his raw material, has not only become difficult or impossible to maintain, it is not only an uncontemporary attitude, it is diametrically opposed to what could be called the central tradition of the European novel. The two greatest novelists of the nineteenth century, Tolstoy and Dostoevsky, had a concern for humanity of a kind which does not exist in Joyce. In some ways *Ulysses* has more in common with *The Natural History of Selborne* than with *The Brothers Karamazov* or *War and Peace*. Human life for them was not merely the raw material of art; it was a strange sea in which humanity thrashed about like a powerful, bewildered whale, harpooned by death, and still consumed with a desire for immortality. These greatest of novelists looked upon themselves and upon all mankind as souls thirsting equally for salvation. Their attitude to category B, the raw material of their art, was an 'I-Thou' relationship rather than the white-coated, rubber-gloved 'I-it' relationship of Professor Joyce pottering about in his human laboratory.

There is a second aspect of Joyce's attitude to the human situation which had an equally powerful effect on Joyce's technique. Eager to reject the facile progressivism of the nineteenth century, Joyce found a view of history which rejected the popular idea of progress and also provided him with the framework of his two great works. This view he found in *La Scienza Nuova* of Giambattista Vico (a little-known Italian philosopher of the eighteenth century). Vico had a cyclical concept of history which did not really admit the possibility of progress. There were three stages through which civilizations moved, and from stage three in a gigantic cyclical movement a society returned to stage one.

I am fully aware that the idea of progress today is very unfashionable among thinking people. But it is a strong element in Protestant Christianity; in fact Protestantism does not make full sense without it. Both individual and racial salvation are not concepts that can be lightly discarded – and, incidentally, I suspect that they are more closely connected than we are usually inclined to assume. A soul cannot make progress *in vacuo*: many men are better for the existence of one good man, and one good man is the product of some kind of progress that was both individual and social.

But it is not with this wider aspect of the idea of progress that I am concerned here. In the strictest technical sense, the novelist who limits himself to a cyclical concept of history (the vicous circle, as Joyce characteristically calls it) deprives himself of some of the main weapons in a story-teller's armoury. Cycles, like circles, do not have a beginning, middle and end; what then of tragedy, where a lifetime leads to a meaningful crisis of disaster? And what is to be the aesthetic significance of death? Indeed, it is difficult to conceive of any dramatic work within Vico's limits. Joyce made no serious use of plot. But plots are far more than pieces of machinery. A plot not only presents the independently living characters of a novel with situations in which they are forced to act, to make a choice, to consider right and wrong, human destiny, their own destiny and salvation; it also reflects the author's understanding of some aspect of his experience of life in which he has been able to catch at least a glimpse of meaning, if not a vision of the will of God.

Neither plot nor any form of commentary, direct or indirect, held much positive interest for Joyce. Indeed, his objection to the use of plot and comment was fundamental to the idea of his art. He deliberately ruled them out. We, with equal deliberation, should rule them in. To put the problem in another way – making use I hope for the last time of the hypothetical distinction between how an artist expresses himself and what he has to express – whereas in Joyce's day how the artist spoke was rather more crucial than what he had to say, by today the difficulty of having something important, vital, to say has become greater than the problem of expression. In our time, the novelist's attitude is more crucial than his manner of expression.

To survive the almost unbearable complexities of his predicament, the novelist must somehow arrive at a balance within himself. If he wishes to establish communication on a serious level today, he must arrive at a positive attitude to the human situation before he can begin to say anything worth communicating. He cannot continue for ever to indulge himself in the quiet sport of technical experimentation, or continue for ever to produce sensitive, nostalgic accounts of the delights of his shining or shadowed childhood.

The artist today needs to exert his intelligence over a wider range than even the most serious Victorians found necessary. Somehow or other he must come to terms with science, and the fantastic powers that science has thrust into man's unsteady hand; with the revolutions our society has undergone and is undergoing. Unless he is graced with the dizzy somnambulism that can ignore it all, he must accept this predicament as a direct and personal challenge to himself. To meet this challenge, the writer's attitude to life, his positive attitude to the human situation, must be grounded on a faith which his reason, his conscience and his experience can accept and serve. It is always true that a novelist's attitude lends its particular significance to his work, and I do not doubt that the serious novel of this mid-twentieth century will be the novelist's response to the challenge he has to meet. But today the novelist needs his faith as a blind man needs his stick. It may be no more than a quiet, persistent, tough humility, but it is a fundamental condition of useful survival. Without it, the novelist is in constant danger of being hamstrung by his own hesitations, his over-cultivated sensitivity, or of having his talents trampled upon by wills stronger than his own.

It is no accident that so much of the writing that has stood the stress of the past thirty years has been the work of Catholic writers. Their religion has given them a firm attitude, a still centre in a turning world. In the case of François Mauriac or Graham Greene, the novel reader feels assured that in questions of behaviour, of good and evil, right and wrong, these writers are able to refer to the unquestioned spiritual authority of the Church whose more or less obedient sons they are. In the last resort, they know where they stand; they know what to accept and what to reject.

But in this they are different from the great mass of readers with whom they communicate. One of the outstanding characteristics of our time is that people in general, and intelligent people in particular, do not know where they stand. The more optimistic cling to what they choose to describe as 'an open mind'; the rest, in the Gallup pollster's phrase, 'don't know'. And how much of the so-called post-war return to religion is more than a search for a more reliable insurance policy that might even cover the hazards of drifting rudderless on a great sea that leads to no certain harbour except death?

Protestant zeal

Protestantism more than any other single force is responsible for the condition civilization finds itself in today. It was our forefathers, having rejected the authority of Rome and the cosmology of the Middle Ages, who embraced a reformed Christianity, a dynamic and romantic force, which laid the foundations of this new world which we go on blindly building. In every aspect of human life the spirit of Protestant zeal entered – commerce, industry, science, philosophy, art – to transform the face of the entire civilized world. The Renaissance and the Reformation are great upheavals in world history that are still active, still working, still progressing, and all of us feel the compulsion to go on, to move forward, even though we no longer know where we are going or why. Few even feel the need to swim against the tide, and if they do it is not surprising how soon they give up trying. It is not merely that we are loath to part with the ease and creature comforts that humanistic science continues to shower upon us; the Protestant Reformer cracked the safe we call the New Testament, and like the spirits of Pandora's box the terrible ideas of justice, brotherhood, equality, love, freedom, service, have infected the whole of mankind and perhaps driven them mad.

The novel is, as it were, a by-product of this same Protestant dynamic. Bunyan, Defoe, Fielding and Richardson were militant Protestants. And, indeed, but for two or three comparatively recent converts, it would be a difficult business to discover a Catholic novelist of any importance writing in English.

Religion got us into the mess we are in and therefore religion should get us out of it. There is truth in such a crude, illogical statement. Every respectable literary critic of our time talks about revitalizing the myth, about the return to reinforced ritual and the subordination of reason and morality to an organic faith. But religions are not bought ready made; they cannot even be taught. Cheerful logic-chopping about the rival claims of Canterbury and Rome or cosy common-room sophistry on the Virgin Birth will not get anyone very far. Religion must embrace what is true in science, because no religion worth the name should be afraid of truth. Religion cannot ignore science on the so-called spiritual plane any more than science can ignore religion on the material.

The intellectual world of our time has been brave and bold enough to declare that it will not accept anything which cannot be demonstrated by experiment to be true: but if this intellectual world has no experience of God, what can it experiment with? It is not by deserting the Protestant principle of personal responsibility that our way of living will recover any degree of stability and meaning. This is something to cling to. It is absolutely right that the writer should be unwilling to become responsible to the state, monolithic or welfare, to the social revolution or to the Ministry of Information, or even to the vested interests of any institution, secular or ecclesiastical; but it is absolutely wrong that he should reject all responsibility. Since Keats and Shelley the demand for absolute freedom has been an obvious weakness in the Romantic writer's position.

Personal responsibility is a Protestant principle – one of the few Protestant principles that still retains its pristine force and power. The great Welsh writer, Morgan Llwyd (a Nonconformist of the most extreme persuasion), described man's conscience as the book in which it pleases God to inscribe his will. Often, in the recent past, the artist has shied away from the crude strength of the Protestant conscience – that constant, hoarse, dynamic whisper. But it possesses an exciting paradoxical combination of simplicity and complexity: an awareness of the great mystery, the infinite unconditional nature of God, and the egocentric solitude and sin of man in his trap of time.

Personal responsibility, conscience, a humble respect for experimental truth – these are aspects of the Protestant principle a novelist in our time should hasten to cherish. But there belongs to the Protestant principle yet another advantage. It belongs to the prophetic rather than the priestly tradition, and professionally the novelist has more to learn, more to gain from the prophet than the priest. A prophet is a prophet because his God has seen fit to give him some key to the insuperable difficulties in which humanity chooses to lock itself from time to time. It is part of the prophetic power to grapple with a contemporary situation and so read in it a meaning which others will learn to regard as some aspect of the will of God.

But what has a prophet to do with plots? It is a paradox of the prophetic view of history that no two identical situations can be found and yet history continues to unfold the one ageless mystery, the relationship between an unconditional, infinite creator, and finite, conditional, created yet aspiring mankind. There is nothing new under the sun, and yet every moment of living must be something unique – the conflict of Parmenides and Heraclitus resolved in the Christian synthesis – so that, in this view, free will and predestination are not so mutually exclusive as the schools have made them. Every situation is not merely an event to be described, or even to be carefully and honestly interpreted: at the heart of each significant situation there is a mystery – like the universe in the grain of sand – which the artist must touch or at least approach, and the mark of his power will be a glow and a flourish about his work that indicate the sureness of his aim.

All art is a transmutation of significant experience. The novel demands an experience which is not confined to the novelist's own living; by means of empathy he must extend his range to include others on the same level as himself. This approach must grow from a love of humanity. This is the only attitude to living that will bring back some kind of music to the tired, overworked vocabulary he picks up like cigarette stubs floating in the gutter, and revitalize the jaded forms of an art always contending with the greed of commerce: a love that refuses to dry up, that begins with the Creation and yearns for the Creator; a conscience that refuses to be muffled; a pursuit of vision to the point of death.

The kind of novelist whom I have called Protestant is required to love the human race at a time when it was never more difficult to love, when it has lost both the guileless spontaneity of the savage and the primitive and the gaieties and sophistication of upper-class culture, and has gained nothing that cannot be obtained in a tin. The New Testament founded the idea of Christian progress on faith, hope and love; and these are the weapons the aspiring novelist needs not only to save his art but also to work out his own salvation.

Under the Yoke

First published in *The New Welsh Review* 3 (Winter 1988), 9–13.

Kate Roberts belongs to that select category of artists whose work emerges from a given landscape and society with the numinous power of a megalith or a stone circle. This is a status not easily achieved. It requires a combination of servitude and revolt which reflects the relationship between the artist and her society. In retrospect, it is the product of a lifelong struggle and a lifelong commitment: the unceasing urge to be both a free artist and a responsible member of a society under siege from hostile historical forces. Kate Roberts is not four years dead but her work has long taken on that unique quality of time-filled timelessness that is the hallmark of the epic in literature. Her achievement is the capacity to dominate the continuing consciousness of her tribe. Wales is still well supplied with men and women of all ages who knew her. She was a forceful character who lived to a great age, and, as one would expect, there are many anecdotes in circulation which testify to a range of qualities from heroic independence to colourful eccentricities. She had a sharp tongue and an incapacity to suffer fools gladly. She was sensitive and thin-skinned and yet enjoyed a robust sense of humour. In the National Library at Aberystwyth there is a great hoard of her letters which will reveal fresh and exciting dimensions to her life story. Nevertheless her greatness resides in her stubborn ability to cherish and develop her unique gift as a storyteller. And it is at this point that the difficulty of dealing with this aspect of her genius in any language other than Welsh begins.

Every literate person is aware of the impossibility of translating poetry. In prose the obstacles are less obvious. Anglo-American English as a world language has always to resist the temptation of exercising an imperial *droit de seigneur*, of plundering the treasures of lesser languages merely in order to enrich itself. I make this somewhat obvious proviso before attempting to put into English a few observations of my own on Kate Roberts's first novel, *Traed Mewn Cyffion*, that were published some twenty years ago.*

* In Bobi Jones (ed.), *Kate Roberts: Cyfrol Deyrnged* (Gwasg Gee, 1969); what follows here is a review, not a translation, of the article. *Traed Mewn Cyffion* (Under the Yoke)

Significantly the opening scene of *Traed Mewn Cyffion* is set in the 1880s. A young woman attends an open-air preaching festival on a mountainside in Caernarfonshire on a hot Sunday in June. It ends during the Great War when this same woman hears that one of her sons has been killed. On the surface the novel would appear to be in the mould of the 'three generations sagas' of popular fiction. But because of the special nature of Kate Roberts's gift and her response to the crisis in the life of her community and the wider upheavals of her time, the novel takes on several of the features of an epic in the classical sense. For example, although her style is bare and her prose is deliberately unadorned, there is throughout the work a note of intensity, a quality of song, that echoes the timeless celebration of tribal and social qualities characteristic of epic poets from Homer to the Hengerdd. Almost in spite of the modern critical mode there is an underlying current of praise poetry. With all their faults and shortcomings these are her people to whom she is tied by indissoluble bonds of attachment.

In the third chapter the grandmother sitting by the fire 'in that expectant attitude of old people, an attitude of expecting nothing' tosses some dried cow dung on the fire and pokes it so that a flame breaks through. She launches into an account of her origin while the younger women take tea. It is here that Kate Roberts exploits the electric current that can pass between the speech of an unlettered peasant woman and the traditional virtues of the literary language – precisely the poetic quality that eludes even the most skilled translator because the distinctive character of one language can rarely reproduce the exact genius of another. 'I came from Llŷn to begin with, you know. But I can barely remember living there. I was four when I came to these parts. But when I was a young girl I went back there one end of season when I was confused in my place of work . . .' The old woman's speech is loaded with that unintentioned folk-poetry that emerges when speech and experience are as close as fruit and flower. The very limitations of the experience enrich the forms of expression which then pass into everyday usage that is a social adhesive as much as a mode of communication.

Through this unique medium the Past speaks of more primitive times before the quarries were opened and a new industrial society sprang up on the hillsides between the mountains and the sea. The people settled in a time-honoured landscape already rich with myths and history. The old woman seems to speak like Nestor of times past and ancient

was first published by Gwasg Aberystwyth in 1936, and translated as *Feet in Chains* by Idwal Walters and John Idris Jones (Cardiff: John Jones, 1977).

sufferings before the heroes came to Ithaca. 'And there was there in those days hardly a house worth calling a house . . . only four walls and a thatched roof was a house then, a peat fire on the floor, two wainscot beds back to back and their heads towards the kitchen floor. With a corpse in the house you had to sleep in the same place as the coffin. Dear me, how things have changed. Now everyone has two fine chambers . . .' The confident instinct of an artist places this episode third in a series of twenty five; a homage to ancestors before moving forward to the birth of the heroine's first child.

The heroine of the epic is Jane Griffith who marries Ifan the son of Y Fawnog. At the beginning of the second chapter we are given the clash between Jane and her unsympathetic mother-in-law. Jane belongs to the category of reluctant heroes unaggressive without a thirst for battle and yet exercising in preparation for the inevitable encounter. Her life as a married woman and mother will be a pitiless warfare against poverty, against a stubborn intractable soil, against illness and misfortune, against fate, against oppression and historical necessity. However humble her circumstances, her spirited response to the daily struggle of keeping house, maintaining a smallholding and rearing a family endows her with the attributes of well-born lineage. She presides over the round table of her kitchen with as much authority as Arthur at his Round Table. Moreover, her life story is governed by a code of honour and a simple morality which is reminiscent of heroic epic form. The honour of the family and the basic virtues must always come first: honesty, truthfulness, good faith, loyalty, charity and the range of virtues which characterize the good neighbour in traditional societies.

A further parallel with medieval Arthurian romance can be discerned in the concept that a flaw is present in the royal line of descent. As Efnisien to Bendigeidfran or Mordred to Arthur, there is a role in this humble epic for the member of a close family circle that cannot be relied on. This part is taken by Sioned Griffith, the mother-in-law. Her weakness is an innate selfishness that allows her at crucial moments to place personal whim and caprice above the well-being of the family as a whole. This weakness appears in the next generation in another Sioned, Jane's daughter, who takes after her grandmother in more than name. At the precise historical juncture when the restrictions of a chapel-governed theocracy are beginning to slacken, it is Sioned who is the first to break away from the round table, the first to be lured by the new fashions of the big town. Her brothers on the other hand are exemplary knights of the round table, constant and reliable and as conscious of their responsibilities as though they had taken solemn oaths. William struggles to establish a trade union among the workers and is constantly engaged in defending the weak and fighting oppression. Owen and Twm are committed to similar 'high ideals'. It is their fate to seek out the Holy Grail of pre-war Wales, namely higher education. The pursuit takes them through the wilderness and dark forests of a foreign education system. There is a friendly character at hand to make the appropriate comment at the school speech day. Ann Ifans sitting alongside Jane at the school speech day gazes in awe at the members of staff in their gowns and murmurs in a way reminiscent of a fragment of extempore verse, 'Da y gŵyr Duw i bwy i roi BA' ('God knows to whom to give the BA'). Owen almost chokes with laughter at the comments of the monoglot Ann Ifans, but there remains a gnomic element in her utterances which foretells the impact English education will make on the theocratic foundation of their way of life in the slate-quarrying district. The novel tells us that this way of life is barely a hundred years old and yet by some mystical process has taken on traditional aspects that seem as old as the mountain itself.

It is, of course, always possible to pursue speculative comparisons so far as to obscure the more modern virtues of the work, the objective and analytical examination of human nature that accompanies the artist's effort to uncover meaning through moulding form. For example, we are shown that a passionate self-respect is central to the character of Jane Griffith. This verges on arrogant pride yet it is kept within bounds by an equal and opposite passion for the well-being of her family. A similar pride in her daughter Sioned has no such restraint. We see her frivolity meet its just deserts in a marriage to the dandy shop assistant Bertie. The author wishes the reader to accept the verdict that the mountain community passes on this light-headed creature. He becomes a convenient symbol of all the shortcomings of the cities of the plain as viewed from the stern moral viewpoint of the mountain people: the shiftiness of the man who cannot be depended upon because of the soft lie that lurks in his soul.

When we say that opening a book by Kate Roberts is entering another world, history itself furnishes the platitude with a new meaning; a fascinating society that flourished in her lifetime in the quarrying districts of Arfon. Now it seems as far away as the age of the princes or even the Romans. The breath of life of that remarkable society continues in the characteristically unadorned style of this author. It is as if she possessed the magic power to recreate living substance in words, to make palpable the most minute details of existence, to exercise the magic power of scooping up water from the river of life and converting it into faceted artefacts. The very first paragraph which takes us with a physical immediacy into the open-air preaching meeting: perhaps the author intended no more than a lively picture of a young woman in an uncomfortably tight corset on a hot summer's day. The result is a portrait and a monument of a lost society. And since this society depended so much on its religious as well as its economic foundation we are obliged to look at yet another epic source of which the Non-conformist founding fathers were continuously conscious. In nineteenth century Wales the chapels with their Old Testament names were civic as well as religious centres, and biblical conflicts between prophets and priests were the stuff of popular gossip and press coverage. Kate Roberts's heroines and heroes are invariably on the side of the prophets and all inclined to lift up their eyes to the hills. When Jane's son Twm has finished composing a piece in the strict metres he turns to his brother and says: 'Let's take a turn to the top of the mountain . . . find the space to shake our feet.' Owen remembers his brother and remembers the excursion: 'The lapwing calling. The reflection of the moon in the peat-pools. The lamps of the town below like a necklace along the straits. The lights of Caergybi winking on the horizon and the summit of Snowdon a clear point in the light of the moon.'

One can hardly claim that human destiny remains the same in Old Testament Palestine or in classical Greece or in Gwynedd during very different epochs of human history, and certainly a twentieth-century Welsh novel is a different medium and measure from Greek or Hebrew poetry. Nevertheless there are sufficient correspondences to deepen our appreciation of Kate Roberts's gift. We cannot claim for her experimental originality, and in most respects her work stands outside the main stream of that modernity which generally characterizes the art of this century. She does, however, possess two instruments which enable her to handle her material in a manner which secures for it the most enduring attributes of modernity. The first is her mastery of the short-story form. Through the English translations of Chekhov and the work of Katherine Mansfield she quickly found her way to a short-story form that was poetic in essence; that flash of light which momentarily illuminates the mists of falsehood and misunderstanding which encompass individuals and their circumstance and is capable of revelation without melodrama, truth without banality and demonstration without assertion. A superficial view of *Traed Mewn Cyffion* might see the novel as a series of twenty-five short stories about the same family at different stages in its history. The second 'instrument' which provides a more significant pattern to the novel is a profoundly feminine understanding of the nature of Time. Because of her peculiar awareness of the passage of the seasons, of the characteristic rhythms of daily life in a given era, it would not be unreasonable to claim that Time itself, Welsh Time, was the chief character in the novel.

The wisdom of hindsight comes easily to us all. Nothing is easier than picking out the shortcomings of our immediate predecessors. The Age of Lloyd George, the years in which he dominated Welsh life, seem to us an epoch blighted with pretentious and pathetic folly. The decay of Nonconformity fostered all its worst aspects. With the exception of dissidents like W. J. Gruffydd and Saunders Lewis, few critical and creative writers in the Welsh language were sufficiently aware of the crisis that had overtaken the civilization of the West. Something of the greatness of Kate Roberts and the importance of her fiction must be attributed to her instinctive understanding of what was going on in the wider world. It is true that she chose to look for the greater part of her material in a quarry which was closed in August 1914 and never reopened. But her approach to this material was objective, modern, almost to the point of being scientific. And yet she treats this material with a tenderness which a loving woman reserves for her memories or a sculptor for his preferred stone. The eye of the author is more than a camera. The details that are picked out always have a depth of significance that sets them in a meaningful relationship to the historical circumstances that surround them.

It is these very circumstances which eventually overwhelm the novel. The concluding pages become more summaries than scenes. The point of view moves from the mother to the son. He is more capable of understanding the catastrophic events that are shaking the foundations of their world. The mother's bewilderment and frustration breaks out briefly when she attacks the form-filling military pensions clerk with a clothes brush. And yet there is a sense in which so much foreshortening is appropriate and part of the essential honesty and integrity of the author. It is difficult for us towards the end of the century to appreciate the explosive nature of the impact of the Great War on the sedate and almost somnolent social order of our grandparents. It was as if a bomb had been thrown into the middle of a Sunday school treat. The world had suddenly gone mad. War machines became synchronized juggernauts that rolled across countries with an insatiable appetite for the lives of young men everywhere. There was no means of controlling these machines or of escaping from them. They seemed bent on creating chaos and confusion – disrupting human existence for ever. Long before the end everyone knew mankind had created a monstrous machine gone permanently out of control. What the end of this novel suggests by its very abruptness is the opening of a technological Pandora's box and an abiding longing for an escape route from the consequences.

It is also worth bearing in mind the author's personal circumstances at the time she was writing the book. In 1935 she and her husband, the printer Morris T. Williams, had moved from the Rhondda and invested all they had in purchasing a weekly paper and publishing house in Denbigh. Their intention was to provide the national movement with an effective voice. Their ambition was to create an independent Welsh view of the world and a platform for views that were still regarded as subversive and heretical. This in itself was a venture of heroic proportions. It is some measure of the woman's indomitable character that her venture succeeded and that she was able to create at the same time a sequence of outstanding works of fiction. She was always a conspicuous figure on the Welsh literary scene. Her work was widely appreciated and discussed during her lifetime. But there remains much more to discover. Her letters reflect a stormier existence than one would have imagined through knowing her in her later years. She was fully aware, for example, of the privileges, of the freedom and independence that education had brought her. She was the first woman of her family to earn her own living. Her rebellious spirit cherished her independence. At the same time she adored her family and even in old age felt guilty about the sacrifices her parents had made in order that she should get on. She disciplined her passionate nature in order to make a more effective contribution to the life and literature of her country. At a time when a good marriage was considered to be the summit of achievement for a woman, she delayed taking this step until reaching her thirty-ninth year and then married a man almost ten years younger than herself. Her letters during that period show how fully aware she was of the problems which confronted her. In the volume of *Eight Short Stories* published the year after her marriage in 1929 and dedicated to her husband there are three brilliant treatments of very different aspects of the problem of getting married: 'Y Golled' (The Loss), 'Rhwng Dau Damaid o Gyfleth' (Between Two Pieces of Treacle Toffee), and 'Dydd o Haf' (A Summer's Day). It is pleasant to reflect that so much more remains to be discovered.

Outline of a Necessary Figure

First published in Alun R. Jones and Gwyn Thomas (eds), *Presenting Saunders Lewis* (Cardiff: University of Wales Press, 1973), 6–13.

I

A narrow white face above a large steering wheel. Recognizable even in a squat car hurtling down an Aberystwyth street. There is a schoolgirl in the back enjoying the ride. And there he is. The necessary figure. The author of books that evoke a more exciting country slaps the steering wheel with his gloved hand. By force of personality he has made the old language a mystery you must struggle to decipher. If there is more to history than a catalogue of classroom defeats he is the one who offers an honourable future. And Welsh is the only true key to open the locked caves where the heroes sleep. The University of Wales doesn't believe this. But he does. That is why they turned him out. But he still exists. And always will. A narrow white face above a large steering wheel.

II

You have been struggling to read *Canlyn Arthur* (In the Steps of Arthur) using a dictionary. It has made you attend meetings and it has made history less confusing. Here at last is a picture of a possible Wales. A viable unit. Written as vigorously as a little Lenin but concerned not with power but with the vital life stream that it is the purpose of power to preserve or destroy. Fundamental stuff but not appreciated by left-wing friends. He's right and they are wrong but you are still slightly torn. You wander into a mass meeting by the back entrance and there he is, waiting in an ante-room, his arms folded, his head lowered and chin extended grimly. He has just been vomiting. He says so. He can't bear public meetings. You see at once he is doing it against his will. Duty. Conscience. Integrity. They exist. He has them. That is what makes him fold his arms so tightly. To prevent himself running away. Or keep down the revulsion. Does that mean he hates or merely dislikes the masses? The Welsh mass in particular singing hymns in an orgy of sentimentality, pointlessly and windily ardent; crafty and cowardly after cooling down.

You decided it is perhaps love after all and that this accounts for the stern measured words when he speaks, a diminutive figure on a distant platform. He is teaching not wooing. Are politicians meant to teach or to woo? No wooing here certainly and no purple patches. Extended reasoning. Flashes of caustic wit. The mass admires but only a small minority adores. He is a leader giving a lead but the path to follow looks ominously like the edge of a razor. Now you say wisely to yourself, 'if only he made a few concessions'. Especially to fashionable left-wing sentiment. A friendly reference to such popular figures as Joseph Stalin or Harold Laski. Then your friends might stop making those hurtful gibes about putting the clock back. A few concessions. He is startlingly intelligent but he doesn't know how to make them.

III

A war has been arranged. But it hasn't started. There are blackberries still on the brambles but the devil has spat on them and they are no longer fit to eat. The west is getting ready for winter. All afternoon in the damp wood he stalks game. Shots are fired but nothing gets killed. Then there is a farmhouse tea before a wood fire. The wind turns and the room fills with smoke. The news on the wireless is minimal and fatalistic. Rain falls at nightfall. Somewhere on the road home the car breaks down. It isn't far from Cwm Cuch and the thick woods that hid the mouth of Hell. This is the moment for the Prince from the Underworld to appear with a crying pack of trained white hounds with red-tipped ears! They could change places for a year or for the duration. The Prince of the Underworld could take over or cast a spell and preserve Wales from extinction during the coming Armageddon. There is nothing unrealistic about this. The Ministry of Information, Thomas Jones, CH, Ll.G., university principals, archbishops, miners' leaders, Mr Chamberlain and Mr Churchill have all in their different ways made it clear that Wales and Welshness are a bit of fancy dress to be put away in a bottom drawer until the serious business is over: along with Welsh broadcasting, the Eisteddfod, sweets, bananas, Sunday school trips, silk stockings and other non-essentials. Couldn't we all hibernate in a Hobbit-like underworld and reappear as fresh as paint when the war was all over? There isn't much point in passing on the bright suggestion. He is concerned with getting the car repaired. He is concerned with his wife at home worrying, and an article he has to write that night. And he knows what's coming. He knows all about war.

Late morning in the intense heat of an Italian army barracks serving as an overcrowded refugee camp. Everywhere there is a stink of displaced persons and stale soup. The man in the corridor still has a kid lying in a broken suitcase lined with filthy straw. The goat died. The mail has arrived. Several copies of *Y Faner* and a copy of Thomas Parry's *Hanes Llenyddiaeth Gymraeg* (A History of Welsh Literature). Outside the camp there are the marvels of the renaissance city. What does it matter whether or not you are Welsh in a place like this? You only need to see his name and you are fascinated by the same old nagging question. Is he seriously suggesting that no good will come of Welshmen unless they have their roots in Wales? All this business about roots is peasant language. Like these men from the Abruzzi impatient for their own soil, land mines or no land mines. Not everyone wants to go back. Not all places are worth going back to. In the long barrack room a party of one hundred Jews, who have somehow spirited themselves down the peninsula, have to be locked up for the night. They are determined to get to Palestine but the authorities don't want them to go. (Who are the Authorities? The Armies of the Occupying Powers. Words for a Cantata.) While you are privileged with a little solitude in your sweaty sleeping quarters in the administration block, you read successive numbers of *Cwrs y Byd* (World Affairs) far into the hot night and the Jews steal away through the high windows. They pass two *caribinieri* fast asleep and bribe their way through the locked gates. They have accomplices in the occupying armies and they are quickly poured towards Brindisi and into the Palestine pipeline. A white-haired Indian Army colonel is very cross, but nobody really seems to mind. There is too much else to worry about. They are off to reoccupy a land they lost more than a thousand years ago. Does he want to turn the Welsh into troublesome Jews? His sermons are always uncomfortable.

V

Why do so many exiles seem to end up in London? You are housed in the wrong end of Chelsea and you have given up sugar because of the Mister Cube campaign: rampant capitalism is trying to prise the dying Labour limpets out of the stone seats of power. The old order is flooding back on a tide of public appetite and the Nonconformity into which you have married would prefer rationing and fair shares for all. Somewhere an English vision has faded and it brings you as near as you will ever come to supporting socialism. All this has to be said to explain the odd fragments of lengthy letters, ungainly and fortunately unposted, unpublished, polemics against his 'Catholic' social and economic policies. As a bizarre intellectual exercise you try to reconcile left-wing reformism and practical Nonconformity and keep in touch with Bohemia as well. Not a bad world when the sun sets behind the black chimneys of the power station and the tugs hoot as they fuss up and down the broad river. Painters live here and work in a bizarre poverty undreamt of in bourgeois or peasant Wales: rooms without carpets, cups without saucers, men without please and thank you and women without inhibitions. Here comes a philosopher, heavy beads about his neck, hand in hand with a piano-playing Pole engaged in a lifelong search for the first Chinese pope. But traffic jams are slowly assembling in the streets again. Armies of cars advancing. The journey to a consumer's heaven has begun. Ration cards, those noble symbols of equality, are being burnt and the long shop windows are gasping with the first pyramids of mass production. The light of austerity is going out and in any case, as the person who is wiser than yourself assures you, London is no longer a place to bring up children. Not Welsh children anyway. All good roads lead back to Wales.

VI

With the excuse that all writers are communicators you find yourself working with the BBC. One of the charms of the position is that you are obliged not to interest yourself actively in politics. Henceforward all struggles must take place on the cultural front. You have a simple policy and it gets blessings all round: get new work out of Welsh writers in both languages; put European drama into Welsh; put the best Welsh dramatists into English and have nothing at all to do with Shakespeare. You guide your uncertain steps across the road to the University. In the library there is a fierce-looking bronze bust of our necessary figure and there he is, not far away, browsing among the foreign periodicals. Now he is not so much necessary as unavoidable. No programme for Welsh drama could avoid having this figure firmly in the centre. It is all so clear but should you conduct business in a series of flashes of intuition? Hardly. He has no idea who you are. The whole library ticks like an unexploded bomb. Any necessary figure is experienced in saying no. You belong to an organization now and perhaps he believes that alien organizations are the devil? You mumble ineffectively but outside the silent library he gives you a fair hearing. He folds his arms and lowers his head. He approves of your purpose and the job immediately becomes lighter and much more enjoyable.

VII

A canteen full of anecdotes . . . Images of actors. Hugh Griffith, in the most inconvenient studio in London, plays the leader of an Eastern European underground movement lying on a sofa, the microphone a few inches from his mouth, because he is recovering from a motor accident. The necessary author is present and he happily writes and plays the brief part of a messenger. Hugh is making a spectacular appearance in *The Waltz of the Toreadors*. He amazes us one evening by limping across the stage with a grown woman on his back and then he takes us out to a late supper where we are surrounded by glamour. Hugh bewilders the wine waiter and the necessary figure smokes the largest cigar you have ever seen. He has an electric effect on actors. They all want him to write plays for them – preferably in English. He is tempted. You are sure he is tempted. Late at night in the West End the Theatres stand like the kingdoms of the earth and the stars glitter in their expensive suits . . . Images of food. *Sole bonne femme* and *Muscadet*. An oasis of France in the Cardiff docks. Seagulls circle around rusting derricks. Elderly Welsh waitresses march in and out of the kitchen with varicose gaiety. They are anxious to please. So are the stockbrokers and the merchant adventurers inside their stiff collars and dark suits bulging into plans for profits and expansion. They want to pay him court over the brandy. What do they see in him? Daring of course. A potential pirate. Like Gwilym Breos he would climb to the top of the ladder and jump without giving a damn . . . Russians. Images of Russians. A delegation on tour under the auspices of the British-Soviet Friendship League. Squat, confident men in the Angel Hotel, Cardiff. More earnest than the businessmen. A very agreeable dinner. They are chiefly interested in heavy industry and peasant poetry. They are led by the secretary of the USSR Writers' Union who looks like Kruschev masquerading as a *bardd gwlad* (people's poet). Your necessary figure is in merry mood. He mentions Pasternak. There is an awkward silence followed by lengthy explanations. It turns out that Pasternak may be quite a lot better off than your necessary figure was when he was sacked from the Welsh University. You mention this to him and he is greatly amused. The Russians look suspicious. You decide not to explain. The meal progresses. The secretary of the USSR Writers' Union announces that he is about to recite Pushkin. He does so with great vigour, thumping the table and flinging his arms about. Your necessary figure pushes back his chair and announces he is about to recite Dafydd ap Gwilym. Respect all round. On the way home he is overtaken by a laughing fit. He recited the middle part of the poem twice over and nobody noticed.

VIII

It becomes acceptable to say that his plays lend themselves beautifully to television. There are many two-handed scenes, many passionate arguments finely constructed and the plots are compelling to the point of being melodramatic. They translate well and for a time they enjoy a vogue and they are televised in Germany, Belgium, Spain, Scandinavia. *Treason* goes particularly well in Germany. But there are legal difficulties. Names of living generals have to be changed. He admits to enjoying it all. With a sudden burst of patriotic zeal a muster of internationally famous Welsh actors agree to take part in a dual production, one in Welsh, one in English. But they are filming all over the place. One has to be in America, another can only work in the evenings. The dual production is transferred to radio. Everyone is marvellous and altruism triumphs. Over a fortnight in a dozen different studios at all hours of the day and night, *Brad* and *Treason* go piecemeal on tape. One lunch hour Emlyn Williams and Richard Burton propose we send a telegram which reads like a loyal address composed in basic Welsh. A further word will be sent inviting him up to a special performance. (It will be a preview of what a national theatre could do.) This goes astray. The special performance never materializes. You return with innumerable cans of tape. He is disappointed but wholly forgiving.

IX

It becomes acceptable to say that a failed politician has been trans-formed into a triumphant playwright or that the idealist who failed to

change the course of Welsh history is finding completeness and fulfil-
ment in Welsh literature. A comfortable doctrine. It fits with the image
of a mellow ageing, a man in his late sixties enjoying his due meed and
fair measure of success. The bomb has been defused. Moguls of the
corporations smile expansively, nod and tell each other how wise they
were to tell each other so. He looks forward to accepting an honour in the
near future from a University college fully Welsh in language and spirit.
There are other offers. In the land of fixers everything and everybody can
be fixed. And it's not just the honours system. But the phase is temporary. A very intelligent Irish actor-producer soon to become a millionaire goes pale one day at rehearsal and says 'so much violent integrity in
one bloody little man'.

X

He is a very private man. In a land where back-slapping and badinage
are tokens of manly cameraderie his dignity is often mistaken for aloofness. And he doesn't suffer from that common Welsh weakness, the
overwhelming desire to be agreeable. He is perfectly aware that the
Welsh nation has rejected his leadership. Even the party he founded
would prefer him to become a silent icon that it could bear up aloft
as it softly circumvents the narrow and dangerous path he would have
it travel. You remember his striking humility. Not the best qualification
for a national leader. A definite lack of Hitlerian hysteria or Lloyd George
capacity for rhetorical deception or even the common egomania of the
romantic artist. You are rehearsing *Esther* in the Temple of Peace. The
acoustics are awful but the sun is shining through the long windows.
Clifford, playing Mordecai, is wearing the first rose of the season in his
buttonhole and the national theatre in his heart. An English actor plays
Haman and wants to cut a speech he can't understand. In the second act
he is talking to Jewish Esther not knowing, of course, that she is Jewish.

> 'It is clear my lady, that you know nothing of subject races. A defeated
> people is paralysed with fear. They will go to their destruction like sheep.
> You can drown their homeland under water and like beggars in a gutter
> they'll whine their thanks for the trouble you are taking.'

'What's all this about drowning homelands?' He has a rich actorish
voice and gestures like aquatints of Edmund Kean. Your author is

leaning against a substantial pillar of the Temple. He gives a grim smile. 'You are lucky enough to be English', he says. 'Leave it out if you don't understand it.'

XI

He moves with unobtrusive skill out of all the niches and down from all the pedestals that are prepared for him. This is very necessary. To a people with overheated imaginations and low thresholds of pain it is always necessary to emphasize that art is not illusion. In an age manipulated by mass communicators truth often belongs to the single voice. Increasingly our intelligentsia is composed of servants in the pay of an alien state. It is not a situation which allows for great clarity of thought. In fact after so many years you have become convinced that every responsible office in Wales is held by a common type of native whose capacity for self-deception, whose delusions of grandeur, are only just contained by his even more powerful instincts of self-preservation. Imagine a collier and a socialist riding in a golden coach with the heir to the British throne, deluding himself into the belief that the staged event is his own Napoleonic coronation, his hour of glory the ultimate revelation of his life's purpose. In the Welsh atmosphere of sulky and shamefaced inertia such men select each other. Their careers often begin in a burst of undergraduate patriotic fervour but before they reach forty their tongues wag their mother tongue for wangling purposes only and their nationalism has shrunk to an after-dinner joke. They are professional embalmers surrounded by their supine monuments. There seems very little that they cannot prevent happening. For the third or fourth time in ten years they have managed to prevent the idea of a national theatre becoming a reality that could threaten their complacency. They have every possible source of finance and every large-scale organization firmly under their control. Their masterly inactivities win for them in London golden opinions and honours. Such nice men. And yet you hope they still tremble when one small foot stamps in Westbourne Road. A very necessary figure.

The Night of the Fire

First published in *Planet* 49/50 (January 1980).

I

In the small hours of Tuesday, 8 September in the year 1936 three men wearing hats and raincoats sat in a car parked in a farm lane a few miles from Pwllheli. Two were smoking cigarettes and all three were staring anxiously towards the south-west. There was a stiff wind blowing and a threat of rain. To pass the time they were discussing a short story the bespectacled non-smoker was trying to finish. The title was appropriate enough. *Dros y Bryniau Tywyll Niwlog* (Over the Gloomy Hills of Darkness) – that is the opening line from one of the better-known hymns of William Williams Pantycelyn. The short-story writer had also cut a finger. It had been carefully bandaged by a doctor friend earlier in the evening and he was playing with it as he peered through the windscreen like a man waiting for a signal. At last the signal came. A red glow in the night sky that grew even as they watched. The man at the wheel finished his cigarette.

'We shan't need to put on the lights. The fire will see us all the way to Pwllheli.'

The car drew up outside the police station at half past two in the morning. The three men asked the yawning constable on duty whether they could speak to the Superintendent. He showed some reluctance to comply with their request until one of the men told him that Penyberth was on fire. Penyberth was the name of the fifteenth-century farmhouse which had been demolished recently to make way for the first buildings of a bombing range in the course of construction for the use of the Air Force. When an Inspector of Police finally appeared, they handed him a letter and asked him to read it. In the subsequent trial this Welsh declaration appeared as Exhibit Number Seven with this translation attached to it.

September 7, 1936
To the Chief Constable at Caernarfon.

Sir,
We, the undersigned, acknowledge our responsibility for the damage inflicted this night, September 7, on the buildings at the Bombing Camp at Penyberth.

From the moment the intention of creating this Bombing Centre in Llŷn was made public, we along with a host of other figures prominent in all aspects of Welsh public life did everything we could to persuade the English government to refrain from establishing in this most conspicuously Welsh homeland an alien institution that would inevitably damage and ultimately destroy its venerable culture and way of life. However, in spite of all our appeals, in spite of humble petitions and protest meetings, in spite of lengthy arguments and letters from hundreds of organisations both religious and secular, and in spite of a petition signed by thousands of electors in Llŷn itself, the English government refused so much as to receive a deputation from Wales to discuss the matter. All this effort conducted in a diligently peaceful manner within the law failed to gain for Wales even a show of common courtesy from the English Government.

Therefore, in order to compel attention to this immoral attack on the well-founded natural rights of the Welsh nation, we have been obliged to resort to this act as the only method left to us by a government that has treated our nation with insulting contempt.

We remain yours in the bonds of Wales,

Saunders Lewis
Lecturer in the University of Wales,
9, St Peter's Road,
Newton,
Mumbles, Swansea.

Lewis E. Valentine
Minister of the Gospel,
'Croeso', St Andrews Place,
Llandudno.

D. J. Williams
Schoolmaster,
49 High St.,
Fishguard.

When he had finished reading the letter, the Inspector showed that he was deeply disturbed. He asked the three men whether they fully realized the gravity of the situation in which they had placed themselves. They had made a most serious and damaging admission. Like the vast majority of his fellow countrymen at that time, Inspector William Moses Hughes was a sober, chapel-going Nonconformist and he was here confronted with three men representing the two things in life for which he had the most profound respect, religion and education. Furthermore the three men were not only confessing to a criminal act. They were also making a political proclamation deliberately calculated to disturb the calm surface of Welsh life, challenging the authority it was his duty and his office to uphold. As he went through the motions laid down by long experience in the service of the law his mind must have been agitated by a sequence of uncomfortable and disturbing questions. The three men were locked in cells overnight. A friendly policeman in attendance was able to complete a quotation from a much loved sonnet by Robert Williams Parry, a close friend of the three. A quiet joke was also made about the old proverb that said 'three tries for a Welshman'. Mr Williams, the short-story writer, had had some trouble with his box of matches. The Inspector followed the Fire Brigade to the scene of the fire.

II

There is a simple sense in which history can be interpreted as the continuing interplay between premeditated acts and a surge of uncontrollable events. The year 1936 is now, of course, part of what is described in curricula as 'Modern History'. These are the events, we say, with the modest confidence of would-be historians, which gave the world in which we continue to live its particular shape and flavour. We like to think that the passage of time opens up the perspective whereby we can discern the patterns of the past with that academic detachment necessary to handle calmly all the mercurial elements involved, so that they mean something and do not vanish like ghostly fool's fire into the mists of irretrievable time.

The letter handed to the Inspector of Police indicates that these three men (of whom two are still alive; the short-story writer D. J. Williams died on 4 January 1970, in his eighty-fifth year) at that point of time saw the course of history as a tidal wave that threatened their nation with a destruction as final as that famous edict, put out by Haman the Agagite in the name of King Ahasuarus, decreed for the Jews.

Not all Welshmen in 1936 were equally worried about their national existence. During the long campaign against the establishment of a bombing school in Llŷn many appeals were made from various bodies for the support of the most influential and celebrated Welshman of that time. The boyhood home of David Lloyd George was no more than ten miles from the proposed site. Throughout his career the former prime minister and war leader had at all times been aggressively Welsh. Even now, with one home in Surrey and another in Cricieth, he compelled all those who came in contact with him, or as some biographers would have it, all who came under his spell, to accept his Welshness and to appreciate with equal force terms of endearment or chastisement in his native tongue. All his life Welsh remained the language of his emotions. The annual renewal of the lifelong love affair with the land of his fathers took place in suitable druidical surroundings every Thursday afternoon of National Eisteddfod week. There could be no doubting the sincerity of his affection. But in this marriage, passionate as it was, the devotion tended to be one-sided: Wales, over and over again, proved more faithful to her wedded hero than he to the indulgent and doting wife of his bosom. At last in the midsummer of 1936, when two thousand bodies representing over half a million Welsh people had made their objections known, the great man spoke. He did so in characteristic fashion. In July the minister of the Calvinistic Methodist church in Cricieth wrote a personal appeal to Mr Lloyd George. Busy as Lloyd George was with plans to re-establish himself as a dominating figure on the world's stage – there were plans afoot for a prestigious visit to Adolf Hitler, and a visit to America to study the New Deal and to confer with President Roosevelt, and possibly a holiday in the West Indies with his second family – he did not neglect to reply, in Welsh, to the minister's letter. His reply arrived on 29 July and on the same day a lucid English translation appeared in all the English-language newspapers circulating in north Wales. (In the case of *The Times*, for example, the letter appeared only in the Welsh editions.) He claimed to have given the problem of the bombing school his close attention. He was in full sympathy with the view expressed by his fellow Welshmen. Nevertheless he felt it was most urgent to link the question of bombing with the larger issue of disarmament. Bombing from the air should be outlawed by inter-national agreement, and, but for the intervention of the British govern-ment, this vital step would have been taken already at the Disarmament Conference. Now as long as aerial bombardment was countenanced by the great powers, it would be inconsistent not to train personnel to reach a level of proficiency in the art and even more inconsistent to expect this to be done in some other part of the country that the air force was created to defend. He himself was disturbed day and night by the noise of military aircraft over his house in Surrey, but he would never be so selfish as to join any movement among his neighbours to remove the nuisance to plague fellow citizens in another part of the realm. If bombing had to be, then there had to be a bombing school somewhere. But of course his answer as always was to get at the root of the problem and work for the abolition of aerial bombardment by solemn international agreement.

When set side by side these two letters, both carefully considered before they were written, throw much light on the characters of the men who composed them in the year 1936: and even more perhaps on the nature of the society which produced and to some extent moulded them. It is not merely that teachers and preachers usually do have greater freedom to demonstrate their tender consciences than politicians. Over this sensitive issue we are witnessing exceptional men operating within the limits of a strictly Welsh context. It is as if Merlin with all his arts and quasi supernatural skills were being confronted and challenged by Gildas, that grim sixth-century Savonarola, and asked to state without the aid of eloquence, in monosyllabic and unequivocal terms, to which kingdom of this world, to which language, to which culture, and to which society he was prepared to give his first allegiance. Although he may not have been aware of it at that moment in the summer of 1936, the former prime minister, and prototype of a twentieth-century dictator, was being faced with a conflict of interest that externalized an even more profound conflict within his own nature And this conflict was made more acute because shared with the majority of his fellow countrymen of his time, and because something of its presence could be traced back in the history of his people for at least a thousand years.

If it had been possible, there is no doubt that his answer to the question of first allegiance would have been 'both'. After all, for most of his career that had been his answer. But self-deception and equivocation are no easier for people with two faces than for people with one. To be two-faced is not merely a defect of character. If you are two men, you are obliged to have at least two faces. Throughout the successful phase of his public life, David Lloyd George had in fact been obliged to be two men. In Wales he was always the great Welsh nationalist (with a small 'n') who more than anyone else had taught his fellow countrymen to lift up their traditionally downcast eyes and to face the world, to challenge it and to conquer it. In Wales he was always the Welsh champion armed like a medieval knight with the breastplate of Nonconformity, as ready as Peredur or Geraint or Galath to enter the list and take on all-comers. But in England he was what Mr A. J. P. Taylor has described as 'the greatest ruler of England since Oliver Cromwell'.

As ruler of England Ll. G. was in control of British imperial policy at a time when it still seemed capable of laying down a new world order. By that strange sleight of hand which seems to be history's continuing legacy to the ambitious Welshman, he was able to use his own fierce private and personal version of national pride as a channel for the abiding patriotism of the English. In 1918 he stood as the chief architect of victory and the architect-elect of a new Europe and a new world. At this point it is fair to say that his attempt to confront the surge of uncontrollable events with premeditated action was on a scale permitted to few men in history. But individuals remain individuals. There is, mercifully, no order of magnitude that allows the great, whatsoever the degree of their megalomania, to reproduce themselves as often as their photographs and images. By the same token, ordinary mortals have no right to expect even the most potent men of destiny to exert that strain of superhuman force that is alone capable of diverting a tidal wave. The best we can do is to record respectfully and accurately the degree of effort made by both the mighty and the weak to alleviate the damage.

One of the signatories to the letter handed to the Inspector of Police in the early hours of 8 September 1936 had already had occasion to make this assessment of the nature of the achievement of the great man; or to put it more precisely, to criticize the great man's basic assessment of his own achievement. In June 1930 an enthusiastic public meeting was held in Caernarfon to celebrate the fortieth anniversary of D. Lloyd George's election to the Parliament at Westminster as Liberal member for the Caernarfon Boroughs. His words were reported in indirect speech in the Welsh-language weekly press:

and he was sometimes reproved for not giving all his time to Welsh questions and leaving other matters to other people. This was a question that did not affect his career alone, but affected also the great number of young Welshmen who were liable to be called to a wider sphere of service. Were they to resist such a call or was it their duty to answer it? There was also something much deeper involved. In this world no man may foresee any more than a river, the course his career may take him. The speaker would not wish to claim for himself anything more than the status of one of the smaller tributaries sprung from the hills of Wales (*laughter*) . . .

Then in conclusion, Mr Lloyd George referred to the Severn and how on his way back to Wales to celebrate this anniversary he had observed the winding course of this river. It began as a little brook secluded in the safety of the mountains and then flowed down the side of Plynlimmon to water the valleys of Cardiganshire and having gained strength there turned eastwards to pass through the sweet meadows of Montgomery and then crossing the border to fertilize with prodigal generosity the broad acres of England. Then we see the river turn westwards, back to Wales – the old land of its birth – (*applause*) before losing itself in the sea. Who would accuse the Severn of turning its back on Wales? The river, Mr Lloyd George said, like everything and everyone else, was in the hand of God. Thus it is that Welshmen must serve their generation as Providence directs them. As for himself, whenever his time came in due season, he hoped to find his last resting place in the bosom of Wales so that on the day of the great awakening his eyes would open to look upon her ancient hills (*loud applause*).

The following month, in the July 1930 issue of *Y Ddraig Goch*, the nationalist paper which he edited, Saunders Lewis published his comments on the Caernarfon speech under the title 'Mr Lloyd George's Confession of Faith'. It is worth reproducing in extended quotation because it demonstrates the polarization of attitude between two generations that had taken place by that date. Lewis was in his thirties. Lloyd George was in his seventies.

The great statesman used the occasion to review his career and towards the end gave us a glimpse of his philosophy of life . . . It is our duty to scrutinise his message and as far as we can to ignore the rhetoric and the loud applause . . . I discern two frightening elements in Mr Lloyd George's confession of faith. The first is the light it throws on his character as a politician and leader. The second and more disturbing is the philosophy he cherishes and now offers freely as a rule of living to the young Welshman of today. About the first element I shall say no more than to invite his electors and fervent followers to consider whether they wish to continue to follow a leader who, on such an occasion and carefully measuring his words, announces that he is not and has never been responsible for his actions: a leader who insists on comparing himself to the river Severn, at the mercy of every wind that blows, twisting and turning, without will, without character, without design, driven on only by the whim of circumstance and his own irresistible instincts and desires . . .

Let us turn to the philosophy Mr Lloyd George offered as a guide to our young people in Wales and what he teaches about the place and the purpose of Wales in the world and in contemporary life. These are the key sentences.

1. 'No man can foresee, any more than a river, the course his career may take him!'

2. 'Who would accuse the Severn of turning its back on Wales?'

3. 'It is in the hand of God, as we all are.'

4. 'Thus it is that Welshmen must serve their generation as Providence directs them.'

The reader will forgive me for repeating platitudes that are in fact old and simple truths well known to everyone, but denied by Mr Lloyd George and forgotten by the audience at Caernarfon that greeted his words with 'Loud applause'.

A man is a responsible being. To this end he enjoys the freedom to choose. He can choose the hard road in life or he can choose the easy way. He can choose and he has the obligation to choose. The man who refuses to make a choice and looks upon himself as a river is lost because he has abdicated his humanity. The river Severn 'loses itself in the sea': but a river can offer no example for the life of a man, and a man is not 'in the hand of God' in the same way as a river. It is true that the Severn begins as a small stream in the mountains of Wales and having gained strength, that it crosses the border to water the fruitful English fields: and it is true (as far as we know) that she remembers nothing of the land of her origin. But, to quote the words of Gruffudd Robert of Milan, an experienced exile, 'The man who denies his father or his mother or his country or his language is never a reliable or a virtuous companion'. 'Who would accuse the Severn of turning its back on Wales?' No one in his right mind. And although Mr Lloyd George only makes the modest claim of being 'no more than a little tributary' we can not allow him this defence nor this frightening denial of his responsibility as a human being and a Welshman. We summon him before the bar of history and reason as every man 'who gained his strength in the mountains of Wales' shall be summoned, and we declare that his excuse is insufficient and feeble, and that he has a responsibility that he cannot throw away and that the Welshman who follows the course of the river Severn in his own life also degrades his own humanity.

Every Welshman must choose. Every man who takes up politics and a political career must choose, must plan, must use foresight. 'In this world no man may foresee any more than a river the course his career may take him', says Mr Lloyd George. This is simply untrue: a person can foresee a great deal more than a river. He can foresee that difficulties and temptations will beset him. Of course what Mr Lloyd George is really saying is: 'if I could have foreseen in 1890 that one day I would have the chance to become prime minister of England, I would not have gone about preaching Welsh nationalism. If I could have foreseen that my own past would one day be thrown in my face, I would not have begun a crusade in Meirionydd against T. E. Ellis because he broke his vow and accepted office in the English government. All my life I have been obliged to eat my words and break my promises – a man can foresee no more than a river.' That is the true meaning of Mr Lloyd George's words. But he does not have the right to transform the story of his own career and the fickleness of his own character into a general example to be followed by the youth of Wales.

We have not come to the end of the sorry articles of faith of 'the most famous Welshman in the world'. We would protest emphatically too against his belief that it is natural for every brilliant young Welshman to turn to England to seek 'a wider sphere of service' and that 'Providence' leads every gifted Welshman into the service of England as effortlessly as the river Severn flows over to the English plain. Let us set aside the comic blasphemy that equates the ambition and lust for power of a man with 'Providence' and 'the Hand of God'. Apart from that, we take leave to doubt the inevitability of the movement from the service of the smaller country to that of the larger. Let us compare Mr Lloyd George's position today with that of Thomas Masaryk. They both set out as leaders of small oppressed nations. The same temptation offered itself to them both, that is, deserting the small country to serve the great empire of the larger. One accepted the offer: the other rejected it. We may ask who is the influence for the good and the inspiration of the best European spirit in 1930? David Lloyd George or Thomas Masaryk? There are too many happy examples in history of the influence of great men in small countries enriching the life of mankind for us to accept uncritically the snobbish servile notion that the size and material strength of a country auto-matically elevates it into 'a wider sphere of service'. We believe it is through Wales that a Welsh statesman can most effectively serve Europe and humanity. And more than that: through the service of Wales that statesman's character will be best formed and his life best fulfilled and enriched. Through England and the service of England, Mr Lloyd George obtained two things that would never have been his had he dedicated himself to the service of Wales: great material wealth and comfort, and the enjoyment of world-wide fame. The effect of these gifts has been to transform him into a hard-faced cynic. Underneath his doctrine of the nature of the relationship between Wales and England we can discern his cold contempt for his own country.

'I hope', he said at the end of his speech, 'to be allowed to rest in the bosom of Wales.' We would prefer men ready to live and work for Wales than a sentimental cynic who wants to return to be buried in her bosom. The evil effect that Mr Lloyd George has had in Wales and continues to have, is to treat her like a bondslave feeding her with lies and rhetoric. His confession of faith at Caernarfon deserves nothing but outright condemnation. There is something terrible in the thought that this is the harvest of forty years' intense political life.

III

Six years later, David Lloyd George was pursuing his political career as intensely as ever. On the night of the fire at Penyberth, 8 September 1936, he was at Berchtesgaden, still basking in the afterglow of two cordial meetings with the German Chancellor, Adolf Hitler. We know from contemporary accounts that both men were much drawn to each other. More than a year before, Hitler had invited 'the man who won the war' to visit him. The newly appointed German Ambassador to the Court of St James, Joachim von Ribbentrop, had renewed the invitation in pressing terms, and by September 1936, Lloyd George could resist the temptation no longer. Many of his more promising schemes to return to power had proved abortive. There was no place for him in the National government in London. His section of the Liberal Party was an ineffective and demoralized rump. The bright promise of the Council of Action had faded. In such a situation, the political dividends to be gained from a visit to Hitler seemed well worth collecting. It would outflank, embarrass and possibly madden Stanley Baldwin. This was a delight in itself. He knew that Baldwin was toying with the notion of meeting the Führer. Furthermore it would capture the headlines all over the world and he would appear once again in his favourite role of conciliator and international peacemaker, and by implication, still fully capable of being the arbiter of the fate of nations. His power base might have shrunk, but his charisma could be shown to be undimmed. If it were true that Adolf Hitler admired him so much, it was not beyond the bounds of possibility that he would take his advice. While spellbinders were not obliged to fall under each other's spells, face to face, they could, as would not be the case with more ordinary politicians, talk as equals. A meeting of exceptional personalities would take place: and this would augur nothing but good for Europe and for the world. With the garrulity of an energetic 73-year-old, Lloyd George enlarged on these themes to his entourage of willing listeners.

According to the published diaries of the ubiquitous Thomas Jones, Hitler himself appeared to consider the visit a historic event. Both Jones and Conwell-Evans record that Hitler could not take his eyes off the Welsh Wizard. Both noted, too, the striking similarity in the magnetic power of two pairs of piercing blue eyes. There were statesman-like exchanges. Hitler declared once again that there was nothing closer to his heart than an agreement with Britain and France. The civilization of Europe had to be protected from the Bolshevik menace. Lloyd George expressed a cautious sympathy with this view but said he was more immediately concerned with the conflict that had just broken out in Spain between 'two sets of extremists'. Thomas Jones records his own irritation at the whirring of A. J. Sylvester's cine camera as the assiduous factotum crept around the cavernous drawing-room taking moving pictures of the historic encounter. Nevertheless, in retrospect, the noise of the camera was the most significant sound being made. The ghostly images can still be seen. Neither of the two pagan heroes was camera-shy. They were both acutely aware of the importance of the new media in the sacred process of moulding the primeval will of the masses. In this sense the meeting at Berchtesgaden was the encounter between the old elected monarch of manipulation and his more fearsome heir apparent – the genial Welsh Wizard on a semi-official visit to Grendel's lair.

Lloyd George regretfully declined an invitation to attend the forth-coming Nürnberg rally. This did not mean his enthusiasm for the constructive aspects of the New Germany were in any way dimmed. Were they not in fact the energetic realization of all the splendid plans he had drawn up himself for the conquest of unemployment in Britain: those new motorways – so essential to a modern industrial nation; the work and welfare schemes; the great building projects; the new popular art; the agricultural settlements; the labour camps? He approved wholeheartedly of all the glossy symbols of a new and energetic national socialist society. But the rally he could not attend. The discarded god of one tribe could not easily find an appropriate role at the organized ceremonial of the god of another. But Thomas Jones attended one session and saw 42,000 polished spades flash in the sun on the shoulders of the brown ranks of the *Appell des Reichsarbeitsdienstes*.

As the evening wore on, Lloyd George showed signs of relapsing into a mood of peevish despondency. He had seen the Führer twice and now the rest of his three-week visit to Germany could so easily develop into a boring anticlimax. He was daunted at the prospect of endless visits

to factories. Thomas Jones recognized the danger signals. He ordered
Pommard 1928 and egged on Lloyd George to tell some of his stories
of the great Welsh preachers for the delectation of Lord Dawson of Penn.
Over the years Ll. G. had collected a large quantity of material about
men like John Elias, Christmas Evans, Mathews Ewenni and John Jones
Talysarn. It was his intention to write a book about them. The emphasis
of the book would have been on the power of their performance and
their ability to arouse vast congregations, to seize the imagination and
emotions of the masses, to mould an entire nation in the image of a
chosen people marching fearlessly in the direction of salvation. It is not
recorded which selection he gave from his repertoire on the evening of 7
September 1936. His preference was always for the Old Testament. As he
said he preferred majesty to meekness. He was extremely fond of
relating John Elias's sermon on Belshazzar's Feast and the writing on the
Wall. He described how carefully John Elias set the scene. He would visit
the chapel before the service and direct that the candles should be
arranged so that his hand, as he stood in the pulpit, would cast a long
shadow on the wall. Lloyd George revelled in describing the alarm and
terror spreading among the congregation when at the climactic moment
the message was actually seen appearing on the wall. Whatever the
choice of anecdotes the result was pleasant. Thomas Jones writes that
they were all in hilarious mood as they made their way to bed.

On 4 October, the Reverend Lewis Valentine was the annual guest
preacher at Salem Chapel, Porth, in the Rhondda Valley. The chapel was
full and there was a higher proportion of men attending the service than
was usual in the Rhondda. They sat mostly in the gallery. They all knew
that the guest preacher, with his two companions in fire-raising, would
be before the Court of Assize in Caernarfon the following week. They
wanted to show some sympathy and solidarity even though many
of them could hardly be classified as Christian believers, let alone
members of the Baptist Church. Lewis Valentine took his text from the
sixth chapter of the gospel according to St John.

> From that time many of his disciples went back and walked more with
> him. Then said Jesus unto the twelve, 'Will ye also go away?' Simon Peter
> answered him, 'Lord, to whom shall we go? Thou hast the words of
> eternal life.'

An eye-witness describes the sermon as deeply affecting, not merely
the content, but even more the calm spirit in which the message was

delivered. The presiding minister referred to Mr Valentine as a prophet and the following morning a large crowd escorted him to the train.

IV

At Caernarfon the Courthouse stands, appropriately enough, in the shadow of the medieval castle. There, because of a persistent rumour that students intended to hoist the Red Dragon on the flagpost of the Eagle Tower the night before the trial, the entrance to the tower steps had been boarded up with planks. The courtroom was gloomy and dominated by the judge's bench. Above his chair a large oil painting caught what little natural light entered the room. It depicted Edward I presenting the first English Prince of Wales to the Welsh nobles, a baby on his shield. Admission to the trial was by ticket and the courthouse was surrounded by heavy police reinforcements. The crowds in the streets and in the square had been gathering since early morning. In the five weeks since the fire at Penyberth, after an initial period of local hostility, popular support had been growing for the three men. The courtroom was packed tight long before the trumpets sounded to announce the approach of the judge's procession.

Before the trial began the traditional words had to be read out: '. . . His Majesty's Justice of Assize do strictly charge and command all persons to keep silence while His Majesty's Commission of Assize is produced and read, upon pain of imprisonment.' The Associate opened a great parchment roll and read out in a loud voice: 'Edward the Eighth, by the grace of God, of Great Britain, Ireland and the British Dominions beyond the seas, King and Emperor, Defender of the Faith, to the Honourable Mr Justice Lewis, Knight . . .' The judge picked up the black cap on the bench in front of him and bowed his head each time the commission referred to him by name. The commission concluded with the words: 'doing therein as to justice doth appertain, according to the laws and customs of England'.

In the case of the King *v.* John Saunders Lewis, Lewis Edward Valentine and David John Williams, the charges were arson and malicious damage to property. The 'Particulars of Offence' stated that they had 'on the eighth day of September 1936, at Penrhos in the County of Caernarfon, maliciously set fire to certain buildings belonging to His Majesty the King.'

In 1937 a full account of the trial and of the circumstances surrounding it was published in Welsh by Dafydd Jenkins under the title

Tân yn Llŷn (Fire in Llŷn) recently republished. Among the illustrations in the book is a photograph of the three men on their way to the trial. They all wear hats and carry attaché cases rather like old-fashioned ministers on their way to a weekend preaching engagement. They are smiling and confident. By the time the book was published they were all three so well known to the Welsh reading public that there was no need for Mr Jenkins to say very much about them.

We can see from the photographs that D. J. Williams was the eldest. He was in his fifty-first year. In the second volume of his lively auto-biography he tells us that he left home at the age of sixteen to work in the coal mines of Glamorgan. Home was a hill farm in Carmarthenshire, where, he says,

> were stowed my notions about religion, about education, about my country, about language and about life before these abstract terms conveyed anything to my understanding. It was an atmosphere and a tradition that came down from generation to generation . . . I believe I was the first ever, of all my line, to leave the land . . . My family's inheritance of land has grown smaller with the centuries, until by my time it has almost vanished. But this does not worry me, because I am aware that I have been allowed somehow to keep something that is dearer in my sight than land or possessions – the consciousness of the ancient values of my ancestors bound with a feeling of responsibility for their continuance.

The story of his life is evidence of the sincerity and the truthfulness of these words, although they were written with the wisdom of hindsight when D. J. Williams was approaching old age. From his autobiography we learn that once in his early twenties he was filled with a sudden desire to emigrate to the United States of America. He had an uncle who ministered to Welsh churches in Kansas and Colorado. This uncle wrote and published in America Welsh temperance novels in which tee-totallers always triumphed. In the depth of the coal mine at Blaendulais, D.J. lowered his mandrel to ask himself a question: 'How long do I have to stay down here punching out my soul in this black hole of hell?' Like so many others underground, the young man dreamed of buying land in the Far West where land was still cheap and building up a ranch that would be a bit of old Wales in the shadow of the Rocky Mountains. In those far-off days, he tells us, he did not stop to think of the tribal rights of the Indian tribes that were in fact not so unlike his own sense of inheritance. But the American uncle, like a recurring character in so many Welsh plays of the period, came home, so to speak, in time for

Act Two. He directed his eager nephew's attention to the alternative nineteenth-century Welsh dream – education. Instead of going to America, Davy John, after many epic trials, most amusingly described, found his way to Aberystwyth and Oxford. But everything that ever happened to him seems to have strengthened that resolute Welsh patriotism so deeply rooted in his native soil.

It seems an ironic parable that his old home today should be buried under the lines of Germanic spruces planted by the Forestry Commission, as neatly mute on the hillside as the crosses of the War Graves Commission.

Llanddulas, the village on the north Wales coast where Lewis Valentine was brought up, has also suffered in the name of progress. What is left of it clings to the side of a motorway that facilitates the annual invasion of the area. What was once a village of outstanding beauty has become as unsightly as the Jersey shore. Valentine's father worked in the quarry and, like Lloyd George's Uncle Lloyd, preached on Sunday in the small chapels of the Baptists in that part of the world. He writes of his father: 'he was the most amiable Puritan I ever encountered. My recollection of his sermons is poor, but his prayers I shall never forget. They preserved me from many excesses in the course of my life.'

In the photograph of the three on their way to the trial, Valentine walks in the middle. He is a tall handsome figure and the idle reader is tempted to speculate about the excesses that could have tempted him. As a theological student he joined the RAMC during the First World War. He arrived in France in time for the first Battle of the Somme. He was one of the thousands who looked up at the leaning Virgin of Albert. In his diary he wrote: 'Formerly with her arms outstretched she offered her Holy Son to heaven, now she looks like a mad woman ready to hurl her child to the ground as a sacrifice to the blind rage of destruction.'

After the war he took a good degree in Hebrew and for a while considered an academic career. He also followed the honours course in Welsh and was elected president of the Student Council at Bangor. It was in this capacity that he organized protests against the use of the Black and Tans in Ireland. To the embarrassment of the prime minister, Mr Lloyd George, in 1920, university students in his constituency paid silent tribute to the body of Terence Mac Swiney, the Lord Mayor of Cork, as it passed through Bangor. This demonstration, organized by Valentine, was condemned by local Liberals as little short of treason. It is not altogether surprising that, when a Welsh political party was at last formed in the course of the National Eisteddfod at Pwllheli in 1925, Lewis Valentine, at the age of 31, should have been elected its first president.

There were in fact only six men present at this inconspicuous inaugural and David John Williams was not one of them. His train from the south was late. He was met on the platform by Saunders Lewis whose first words to him were, 'the thing has been started'. By 'thing' he obviously meant that a new political party had been established by the union of the two or three spontaneous movements that had already come into being among the workers and students in the north and the academics in the south. But the reverberations went much deeper. The 'thing' was nothing less than an attempt to hold up and even reverse what the majority of Welshmen were coming to accept as an inevitable historical process: even that redoubtable nationalist with a small 'n', David Lloyd George.

The third accused, John Saunders Lewis, was born in Wallasey, Cheshire, in 1893. His father was a Welsh Calvinistic minister. And so for that matter was his grandfather, Dr Owen Thomas of Liverpool, as he was known throughout Wales. And his great-grandfather, William Roberts, Amlwch, the friend and companion of John Elias and John Jones, Talysarn, was among the galaxy of great preachers that Lloyd George so much admired. Merseyside at the turn of the century was to Welsh minds no more than a convenient extension of north Wales. (The exact opposite one might say, of the present-day situation.) More than a hundred thousand Welsh-speaking souls earned their living in and around Liverpool. A high proportion of them were virtually monoglot Welsh. A recurring theme in the memoirs of nineteenth-century north Walians was the experience of arriving in the metropolis and being unable to ask the way. (A variant on the same theme was the parallel arrival in Philadelphia or New York. Before the 1880s very few Welsh emigrants would have acquired English before leaving home.)

Lewis was educated at home and in chapel entirely in Welsh until at the age of eight he was sent to Liscard High School and from that moment we can only assume that, like any other immigrant, he was made conscious of the dualism of belonging to two worlds. Home and chapel were Welsh, school was English. Under such circumstances a boy is obliged to shine or go under. It is quite clear that the young Lewis, small and frail as he was, shone.

He attended Liverpool University, reading English and French. On the morning of 4 August 1914, crossing the Mersey by ferry boat he opened his morning paper and learnt that war had been declared. He volunteered that day for military service. He was commissioned and served with the South Wales Borderers throughout the war in France and in Greece. He was wounded but he survived. The great war had a grim appetite for poets: Apollinaire, Wilfred Owen, Péguy, Edward Thomas, Alain Fournier, Hedd Wyn, Jean Pierre Caloch, Isaac Rosenberg. But some escaped. Men like Ungaretti, Robert Graves, Bert Brecht, David Jones and Saunders Lewis. War seems to have disturbed him rather less than most writers. In all his work, plays, poetry, novels, literary criticism, there is hardly any mention of his personal war experience, unlike the work of his friend David Jones, for example.

Nevertheless the war changed his life. During the grim Battle of Loos he read Maurice Barrès for the first time and was given a new vision of the nature of the relationship of the artist to the society to which he belonged. Then came the Easter Rising in Dublin. This seems to have affected him no less than it did the Irish poets. And in the same fateful year, home on convalescent leave, he wanders into a bookshop in Swansea and picks up a biography of Emrys ap Iwan, that lonely voice in nineteenth-century Wales, a European Welshman who lived in France and Germany and Switzerland and urged his fellow countrymen to look to Europe and not be mesmerized by the cultures of England and America. This was the deepest resistance of all. The language barrier could be more formidable in the end than the bullet or the barricade. From this time forward he took the path that led inevitably to the trial at Caernarfon.

V

'How say you, John Saunders Lewis, are you guilty or not guilty?'

Lewis answers in Welsh. 'Yr wyf yn ddieuog.'

The judge leans forward. His name too is Lewis. Sir Wilfred Hubert Poyer Lewis, grandson of a former bishop of Llandaff, educated at Eton and Oxford and a captain in the Glamorgan Yeomanry during the war. Captain Lewis faces Captain Lewis. Not so much two sides of the same coin as two aspects of Welsh life now placed in positions of open conflict.

'Is John Saunders Lewis the person who is described in the indictment as a lecturer?'

He gives sarcastic emphasis to the last word. Lewis in the dock continues to speak in Welsh.

'Ie, darlithydd wyf i, yn Llenyddiaeth Cymru, yng Ngholeg y Brifysgol, Abertawe.' ('Yes. I am a lecturer in Welsh literature at the University College, Swansea.')

The judge is irritated. Not only is it inconceivable that an educated man anywhere in the British Isles should claim not to be able to speak English. There is also the alarming possibility that some obscure disrespect is intended, perhaps to a judge only recently knighted and on his first circuit as a member of the King's Bench Division of the High Court. Breathing deeply he prepares to assert the dignity of the law and the authority of the Crown.

'Listen to me. Do you tell me that you cannot speak or understand English?'

The defendant continues to speak Welsh.

'Mi fedraf Saesneg, ond Cymraeg yw fy mamiaith.' ('I can speak English [lit. I can manage English] but Welsh is my mother tongue'.)

The judge adopts the style of a barrister cross-examining an unreliable witness.

'Do you mean to tell me that you cannot understand or speak English?'

There is a moment's pause while Lewis considers his reply. He speaks again, in measured tones, in Welsh.

'Yr wyf yn gofyn yn ostyngedig i'm Harglwydd ganiatáu imi ateb yn Gymraeg, am mai hi yw fy mamiaith. Gofynnaf i'r cyfieithydd gyfieithu hyn.' ('I ask humbly that your Lordship permits me to answer in Welsh since that is my mother tongue. I ask the translator to translate this.')

'Do you understand and speak English?'

At last Lewis speaks English. 'I can understand and speak English, but Welsh is my mother tongue.'

The judge remains acutely dissatisfied.

'Do you understand and speak English? Answer me. Yes or No.'

'Yes, my Lord.'

'Very well then. You will plead to the indictment in English.'

The indictment is read again in English and the accused is asked whether he pleads guilty or not guilty. Lewis replies in Welsh.

'Yr wyf i yn ddieuog.'

The judge leans forward menacingly.

'I will give you one more chance. Do you speak and understand English?'

VI

Sir Wilfred Lewis was ready to administer the law of England with all the confidence of a man called to the bar by the Inner Temple in 1908.

Every law book he had ever read began by extolling the supreme
virtues of the Common Law and the English Judicial System. What was
left of the law of Wales had been abolished by the Act of Union exactly
four hundred years ago in 1536, along with most of the trappings of
independent existence. The twentieth section of that Act declared:

> Also be it enacted that all justices, sheriffs, coroners, escheators . . . and
> all the other officers and ministers of the law, shall proclaim and keep the
> sessions, courts, hundreds, leets, sheriff's court and all other courts in the
> English tongue: and all oaths of officers, juries, and inquests . . . be given
> and done in the English tongue: and also that from henceforth no person
> or persons that use the Welsh speech and language shall have or enjoy
> any manner of office or fees within this realm.

The Act of Union offered the learned judge no compromise. King
Henry VIII could express a profuse and 'singular zeal, love and favour
towards his subjects of this Dominion of Wales'. His dynasty owed the
throne to the singular zeal, love, favour and sacrifice of the people from
whom they sprang and to whom his father had appeared as the *Mab
Darogan*, the national saviour whose coming had been so vividly
prophesied by the bards and poets. But Henry VIII was always a
demanding lover. Too often his tender embrace could end in a kiss of
death: 'his said country or dominion of Wales, shall be, stand and
continue for ever from henceforth incorporated united and annexed to
and with this his Realm of England.'

Mr Justice Lewis must have been aware that the trial would develop
into a political occasion. The three men had deliberately set fire to the
sheds and materials in order to draw public attention to their cause.
They had presented themselves at the police station with a letter already
written, carefully setting out their motives for committing the offence.
The three had appeared twice before the magistrates before being sent
to trial at the Caernarfon Assizes. But they had not given evidence or
called witnesses. Although the Crown solicitor had pointed out that the
maximum penalty for the crimes of which the three were accused was
penal servitude for life, the magistrates had allowed bail on condition
that they would not make propaganda in relation to the case. On
submission by his solicitor, it was agreed that Mr Valentine should be
allowed to keep his preaching engagements.

It is doubtful that Mr Justice Lewis would have been aware of the
warmth of the reception the preacher received in the chapels he visited

up and down Wales. But he would have known that the defendants had engaged W. H. Thompson, a company of solicitors well known for their expertise in political cases. And he would also have been aware that the protesters against the bombing site in Llŷn had made much use of the fact that the Air Ministry had abandoned similar projects on Holy Island, Lindisfarne, and Abbotsbury, Chesil Bank, in deference to local sentiment. Their claim was that Llŷn, with its historical and religious traditions and its living language and unique culture, was entitled to at least the same degree of consideration as bird sanctuaries in England. His summing up at the end of the trial showed that Mr Justice Lewis had been prepared for this: 'Let me say this. It may be that you and I and everybody in this court – I do not know – it may be that we all think it is a pity that the aerodrome was placed at Penrhos – we may all think that – I do not know – but that fact does not in law justify the act of burning it down . . .'

What seems to have taken him by surprise was the demand of three educated men to be tried in their mother tongue and not the official language of the court. This simple fact reveals a great deal about the strange course of Welsh history after the Act of Union. It is true that the old aristocracy, who throughout the Middle Ages had been the chief defenders of Welsh culture and national identity, for the most part had responded with alacrity to the Tudor policy of merging Wales into the centralized English state. A new middle class emerged to exploit the new system. A breed of lawyers appeared and multiplied. The profit motive and the new law walked hand in hand. But even in the legal system there were men prepared to speak up for the old language as they might have done out of charity for a ragged beggar-maid pleading for entry at the gates of justice. In 1575 we find a judge of the Great Sessions writing to Walsingham urging the appointment of at least one judge able to understand Welsh,

> since now a judge must needs use an Interpreter, and therefore the Evidence is told according to the mynde of the Interpreter, whereby the Evidence is expounded contrary to that which is saide by the examynate, and so the Judge gyveth a wrong charge.

The Great Sessions absorbed the bulk of the more considerable business formerly conducted in the old Marcher courts and also relieved the work of the Court of the Lord President and Council for Wales and the Marches. The four English shires that came under this jurisdiction much resented their position under the Lord President. It seemed to lump them in with the Welsh and deny them the full privilege of being Englishmen of the first quality. The Marches that were of mixed population and had for so long belonged to neither Wales nor England were now overwhelmingly eager to be in every respect completely English. During the Commonwealth, the Council declined in importance and after the Revolution of 1688 it was abolished. But the Court of Great Sessions continued in active operation until 1830.

At that time, again after much agitation in English legal circles in London, a bill for the more effectual administration of justice in England and Wales proposed the extension of the jurisdiction of the Superior Courts of England to Chester and Wales. In the Commons, Sir John Owen, MP for Pembrokeshire, John Jones, MP for Carmarthen, Rice Trevor, MP for Carmarthenshire and later the second Lord Dynevor, and one or two others, opposed the bill vigorously. They urged that the bill would entail great additional expense on Welsh suitors. The lower classes were almost entirely Welsh-speaking and the complete incorporation into the English system would put them at a grave disadvantage. They were only voices crying in the wilderness. The bill became law. In 1830 the majority of Welsh members were country gentlemen who rarely took part in debate. They sat in mute and comfortable agreement on the government side. For some years the Act inflicted much hardship on Welsh suitors. Writers of the time complained of the want of sympathy shown by English judges going on the new Welsh circuits. They made no attempt to conceal their assumption that Welshmen were beings inferior to Englishmen, and the Welsh language an encumbrance of the ignorant. It was not until the new Welsh Liberals entered the House of Commons in 1868 that matters showed any improvement. This, we are told, was due to the arrival of a new generation of Welshmen in the ranks of the legal profession imbued with the new spirit of pride in their language and nationality. However deep this new spirit may have been, and there certainly was a great political assertion of nationhood, it had little effect on the law courts or on conservative legal custom and practice. Lloyd George, the politician, for example, was a far more fervent devotee of his native language than Lloyd George, the Porthmadog solicitor. The educated Welshman of the great Liberal era was only too anxious to display his English education and his brilliant command of the English language. His aim in life was to excel in all the courts of the English and to climb as high as he could to attain the commanding heights of the Imperial English System. It was a miraculous change to look down instead of being looked down upon. The word 'British' had come into common usage, Matthew Arnold had decreed that the Empire needed the vital spark of Celtic imagination to extend the power of the Empire and complete its superiority in every sphere over all the nations of the earth. So be it. Platoons of bright young Welshmen lined up to offer their services. The language was left at home to remain a suitable vehicle of religious devotion (hence the cant phrase so widely in use 'the language of heaven'), for nostalgic songs, for eisteddfodau and for the cloistered delights of Welsh childhood, and for watered-down praise poetry. It was not wanted for the sterner pursuits of building and maintaining the great Empire in the world. And since English Common Law was one of the more obvious benefits bestowed by the Imperial System on unruly lesser breeds scattered about the globe, it was patently clear that English was the only possible language for the proper dispensation of the law wherever a court should find itself in session. There is very little evidence that the Liberal Welsh nationalists with a small 'n' ever contested this proposition except to defend the rights of interpretation for their less fortunate fellow country-men who had not enjoyed the manifold blessings of an English education.

VII

The effect of Mr Valentine's speech in his own defence was completely spoiled by the mechanics of translation and to a lesser extent by frequent interruptions from the judge who insisted that much of the substance of the speech was irrelevant to the case in hand. The interpreter rendered each sentence as it was delivered.

'My denomination takes the point of view I do on the matter of the bombing school and so do all the Nonconformist denominations in Wales today. Let me quote the declaration made by the Archdruid of Wales from the presidential chair of the Union of Welsh Congregation-alists at Bangor this summer.'

The judge interrupted.

'I am not going to allow you to quote what any Archdruid or anyone else has said.'

Valentine stretched an arm towards the bench.

'I plead with you, my lord, in my difficulty'

'I see no difficulty. You describe yourself as a minister of the Gospel and are presumably a man of intelligence. You will address the jury solely on the matters which are relevant to the charge.'

In spite of its dignified and impressive content, most people in the crowded court room appeared relieved when Valentine's address at last came to an end. The ventilation was bad. The High Sheriff, Mr Ronald Armstrong Jones, father of the distinguished photographer, could be seen leaning back in his chair, stifling yawns and staring fixedly at the ceiling. During the fractured progress of speech and translation the sound of singing rose and fell in the streets outside. There were hymns and repeated renderings of 'Hen Wlad fy Nhadau': also the undergraduates had a series of new verses about the burning of the bombing school. Porth Neigwl, the bay where the bombing markers would be placed, was for some reason called Hell's Mouth in English. The lampoonists were able to make great play with all the infernal implications. A powerful myth was being sent on its way, even as the trial was in progress. Friendly policemen beguiled the singers away from the court by subtle appeals. An inspector said, 'Now then, lads, now then good friends, don't disturb the court. Saunders Lewis is speaking and he's speaking marvellously too.'

The tactics of the defence had been worked out with a certain skill. There were several issues at stake. While they were all related it was important that the progress of the trial should reveal the intrinsic importance of each one in turn. The question of the inferior and disenfranchised position of the national language came first. The natural eloquence of the Reverend Lewis Valentine was as it were sacrificed for this cause. His difficulty demonstrated a fundamental point. Language, these men were saying, was central and fundamental to human dignity. All forms of behaviour, positive or negative actions, even questions of guilt and innocence, were defined by the language used to express the experience. Something of the value of the experience was inherent in the value of the language. If the language was treated with contempt, so were the people to whom the language belonged. They were on trial for wilful and malicious damage: the nature of the proceedings would be made to show just how much wilful and malicious damage had been and was being inflicted on their native language; and by the same token, how the native culture was still being eroded by an alien system of law and authority.

When he had made his formal protest about the way in which Mr Valentine's statement had been ruined by piecemeal translation, Saunders Lewis proceeded to address the jury in English. Of the three defendants it had been agreed that he was the one best capable of expressing their case with the necessary clarity and vigour in the English language. His style of delivery was cool and measured. He admitted the facts, explained the background of constitutional opposition to the bombing school, and outlined the cultural and religious traditions of Llŷn.

It is impossible for one who had blood in his veins not to care passionately when he sees this terrible vandal bombing range in this very home of Welsh culture. On the desk before me is an anthology of the works of the Welsh poets of Llŷn, *Cynfeirdd Llŷn, 1500–1800 (Early Poets of Llŷn, 1500–1800)* by Myrddin Fardd. On page 176 of this book there is a poem, a *cywydd*, written in Penyberth farmhouse in the middle of the sixteenth century. That house was one of the most historic in Llŷn. It was a resting-place for the Welsh pilgrims to the Isle of Saints, Ynys Enlli, in the Middle Ages. It had associations with Owen Glyndŵr. It belonged to the story of Welsh literature. It was a thing of hallowed and secular majesty. It was taken down and utterly destroyed a week before we burnt on its fields the timbers of the vandals who destroyed it. And I claim that, if the moral law counts for anything, the people who ought to be in this dock are the people responsible for the destruction of Penyberth farmhouse.

At this point, the spectators could no longer restrain themselves from applauding. The judge ordered everyone to be quiet, and the officers of the court to remove anyone who dared to break out into further cheering. One or two learned genealogists present at the trial were much taken with the hidden irony that the judge himself, Sir Wilfred Lewis, belonged to just such a family of Welsh *uchelwyr* as had lived in Penyberth for so many centuries. And now the judge had been so thoroughly Anglicized that he was hardly aware of the true nature of the culture the three men were claiming to defend. Even had he wanted to, he lacked the ability and the means to relate all the spiritual values that were being described to any moral law that his mind could usefully connect with the law of England it was his duty to administer. In a sense of course this made his task much simpler, and the private thoughts of genealogists were not available to him. But it was clear that he very much resented being looked upon, by so large an assembly, on his first circuit as a High Court judge, as some latter-day manifestation of Pontius Pilate. And he resented, too, the disturbing possibility that the jury were paying more respectful attention to the defendant than they were to him, in spite of all the traditional courtesies he had extended to the twelve good men and true. His interruptions were the more forceful because they were needed to concentrate attention on the proper seat of appointed authority. The defendant Lewis was coming to the end of his statement. It seemed perilously close in tone and argument to a judicial summing up:

> You, gentlemen of the jury, are our judges in this matter . . . We ask you to have no fear at all. The terminology of the law calls this bombing range 'the property of the King'. That means the English government. It means these bureaucrats in the Air Ministry to whom Wales is a region on the map, who know nothing at all of the culture and language they are seeking to destroy.
>
> But there is another aspect to this trial that gives it special importance. We have said from the beginning, and it was the point we emphasized in our letter to the Chief Constable of Caernarfonshire, that our action was a protest against the ruthless refusal of the English state even to discuss the rights of the Welsh nation in Llŷn. Now, everywhere in Europe today we see governments asserting that they are above the moral law of God, that they recognize no other law but the will of the government, and that they recognize no other power but the power of the state. These governments claim absolute powers; they deny the rights of persons and of moral persons. They deny that they can be challenged by any code of morals, and they demand the absolute obedience of men. Now that is Atheism. It is the denial of God, of God's law. It is the repudiation of the entire Christian tradition of Europe, and it is the beginning of the reign of chaos.
>
> The English government's behaviour in the matter of the Llŷn bombing range is exactly the behaviour of this new Anti-Christ throughout Europe. And in this assize court in Caernarfon today we, the accused in this dock, are challenging Anti-Christ. We deny the absolute power of the State-God. Here in Wales, a land that has no tradition except Christian tradition, a land that has never in all its history been pagan or atheist, we stand for the preservation of that Christian tradition and for the supremacy of the moral law over the power of materialist bureaucracy. So that whether you find us guilty or not guilty is of importance today to the future of Christian civilization and Christian liberty and Christian justice in Europe.
>
> If you find us guilty the world will understand that here also in Wales. an English government may destroy the moral person of a nation.

At this point the Judge interrupted.
'That is absolutely untrue.'
Lewis ignored the interruption.

You declare that the government may shatter the spiritual basis of that nation's life, may refuse to consider or give heed to any appeal even from the united religious leaders of the whole country, and then may use the law to punish with imprisonment the men who put those monstrous claims of Anti-Christ to the test. If you find us guilty . . .

The judge broke in again. 'That is untrue. Will you stop? I am not going to allow you to make statements which are not only untrue but almost blasphemous.'
'If you find us guilty . . .'
'You are not to say that again!'

I wasn't going to. If you find us guilty, you proclaim that the will of the government may not be challenged by any person whatsoever, and that there is no appeal possible to morality as Christians have always understood it. If you find us guilty you proclaim the effective end of Christian principles governing the life of Wales.

On the other hand, if you find us not guilty, you declare your conviction as judges in this matter that the moral law is supreme; you declare that the moral law is binding on governments just as it is on private citizens. You declare that 'necessity of state' gives no right to set morality aside, and you declare that justice, not material force, must rule in the affairs of nations.

We hold with unshakeable conviction that the burning of the monstrous bombing range in Llŷn was an act forced on us for the defence of Welsh civilization, for the defence of Christian principles, for the maintenance of the Law of God in Wales. Nothing else was possible for us. It was the government itself that created the situation in which we were placed, so that we had to choose either the way of cowards and slink out of the defence of Christian tradition and morality, or we had to act as we have acted, and trust to a jury of our countrymen to declare that the Law of God is superior to every other law, and that by that law our act is just.

We ask you to be fearless. We ask you to bring in a verdict that will restore Christian principles in the realm of law, and open a new period in the history of nations and governments. We ask you to say that we are Not Guilty.

Thank you, my Lord.

The defendant finished with a courteous bow in the direction of the bench as if he had borrowed the authority of the court for the duration of his speech and was now handing it back to its legal owner.

VIII

The judge's summing up, when it came, was complex and repetitive: as
if he had become a little uncertain of the jury's capacity for following
a legal argument in English. Even as he spoke the centuries seemed to
be rolling back and the men who listened to him identified with their
ancestors: as if they had just received from a beneficent monarchy the
bewildering gift of English citizenship and a more experienced adherent
of the Crown was guiding their uncertain steps in the complexities of
English Common Law.

> I am here to do to the best of my ability the duty which I have sworn to
> do, namely to administer the law of England. You when you went into
> the jury box took an oath to administer the law of England and it is your
> duty to accept from me what the law of England is.

Their reaction seemed to waver between appreciation and resentment as
they struggled to forget the stirring call of the defendant and concentrate
like well-behaved pupils on their first morning in a new school.

'This case has lasted some time. It is really as simple a case as ever it
became the lot of the jury to have to consider.'

The frowns on the faces of the jurymen as they struggled to follow Sir
Wilfred's increasingly complicated exposition suggested they found the
case anything but simple. The testimony of a nightwatchman had to be
disposed of. He had claimed that he had been set upon by two or even
three unknown assailants. They had held him down while the fire was
started. All three defendants had testified that the nightwatchman was
lying. The man was a one-armed veteran of the Battle of Ypres and the
London press had given great prominence to his story. The judge went
over it all in great detail. He was not prepared to say whether the nightwatchman's evidence was true or false. He was not even prepared to tell
the jury whether or not they should take any notice of it. At one point he
seemed to be saying that it was irrelevant: nevertheless he had just gone
over it in considerable detail and this seemed to imply that it was a
central issue. He also dwelt on the individual characters of the three
defendants for some time before suggesting that those considerations
too were not for them to consider.

> Members of the jury, let me only say this one other word. You have heard
> from the lips of two of the accused a suggestion that the whole of Wales

approves of this act. You may know, I know, that there are many many
patriotic Welshmen – real patriotic Welshmen – who would shudder at
the thought of such an act of violence as this. I only mention that because
the accused have suggested to you that this act which they have done is
an act which has received the approbation of the whole of Wales.
Whether it has or whether it has not, you may know better than I; but
whether it has or has not the approbation of the whole of Wales has got
nothing whatever to do with this court; and if you are satisfied that this
was done it is your duty, unpleasant though it may be, to find a verdict of
guilty.

Now members of the jury, will you be good enough – I have no doubt
you would like to retire – to consider your verdict in this case, and to let
me know whether or not you find the prisoners guilty of both or one or
other of the two charges, or whether you find them not guilty on both?
Will you now retire and consider your verdict?

The jury took three-quarters of an hour to consider it. They returned
to the court and stood in their places while the clerk asked them:

'Members of the jury, are you agreed upon your verdict?'

The foreman of the jury, by name Harlech Jones, replied, 'We are. We
have failed to agree.'

The judge intervened. 'Is there any chance of you agreeing?'

Harlech Jones answered. 'I am afraid, my lord, there is no chance.'

'Very well, then the case will go over to the next Assizes.'

For a moment there was silence. The news reached the crowd outside
and they reacted immediately as if a great victory had been won. They
began to sing 'Hen wlad fy nhadau' so loudly that the proceedings in
the courtroom were thrown into confusion. The formalities of bail were
gone through, but the defendants remained in the dock as if they had
still not realized that they were free to leave. Once outside the three men
were hoisted on the shoulders of young supporters and carried through
the town. The police appealed to Saunders Lewis to help restore order
and he did so. He spoke from the steps of the Welsh Nationalist Party's
offices and within minutes the crowd had dispersed.

The judge had directed the jury to ignore the defendants' motives, but
it was clear from the verdict that they were unable to do this. It has been
recorded that five wished to return a clear verdict of 'not guilty' and
seven were in favour of 'guilty'. In present-day terms, the verdict was as
accurate a reflection of Welsh public feeling as an opinion poll. Certainly
this was the view taken by the office of the Attorney-General and the

government in London. It became clear to them that a verdict of 'guilty' would be difficult to obtain in any Welsh court. No Welsh jury would be capable of distinguishing between the defendants' motives and the offence committed. On 7 December, the Crown made application before the Lord Chief Justice for the trial to be moved from Caernarfon to the Central Court in London. The Law of England and the spirit of the Act of Union were not to be lightly set aside. Welsh national sentiment could well be glowing, as the American magazine *Time* put it, with a refulgence not seen for 400 years; it was less than dust in the balance of the well-tried scales of English justice.

But the glow was bright enough to awaken an ageing giant dozing fitfully in the Jamaican sun. When Lloyd George heard the news of the transfer of the trial to the Old Bailey by a writ of certiorari, he was moved to write angry protests to his daughter Megan in telegrams and letters.

> I think it is an unutterable piece of insolence, but very characteristic of this government. They crumple up when tackled by Mussolini and Hitler, but they take it out on the smallest country in the realm which they are misgoverning . . . In the worst days of Irish coercion, trials were never taken out of Ireland into the English courts . . . This is the first government that has chosen to try Wales at the Old Bailey. I wish I were there, and I certainly wish I were 40 years younger. I should be prepared to risk a protest which would be a defiance. If I were Saunders Lewis I would not surrender at the Old Bailey: I would insist on their arresting me, and I am not sure that I would not make it difficult for them to do that . . . It makes my blood boil.

Lloyd George bore no resentment against Saunders Lewis for the fierce attack printed against him in Y *Ddraig Goch* in the summer of 1930. An inability to bear a grudge was indeed one of the most attractive aspects of his character. In the mean time he had had occasion to collaborate with Saunders Lewis on the Advisory Committee of the University of Wales on Broadcasting. It was this collaboration that secured some measure of recognition from the BBC of Welsh nationhood and led to the creation of a BBC Welsh region. And we know from his brother William's memoirs that the great man had formed a high opinion of Lewis's character and capacities.

But in the case Rex *v*. Lewis, Valentine and Williams, Lloyd George could do nothing: any more than he could prevent Stanley Baldwin from forcing the Rex in question to abdicate in order to marry Mrs Simpson.

Guided by the government, the Law of England took its inexorable course. At the Old Bailey on 19 January 1937 the three were found guilty and sentenced to be kept in prison for nine calendar months.

It was a comparatively light sentence and commentators at the time saw in it a measure of political sagacity: too much should not be done to exacerbate and inflame Welsh feeling. Whatever this new phenomenon of Welsh Nationalism with a capital 'N' might be, there was no sense in going to extremes and helping it to 'catch on'. The Imperial government was saddled with enough problems in Ireland and India and even in darkest Africa; it would be too provoking if the ghost of ancient national sentiments across Offa's Dyke suddenly took on the too solid aspect of flesh and blood.

At the end of their sentences, Lewis, Valentine and Williams were given a tumultuous homecoming. More than twelve thousand people filled the old Pavilion in Caernarfon – where Lloyd George had held so many memorable meetings – at the welcome meeting organized by J. E. Jones, the indefatigable secretary of the Welsh Nationalist Party. It must have seemed to them then that there was a rich political harvest to be gathered. Were they not the inevitable successors to the kingdom of Lloyd George? But the new-found zeal and enthusiasm quietly melted away. Although Williams and Valentine returned to their old posts, Lewis had been dismissed from his by the Council of the University College of Swansea. There was not enough power in the new head of Nationalist steam to reverse this decision. It only needed a couple of committees to rule the motion out of order for the new leader to be left out in the wilderness like a sacrificial goat. In the valleys of the south, the quick sympathy of the Welsh workers, employed and unemployed, was being rallied to the support of Republican Spain. It became the overwhelming issue of the day. The Left Book Club made rapid headway in the colleges. Side by side with Pacifism, Utopian Internationalism, and a heady variety of idealism difficult to imagine today, there was also a growing sense of fatalistic foreboding. The threat of another world war was a black cloud growing on the horizon.

It was not a good time for reflection. Events were moving so quickly they collided against each other as if the increase in the world's output of machines was taking a hand in history, and speeding up the process. Each new machine increased by a thousandfold the capacity to destroy and forget.

All that could be recorded was that three men had been willing to act as though a Welsh nation existed in the modern world and needed saving: and that when they so acted, a large section of their fellow countrymen, including Lloyd George himself, for so long the hero of the people and the wizard of British politics, rallied to their support. Politically, at the time they gained very little. But their moral victory was great. They had reaffirmed the existence on the plane of reality of a nation that was on the verge of becoming an unsubstantial and sentimental shadow. And it was the language that made them do it.

MWT: In one of your essays you refer to the First World War and say: 'It was as if a bomb had been thrown into the middle of a Sunday-school treat.' That catastrophic disruption of a familiar, established world would seem to have been a very important point of historical reference for you as a novelist.

EH: Oh, yes, it must be for my generation – I was born just a year after that war. My father was in and out of hospital for years, and I remember a nurse coming to treat some kind of damage he had had to his ribs – it was the result of something very unromantic, like falling off a truck or something. He had also suffered gassing, so his breathing was very bad as a consequence of that.

MWT: In that way it was literally brought home to you that the Great War had been a turning point in modern history.

EH: Yes, it was a huge event that had taken place and marked off a way of life that was totally different. That was when a new, modern world began, with innovations such as bus services that marked the departure of the pony and trap. It was a huge watershed really. But it was only later – much later – that I came to understand its implications for Welsh culture, although I think I held it responsible for the fact that I was not brought up Welsh-speaking. When he was in the Army, my father turned away from the Nonconformist religion in which he had been raised and became an Anglican. I think it was something to do with what he called 'the padre', with whom he had good relationships. He had been quite old when he went to the war. He was already married, and my brother, born in 1915, was already there, so to speak. I was born afterwards, in 1919. The whole trauma of the experience affected my father very deeply: he came out of the war a very different person from what he had been when he went in.

MWT: What sort of person had he become?

EH: I always remember him as an invalid, a wounded man in every sense. There was a quality I noticed both in him and in some of his friends who had gone through the same experience: there was a blue tinge to their complexions, which I always supposed was the result of the gas. A lot of them had been gassed, and if they survived then they survived as a damaged generation.

MWT: That brings to mind the number of damaged men in your fiction, who not infrequently seem to be dominated by women far stronger than themselves.

EH: That was certainly true of my parents. My mother was much younger, and much stronger physically, and a very headstrong, impulsive woman. Whereas he was very cautious. I suppose I had a weird upbringing in many ways; but many did of my generation.

MWT: Would that help explain why you developed, through your fiction, such an admiration for women's role in the running not just of the home but of society at large?

EH: No, I don't think that's due to my parents. That's much more due to my own mature self. As a child, you accept everything that surrounds you as natural. And, according to my brother, I was spoilt, although only within firm limits. My father had a whistle, which he would blow if we wandered too far. In many ways I had an idyllic childhood. You've seen Trelawnyd, and know what a beautiful spot it is, with that hill, the Gop, above the village, which was our playground; and there was a river down in the bottom, so it was a magical place.

MWT: But not a home full of books, I take it?

EH: No, not really. Although I took to reading quite early. I used to love being read to. We had a maid, and she used to read in exactly the way I depict in *A Toy Epic*. She would read in a perfectly flat tone of voice, she didn't take any notice of punctuation, and she didn't understand lots of the words she was reading. So I was fascinated by that. And they were also the kinds of books I mention in *A Toy Epic* – English public-school adventures and the like. I never saw the more standard classics – although my father did make an effort to get us to read *The Children's Newspaper*, but that didn't go down very well.

MWT: But then your exposure to more serious, substantial literature happened at school?

EH: It wasn't school so much as the public library, although I did have a couple of very stimulating teachers – Moses Jones, and Silvan Evans, who was the English teacher. But I should imagine that they influenced me only quite late in my school career – when I was sixteen. I was a very backward child in many ways, I think partly due to this strange dichotomy between the idyllic surroundings where I was brought up, where I enjoyed considerable, though limited, freedom, and then this fancy world of reading, which was entirely English. So there were two worlds really: there was the local, natural world, in which I was deeply rooted, and there was this other, foreign world in fiction. And I didn't really make any connection between art, or literature, and life until quite late, when I was about sixteen. That was when I woke up. Until then I was very slow – I think I had an illness of some kind, possibly quinsy, when I was supposed to be doing the School Certficate, so I had to do it some six months later. And I remember being aware, by then, of things in a different way.

MWT: You've said that your awakening to the Welsh language and your awakening as a writer happened simultaneously.

EH: I think it had to do with the burning of the Bombing School, at Penyberth, in 1936, when I was sixteen or seventeen. That was a kind of explosion in my mind, and I became a nationalist before I had learnt Welsh. Then, having acquired that point of view, I realized that the language was the essential piece of equipment in order to make this commitment a real, substantial thing.

MWT: So you became a nationalist as a result of the actions of Saunders Lewis, D. J. Williams and Lewis Valentine at Penyberth, but can you recall what nationalism meant to you, intellectually and ideologically, at that time?

EH: I was committed only to Welsh nationalism, and not to any other; and for me this related to the recovery of a Welsh identity that had been lost in my family. I had no intellectual preconceptions about nationalism: it was just an awakening to being Welsh, as it were. Because in the general tone of the thirties, the political outlook was, of course, anything but sympathetic to nationalism in general. My brother, for example, belonged to the Left Book Club, and he used to have these strangely bound books every month or so. This was very fashionable at the time – he was already a student at the University College of Wales, Aberystwyth. It was natural for young people of that time to be drawn in the direction of the Left, whereas Welsh Nationalism inclined in a different direction completely. The papers and magazines Moses Jones used to give me were *The New English Weekly* and *GK's Weekly*. There was a movement called Distributism that was very prominent at that time, because it was supposed to be the antidote to Communism. So that was the way that political thought at that time tended to polarize.

MWT: In 'The Night of the Fire' and other essays, as well as in your fiction, you as a mature writer have interpreted Penyberth for us. But can you go back and remember what, at the time – in 1936 – the event meant for you?

EH: Reassertion of a national identity. It made you feel that after all there was something important in being Welsh – there was a value attached to it: it wasn't something to turn your back on, it was something to adopt and to cherish and to defend.

MWT: The picture you've given me leads me to wonder whether there may not have been an element of adolescent rebellion in your espousal of Welsh nationalism, given your father's attitudes.

EH: Oh, quite likely. Not that I was a rebellious youngster by nature, but I was repudiating my father's political beliefs. He was a National Liberal, and all my mother's family were the same, or Lloyd George Liberals. They were never Socialist.

MWT: So how did your father respond when it emerged that you'd thrown in your lot with the Welsh Nationalists?

EH: I think he groaned a bit. But, partly because they did spoil me to some extent, they didn't repudiate me. They didn't agree, but they wouldn't have the heart or the will, so to speak, to cast me out. Neither my father nor my mother was particularly politically aware. What counted were things like the choir – my father had a choir, and along with being the headmaster of a country school, this took all his energy, since he was an invalid. Both of them adored sport – both went to watch football, not in Liverpool but in Rhyl! They were appalled later by the fact that I was a conscientious objector; then they thought I'd gone completely off the rails. But they were very kind. My father – who hated to travel – came by train all the way to Aberystwyth to try to persuade me to continue with my course of study there. I was intending at that time to be an ordinand in the Church in Wales, but then I decided to go off, with Robin Richards, to live on this farm in Pembrokeshire. We thought that the world was going to come to an end, but that there would remain remnants of Welsh affiliation on the land. It was a theory as much as a practice. I left university, to my father's dismay, before ever I was called before a tribunal as a conscientious objector. I felt, by then, that I hadn't the vocation to become a clergyman, although I'd been offered a place in St Stephen's Hall, at Oxford. That had pleased my father no end, but I thought that was all wrong – I was a bit confused, really. I do remember the feeling that the only thing to do was to get back to the land, and I was already working on this farm when I was given the exemption to stay there by the tribunal – and later I had to get another tribunal to get off it, because the traditional exemption was for working on the land, so when I wanted to go to London to work for the Save the Children Fund I had to have the permisson of a tribunal to be allowed to change. I don't regret it – it was a huge education to do these things. I didn't grow up until this started. If you were born in 1919, as I was, the entire period between the end of the First World War and the beginning of the Second World War was the time you needed for growing up. Nothing really resolved itself, for me, until the end of the Second War: it was then, really, that you had your compass bearings. I was a very slow developer, not only as a child . . .

MWT: I don't think that's unusual for artists, because there is a different incubation period for different gifts.

EH: Yes, and there's also a kind of essential naivety when faced with life's dilemmas. Although I was scribbling away all the time, one way or another, I don't think that much of what I'd been writing was of any consequence, with the exception of my early drafts of what, more than a dozen years later, became *A Toy Epic*.

MWT: Why scribble?

EH: I don't know, it's a strange compulsion. Even when I was working in the fields I would usually have a piece of paper and pencil, and when it was time to sit in the hedge and have a bite to eat – we were working with horses, because at this early stage of the war tractors hadn't arrived – I would try to scribble something, even then.

MWT: Later, you became renowned for your advocacy of the social and cultural role of the Welsh writer, but you didn't have that concept of what it was to be a writer when you started, did you?

EH: No, not at all. I had no concept whatsoever of the role of the writer at that time, just the urge to self-expression, a desire to put something into words all the time, to communicate to yourself before communicating with anyone else, to clarify your mind. I think the impulse was purely poetic at the beginning, and what I needed more than anything else, as time went on, was some kind of objective correlative. Communication became increasingly impossible for me until I found a story. I found my form when I found fiction, and I could have jumped up and down for joy at discovering this, because I had the other problem as well: I wanted to write in Welsh, but I didn't have enough Welsh for that purpose. I can remember performing certain exercises in order to improve my command of the Welsh language – I can remember trying to translate poems by C. Day Lewis. So I was in a real cleft stick, and the discovery of fiction was a great blessing.

MWT: Can you remember when exactly you discovered yourself to be a fiction writer?

EH: I think it was when I began to work on what later became *A Toy Epic*. That fired the possibility. And, of course, you do have vague, amorphous ambitions – a searching for you know not what – and then you stumble on what you didn't really know you were looking for. It doesn't change very much throughout the years, really, when you're the kind of writer I am. The problems remain the same, the process remains the same, and the need remains the same – over a period of sixty years. The need never really abates: it is an obsessional necessity.

MWT: Since storytelling has been so important to you as a fiction writer, has it also played an important part in your ordinary life? Are you the kind of person who weaves experiences into a narrative?

EH: No, writing stories is quite separate from that. My impulses in ordinary life have nothing at all to do with fiction. My interests and my urges are towards religion and philosophy – those are my normal dynamics. Going into fiction is a release, or relief.

MWT: Are you surprised by the fiction you produce?

EH: Always. If I'm not surprised, the work probably isn't very good. And there's a quality to your writing that, when it's achieved, you instinctively feel, 'That's OK: I can go and do something else now.' If that doesn't mysteriously come, then you tear up what you're working on. I don't want my failures to be exposed – and you have to fail, quite often. When you embark on a fiction, it can take you quite a long time to find the door that opens to where you want to get to. So there are bound to be lots of false starts.

MWT: I know of the Welsh-language writers you admire – they'd include Kate Roberts, John Gwilym Jones (who was a close friend), and obviously Saunders Lewis. But if we move outside the field of Welsh-language culture, what other writers have been important to you?

EH: In my youth, T. S. Eliot was the twin deity with Saunders Lewis. I didn't realize at the time how closely they coincided intellectually with each other. Then I actually came to know Graham Greene, and that became a very good spur towards realizing the possibilities of fiction. I did cherish, when young, the hope of being a reasonably successful novelist commercially, but it didn't really happen – and now I can see why! And then I very greatly admired D. H. Lawrence always, and always very greatly admired James Joyce. And on top of that there were all the great novelists – Tolstoy, Stendhal and their like – I was devouring novels at one time.

MWT: When would you have been doing that?

EH: During the war a lot, because there was nothing else to do, when you weren't working or on duty in some way. I was very lucky that when I joined the Save the Children Fund we were given a house in Chelsea – by Quakers, I think – which was a very cultured house, full of books in several languages. Then I became friends with Basil McTaggart, who was a master of five or six languages, so that other doors opened in many ways from then on.

MWT: So in a sense you had two kinds of education, formal education from grammar school to university, but also that other kind of education, which has been much more important for you in the long term.

EH: Much more – not that that is any reflection on the education system, it's just that I was a poor pupil. I think what I enjoyed most in formal education, during my two years at Aberystwyth, was history, particularly the medieval history taught by the history professor. I didn't enjoy English so much – Anglo-Saxon I didn't like, because it involved discipline and hard work, which I wasn't very good at! And Latin and French were fine, but I was not a good student.

MWT: Whereas some readers might feel they could trace the influence of Kate Roberts or Saunders Lewis or T. S. Eliot on your work, it would be difficult to trace any sign of D. H. Lawrence. So how did he matter to you?

EH: First of all, I loved his poetry, more than his prose. But what I liked about his novels was something I haven't got myself at all: the ability to make the whole of nature come to life off the page – not so much characterization in the ordinary sense but this wonderful vision of a living world. I think that the more traditional forms of fiction would have had much more influence on me when I was young – the novels of Tolstoy or Balzac: I've always thought enormously highly of Balzac. Mind you, I was reading these in translation, and my friend Basil would always say, 'You should read them in the original'. And I think it was absolutely true. Although fiction does translate far more easily than anything else, there are no two ways about it, to appreciate any writer you need to read the original. So I've dabbled in trying to read in Italian and German poetry, but always with a crib.

MWT: Those experiences of the inadequacy of translation have clearly influenced the way in which you've written, in your essays, about translating, and the misgivings that are expressed there.

EH: Yes, I was just thinking now about the story I'm currently trying to write. It may well not come off. It's called 'Nightmares', and in the text the nightmare of the child, and the nightmare of his parents, and the nightmare of his grandparents are all coexisting but conflicting. And this is actually true – when you adopt the language of the oppressor, the imperial power or whatever it may be, you are taking part in the oppression. You yourself become guilty. You therefore have this terrible nightmarish conflict, which has been with me all my life in the form of an inner tension. And in the case of the story on which I'm working, it becomes connected with the struggle against globalization – if you object to globalization you must flourish in the local; if you flourish in the local, you must flourish in the local root; and the local root is the language that belongs to the landscape; and the language that belongs to the landscape here in Wales is Welsh. That is the theorem on which I base my work, and it enables me to understand the agony of a Jewish poet like Paul Celan, who was writing in German. It is, for the artist, a suicidal situation, a situation which in Celan's case resulted in actual physical suicide. One of the escape routes is fiction, because story is a language of its own, a music of its own, a supranational language which is detached from the cultural problem. And that may be one reason why, culturally situated as I am, I find fiction such a very attractive form.

MWT: One aspect of the cultural situation in Wales on which you have insisted in your essays is that it faces the writer with a fateful choice between serving the native, indigenous culture or of participating in the worldwide cultural empire of the English language.

EH: Yes, and in my own personal experience Saunders Lewis and Goronwy Rees were two charismatic figures who dramatically exemplified these two options. The contrast between the two is quite striking. Both of them were sons of Welsh Calvinistic ministers and therefore came out of the same cultural milieu, but they very deliberately took very different paths. I knew them both reasonably well. I remember doing a play with an actress called Beatrix Lehmann, the sister of the novelist Rosamund Lehmann – she and Goronwy Rees had been lovers in the thirties. I recall Beatrix Lehmann going on about Goronwy because she remembered him from the thirties as a rabid Welsh nationalist who had a big chip on his shoulder. That didn't at all coincide with my own, later, experiences of him, so obviously he had been a very different character in his youth, a rebel in a number of directions, because he had great sympathies with the Left as well. By the time I came to know him well, he had left Aberystwyth under a cloud – it was a terrific cause célèbre of the fifties, and the Welsh intelligentsia had been divided on the subject. So by the time I was working in the BBC in London, alongside producers such as Louis MacNeice and others, their attitude was that Goronwy had been badly treated by these philistines in Wales. I also remember Goronwy coming to stay the night with us in Penarth in the sixties, because I was doing his translation of Brecht. I thought this would be a good opportunity to see how Goronwy and Saunders Lewis would react to each other face to face. So I rang up Saunders and invited him over to dinner. But he refused, explaining that he had no wish to meet a man 'sydd yn elyn i'r iaith Gymraeg', who is an enemy of the Welsh language. I was very embarrassed at the time, because I felt I was like a circus performer with one foot on one horse and one on another, and I was bound to come a cropper! I'm only telling you the story because it illustrates the situation that Welsh writers and intellectuals are always confronted with. And Goronwy Rees and Saunders Lewis both belonged to the generation before this situation, this choice, had made itself abundantly clear. Each of them followed his own path, which in Goronwy Rees's case led to All Souls, and in Saunders Lewis's case led to Wormwood Scrubs. To me this seems the prototypical Welsh situation, and it is going to recur, because you have a bilingual society, with allegiance to two different cultures, two different social, economic and political structures. Writers therefore have got to find some way of living with it. In an ideal world, it would be possible to abandon English altogether, and do what the Israelis have done – create an independent society which is entirely Welsh-speaking and where English is learnt only for convenience. To me, this would be an ideal, but I can quite see that it wouldn't be for 99 per cent of the population. This is the situation I have to live with, and therefore as an independent writer I have become an author who exerts his own authority, since in fiction I can control the circumstances in a way that would be totally impossible in real life. So, it could be that writers of my kind are propelled by, and find a great creative dynamic in, the fact that the very world they would like to have lies beyond their reach. Indeed, it is going increasingly, and further, beyond their reach as time goes on. So a dark and pessimistic way of looking at such a writer would be to suggest that the ultimate logic of his career is that it will end in silence.

MWT: You mentioned that Goronwy Rees and Saunders Lewis belonged to a generation for whom the choice you've outlined was not as yet brilliantly clear. Would it be fair to say that, for writers of your own generation, it was Saunders Lewis who, through his writing and actions, highlighted that choice?

EH: Yes, it was his own clarity of vision that made the choice clear to us. He has a book which I think ought to have been translated into English a long time ago, called *Canlyn Arthur*, where he does put down some very extreme points of view. He has one essay which is both brilliant and uncomfortable – 'Carthago Delenda Est' – where he makes it perfectly clear that the only salvation for Wales is to do away with English. There is a frightening logic about it. If you want to maintain an identity, the first step you must take is linguistic, and unless you have the supreme power invested in the language, you have no hope whatsoever of maintaining your identity. I think Israel is the classic example of this in the modern world. Whether it is desirable or not is another question. But it is a practical truth, and it is a practical truth that all the European nations have got to come to terms with in the twenty-first century, when American English is set – perhaps along with Chinese – to dominate the world. Neither of these is European in its centre of gravity, and therefore the European situation is a very special one, which is going to become ever more apparent. Because insofar as language is fundamental to identity, every European nation, large or small, will have to grapple with this question. The only alternative is a kind of globalization which will eventually extinguish their separate identity, and I cannot see any other outcome in western civilization myself. As you put it in your book about America, the only choice is whether this is going to be a European Wales or an American Wales. If it's going to be an American Wales then it's going to be in even greater danger than it is in being a minor part of Britain.

MWT: You have long regarded yourself as a Welsh and European writer. When did that awareness begin? Does it go back to wartime, or is it post-war?

EH: I think it's something to do with becoming a commercial failure, because it took a long time for me to realise that the English reading public is not terribly interested in knowing about Wales. They've got far greater interest in Papua New Guinea, or the Solomon Islands, or anywhere. Therefore anybody with the ambition of being a successful commercial novelist would have to make a choice. It became clear to me by about the middle fifties that the subject that interested me, that gave me a reason for writing, was not a subject that interested the reading public outside Wales to any meaningful extent. Not many of my books have been translated into European languages – some into French and some into Swedish, but not much. I think the European literary market has not awoken to some of the problems that we're already aware of: they are very anglophile in their outlook, and the European choice is the false one between British English on the one hand and American English on the other. They've come to the conclusion that America is the more interesting, but they have yet to face the problems of how to maintain their own distinctive, indigenous cultures in the face of this challenge from the culture of the USA.

MWT: Europe may be slow to recognize writers such as yourself, but you have certainly been interested in European culture, in particular the culture of Italy, where you served during the latter stages of the Second World War. What is it about Italy and its writers that appeals to you?

EH: I think Italy is in many respects the home of European culture as a whole – the source of Latin, the source of medieval civilization, is Italy. You feel that the minute you're there. And of course I have got to know a number of Italian writers. I met and liked Vittorini very much, and I also admired Sciascia, the Sicilian writer. Montale and Ungaretti are two of the Italian poets whose work has meant a great deal to me. Pirandello and Verga were modern writers of the novella tradition that stretches back to Boccaccio. And I've also loved the rootedness of Italian life – the *paese* idea, that Italy is in itself a continent not a country and that it includes an infinite number of regional variations and of local dialects which sustain their own thriving literatures. Writers like Primo Levi and Italo Calvino remind us that the Italians are a defeated nation, who experienced a terrible war and have recovered. They are very important to European life. They haven't got the pretensions of the French, who are much more like the English in being imperialistic and convinced of their own superiority. The Italians haven't got that at all, and neither do the Germans: these two great defeated nations seem to me to be the two most civilized European nations of our days. France is a much more difficult question, because they can't come to terms with the fact that they ever were defeated, and so have great difficulty in coming to terms with what they think they are. Whereas there can be no question that the

Germans and the Italians have been through the fire and have come out as something different.

MWT: Have any of the Italian writers you've mentioned influenced your actual manner of writing?

EH: No, I don't think so. Italy has functioned in my writing only as a source of fictional raw material. I do, of course, have a particular interest in the Etruscans, in part because of the parallel between their history and that of another vanished civilization, the Celts. These were the two great pre-classical civilizations of Europe, and they actually had quite a lot to do with each other. The mysterious thing about the Etruscans is that they developed a very high civilization, probably on a par for sophistication with that of the Greeks. Yet they left virtually nothing in the way of writing. What they left were grave goods, and these have been systematically exploited down the centuries, down to this very day. And it's a huge area, stretching from the gates of Rome to Florence and beyond – it's much more than just Tuscany – and it exerts a mysterious fascination. You can still feel their presence. Their graves are houses, and when you go into their necropolis it's like going into an empty house where the occupants have left all kinds of objects of ordinary everyday use but the occupants themselves are no longer there. There's a strangely contemporary feel to the experience – there's no sense of antiquity, of life lived two or three thousand years ago: it feels as if it's happening now. And it's as if you're offered a parable of the fate of the human race itself. They've deserted the planet, so to speak, leaving behind almost living evidence of their presence: but where have they gone? Etruscan remains have all sorts of numinous qualities, I think.

MWT: Your interest in European writing took a different form back in the fifties, when you joined the BBC, because you made a conscious attempt at that time to bring European drama to Wales. Did that prove significant for your future writing – did your work in radio and television at that time result in any change in technique?

EH: I think it had quite a lot of influence, more than I realized myself. In the first instance, I was lucky to start working in radio at the very end of a golden era, and so I met very interesting writers and thinkers and producers who must have had a considerable influence on me. I mentioned Louis MacNeice earlier, but there was also Martin Esslin, the man who brought Brecht into the English-speaking world, and I had quite a lot to do with him. He was very much a Central European in his outlook on everything. He was a great admirer not only of Brecht but also of Beckett and of Pinter, so he was a pivotal figure in many ways. As a writer, I had to measure up what I was trying to do with what these much better writers were doing. So there was a benchmark of method and of style and of content. I was only in the BBC for ten years, but it was an important period for me.

MWT: Would that help explain why one of your major novels, *Outside the House of Baal*, appeared during that period?

EH: Absolutely. I remember having a conversation with John Ormond – I was working in television and he in film – and he asked me what I was writing. I explained that what I wanted to do was to write a novel where you only put down either what people say or what they do. He was very intrigued with this, because it corresponded with what a film-maker would do. So it's obvious that that urge came from working in the media. But it also came through another door. I had a colleague in the BBC called Walter Todds, who became a close friend: he was a music producer who was very interested in philosophy and it was through him that I began to read Wittgenstein. And of course some of the famous pronunciations of Wittgenstein appealed enormously to me at that time as methods of writing. 'The world is that which is the case'; 'It's not how a thing is but why it is' – all these aphorisms reverberated in my mind and led me to feel that this was a valid way of writing fiction in one language about a life that had happened for the most part in another. So the time at the BBC was a vital, inspirational period, although I wasn't so aware of that at the time: a lot of my conclusions now are a case of being wise long after the event. It was a subliminal influence.

MWT: And then another long period, after you'd left the BBC, was dedicated to the writing of that remarkable seven-novel sequence, 'The Land of the Living'. Where did the idea for that project come from?

EH: The original ambition was to try and make a companion novel to *Outside the House of Baal*, where the leading element would be space rather than time. That sounds terribly pretentious now, but these are the kind of formulae and theories that I need in order to get to grips with materials. This is the scaffolding, so to speak, that's needed. Then that novel grew into a sequence, partly because space had to give way to time. Once you adopt a chronological narration, time must take over, and that's the difference between the structure of *National Winner* and the other six.

MWT: Did you have any models of the saga novel in mind? I'm thinking of Anthony Powell's *A Dance to the Music of Time*, for instance.

EH: No, I was struggling hard against making it a sequence in the first instance, because I happened to be in very close contact at that time with C. P. Snow, who was writing a sequence, called *Strangers and Brothers*, and the early volumes were quite good, but they got progressively more wooden and pedestrian as they went along. He'd become caught in the whole scheme, and it had blighted the effort. So I wanted to avoid that at all costs. In the case of Anthony Powell, who is a more light-hearted ('gay' in the old sense), more confident, more subtle and more amusing writer, it seemed to me that he was dealing with a very restricted stratum of social life. It was delightful to read, because it was a *roman à clef*: you knew who all these characters were, since they were all part of the Bohemian upper-class literati in London, which is fine: that was his field. But anything of that sort was useless to me, because I have no experience of that kind of life, and have even less affection for it, so I would have to deal with the kind of society with which I was involved and knew intimately. The shape of the sequence therefore imposed itself upon me, against my wishes.

MWT: So when did this fiction make it clear to you that it required a sequence in order to fulfil it? You started with *National Winner*, but then moved back, in *Flesh and Blood*, to begin at the beginning of Amy's life. By then was it clear that you were embarking on a sequence?

EH: Yes, once I'd started that novel I was committed; but it was extremely difficult material, because I had to earn a living – I'd left the university and re-entered the world of television, and the trick was to earn enough in that medium and carry on the series. So there are quite big gaps between the publication of the novels, which is why the writing of the sequence extended over a period of twenty years.

MWT: The role of Amy in the whole sequence, does that seem to you to be central? Or would you argue that interest is dispersed across many characters?

EH: I think she is the central character, the dominant female, and John Cilydd a weak male, and this correspondence between the sexes seems to be a fair reproduction of Welsh experience in the twentieth century. Everything flows from that. She's like a mirror walking down the street, but not the only mirror, so you have a multi-perspective portrait. Many of the characters are marching down the street of history, the march of time, and each one reflects something of the times. So, in pictorial terms, it's the juxtaposition of these different colours that make up the complete image. The whole is greater than the sum of the parts.

MWT: So here again you're indicating the importance for you of abstract painting as a model for your work. The sequence resembles a Cubist painting, for instance, in the way it offers a simultaneity of many different points of view, or angles of vision.

EH: That's very important, because of the fractured nature of civilization in the twentieth century. It's a better reflection of the pain and agony, the splendours and miseries of the whole period.

MWT: The writing of such a sequence presumably presented you with another problem, since each of the novels had to be free-standing and self-sufficient in order to be sold as one-off novels to readers who might not be interested in the series as a whole.

EH: Yes, that was a convenient problem in a way, because it coincided with my working situation. I was never under any compulsion to finish everything within a given time. So I had plenty of time to think about how things developed, so the weaving of this pattern took a long time, but it made it possible to build up the separate units in a viable form. I hope there's not too much overlap and wastage in the whole.

MWT: How much of the course of Amy's life, as the sequence now shows it to us, was clear to you when you started *Flesh and Blood*?

EH: *National Winner* had of course already been written, and in that novel she was Lady Brangor, an elderly lady who had already been married twice and had accumulated a family and experience and wealth. So if she began in fairly poor surroundings that would make the story a fairly simple, classic Catherine Cookson pattern; an elementary plot!

MWT: But then you presumably kept discovering along the way aspects of Amy's character, people in her life, actions of hers that you hadn't been able to foresee?

EH: Oh, yes. There is a sense in which novels begin by being gaseous clouds that coalesce, firm up, and then become palpable qualities. So you have to leave space for intuitive creation. You don't know whether the thing is right until you've actually done it. It's only when you know it's working that you can be sure.

MWT: Since it took you so long to write the whole sequence, many things changed while you were at work upon it. You changed in that time; the world changed in that time; and the world of publishing changed in that time. Did those changes leave their mark on the sequence?

EH: Fortunately, the sequence ends about 1970, just after the Investiture, so some of the great transformations that have happened since didn't impinge. One of the central things is the contraceptive pill, which has made an enormous difference to the novel as a form. The other is the mobile phone. These have transformed social life in a way novelists have still to come to grips with. And I think that's one of the undeclared reasons why so much explicit sex has become part of the structure of the modern commercial novel. It has to do with the fact that novelists cannot cope with the intricacies of social interaction, since society has been subjected to centrifugal forces, blowing it apart. So that there's nothing left except the sexual connection to provide the fulcrum of the story – the whole narrative hangs on a penis, as it were, instead of on a pen. The only notable exceptions are writers, such as black writers, coming from a society shaped by stress. But in the prosperous societies such as England, they've lost touch with these elements in the novel, so what has happened is that creative writers are attracted to the biographical. One work that I enjoyed very much reading recently was Penelope Fitzgerald's novel based on the life of the German poet Novalis – an example of biography being used as a prop to sustain the novelist's form. The other thing is the huge increase in popularity of biography itself. It has virtually taken the place of the novel over the last twenty or thirty years. And I think that these great cultural shifts are due to social revolutions brought about by things small enough in themselves, like the pill and the mobile phone. It's as if the novel in England is in the same condition as the Tory Party: it doesn't know really what it wants nor where it's going. So the people who practise the form with the greatest success are outsiders, such as Salman Rushdie, whose real source of inspiration is India. There's much more exciting writing being done in English by non-English writers than by the English in England. And this is an extraordinary state of affairs to me. So I consider myself to be very lucky, in that I have a parish and a subject matter which I can explore without having to worry too much about the social context. Our problems in Wales are comparatively simple in a way, and we've lived with them for a long time. We're bilingual and we're schizophrenic culturally, and we know that we are, and we know that this is one of our major challenges. The challenge for an invalid is to be interested in the nature of his complaints without becoming a hypochondriac.

A Lost Leader?

First published in *Planet* 83 (October/November 1990), 3–11.

Even at the end of the twentieth century, the language, absent or present, remains the key to the Welsh condition. A biographer such as Paul Ferris, with a penchant for Welsh subjects – Aneurin Bevan, John Jenkins, Evan Roberts, Dylan Thomas, and now Huw Wheldon – needs to be able to read Welsh. Otherwise the language lurks in the background like a mythological mist, liable to become a source of unstable speculation, obscuring those elements of abiding truth that in the end justify the existence of biography as a literary form. In *Sir Huge,** Paul Ferris has made a gallant effort to trawl the depths of his subject's ancestry, but as a result of his ignorance of Welsh literary tradition (an ignorance, as I am sure he would hasten to point out, he shares with about 80 per cent of the population), the biggest fish in those Methodist-ical waters escapes his net.

Huw Wheldon's great-great-great-grandfather was the redoubtable Robert Jones, Rhoslan. Even among mountain folk who are known to possess geological affinities that attach them more closely than the rest of us to the rock from which they are hewn, it may seem absurd to require research of such genetic particularity. But the reader should know that Robert Jones, Rhoslan, was a founding father of that Welsh Calvinistic Methodist Connexion that created the close and dynamic social order in which generations of Wheldons and Joneses were brought up. In many ways the Welsh Nonconformist world was a tighter and more demanding polity than some of the eastern European communist states we have seen crumbling rather than withering away over the last eighteen months: and it was more durable, it could be argued, because it was based on a deeper intuitive understanding of the strengths and weaknesses of human nature than the more abstract intellectual analyses of Marx and Engels. Robert Jones was a carpenter who only enjoyed six weeks' formal schooling: but he was caught up in the spiritual upheaval brought about by Harris, Pantycelyn and Rowlands and thereby given the power to compose eight books, the last of which, *Drych yr Amseroedd* (A Mirror of the Age) he published at the

* *Sir Huge: The Life of Huw Wheldon,* by Paul Ferris (Michael Joseph, 1990).

age of seventy-five in the year 1820. This book is rightly considered a Welsh classic in a tradition of historiography that reaches back as far as the sixth century and Gildas's *De Excidio et Conquestu Britanniae.*

In Robert Jones two archetypal myths meet and mingle: the Loss of Britain, that Welsh obsession with their imagined loss of sovereignty of 'The Island of the Mighty', that can be traced through Theophilus Evans, Charles Edwards, the Protestant reformers and translators, to Geoffrey of Monmouth, Nennius and Gildas; and the biblical captivities of another chosen people who were punished for their sins and shortcomings. In its own inimitable anecdotal way, *Drych yr Amseroedd* gives the myths a fresh twist and a new lease of life. It takes the form of a first-hand account of 'the wondrous work of the Lord, in his great mercy, spreading the light of his Gospel through Wales in these latter days'. In the course of his long life Jones had seen his 'society', his 'people', transform themselves from a persecuted and faintly subversive minority into the first fully-fledged indigenous institution to emerge in Wales since the fifteenth century. In 1811 the Welsh Calvinistic Methodists incorporated themselves as a separate church and a theocratic society. (In 1819, Iolo Morganwg, in temporary alliance with Bishop Burgess, launched Gorsedd y Beirdd in the garden of the Ivy Bush in Carmarthen. The carpenter and the stone-mason are obliged by either the music of the spheres or the Spirit of the Years to join the same dance. This decade marks the emergence of the Welsh from the darkness of provincial obscurity to a condition of renewed, if flawed and at times feverish, nationhood.) A national existence on the bright uplands of Renewal could only be sustained by careful organization. A dense network of Nonconformist chapels needed to be built where the hungry sheep could look up and be fed. In addition to an option on eternity, the Welsh would be given a social order, stability and a measure of material security that had been denied them throughout the long centuries of defeat and loss and oppression and superstitious darkness.

To understand Wheldon and the force that through the green Welsh fuse drove him, it is essential to read Robert Jones's modest masterpiece. I say 'modest' because Jones himself stressed the imperfections of his work and because his character was notably modest and unassuming. In his own day his reputation rested on his missionary zeal, his elegant prose style and his loyalty to men like Thomas Charles and John Elias whose talents he considered to be so much greater than his own. This self-educated artisan was equipped with the sonorous Welsh of the Tudor Bible. The dignity of the language as much as the sobriety and puritanical mode of methodism (with a small 'm') required that this renewed nation should become bourgeois as rapidly as possible. It was the Calvinistic Methodists (*Y Trefnyddion* – The Organizers) who set the pace. What had been an inexplicable release of spiritual energy was transformed into a social order with all the trappings and inhibitions of 'tradition' in a matter of two generations.

Huw Wheldon's grandfather, Thomas Jones Wheldon, was born in 1841. His *Cofiant*, that specialist form of biography propagated throughout the nineteenth century for the edification of the faithful of all denominations, was published in 1925 at the instigation of his son, Major Wynn Wheldon DSO (later Sir Wynn), then registrar of the University College at Bangor. It specifies the concerns and causes to which T. J. Wheldon dedicated his considerable energies: building bigger chapels; the imperative disestablishment of the Anglican Church in Wales; free education, primary, secondary, higher; pension schemes for ministers; Presbyterian management of the affairs of the denomination; teetotalism; the establishment of English-language chapels controlled by the Connexion, even in Welsh-speaking areas; and a sufficient degree of self-government for Wales to ensure that neither English governments nor Welsh politicians should exercise those powers over the lives of the people that properly belonged to Nonconformist ministers in general and Calvinistic Methodists in particular. Even in 1926 it appeared that his had been an energetic and exceptionally fruitful career. True, it almost came to grief over his determination to build a chapel in Bangor big enough to celebrate his vision of the importance and power of a Presbyterian Church of Wales.

The characters and the careers of the grandfather and grandson bear sufficient resemblance to each other to remind the thoughtful reader of the Calvinistic origins of the denomination to which the family owed a fierce and hereditary loyalty. This was a sect which aspired to be an established church. In Thomas Wheldon's day, his *Cyfundeb* cherished a thinly disguised ambition to exercise its authority in every aspect of Welsh life. When this ambition was thwarted the urge for power was turned in upon itself, so that the lives of members of the denomination were governed and circumscribed to an even greater degree than the other sects of the Nonconformist world. Here again *yr Hen Gorff* set the pace. Certainly, it provided sufficient outlets for all Thomas Wheldon's considerable energies. He is described as a thrustful, positive, restless, impatient, argumentative, eloquent man with an irrepressible urge to get things done. He was explosive and yet serious, bold and yet puritanical, adventurous with a love of responding to a challenge, moderated by a fierce loyalty to the organization to which he belonged. As Mr Ferris's biography demonstrates, *mutatis mutandis,* much the same could be said for Huw's devotion to the BBC: 'He was committed to the BBC as if to a Cause . . . He thought of it as a jewel of Western civilization . . . It provided a context for him to flourish in.'

It is clear that as a family the Wheldons were brought up to accept responsibility and revere tradition. The men appear upright, loyal, brave and given to marrying late. They have no desire to make radical changes to existing constitutional structures and therefore no great interest in party politics. At the same time their combative natures relished causes for which to fight and took trouble to find them. This biography shows, for example, how long it took Huw Wheldon to find the cause to which he could devote all his energies, and how well he fought for it as long as he could. There can be no questioning the loyalty and devotion and courage that these men were prepared to lavish on the institutions for which they worked. What they seemed to lack is that breadth of vision capable of redirecting power to meet great historic change. They needed that degree of sensitivity and creative originality that had been so evident in the writing and personality of Robert Jones, Rhoslan. In the life of European nations it seems inevitable that there are moments when the fate of a people depends more on the sensibility of a poet than on the dedication of a civil servant. In our own experience we can turn to another Robert Jones in order to discover this principle in operation: the vision of an inconspicuous man of letters working as an antidote to the provincial dogmatism and legalistic orthodoxy that restricted the lives of dedicated pastors like T. J. Wheldon.

Robert Ambrose Jones (Emrys ap Iwan) was ten years Wheldon's junior. As that valuable compilation, *The Oxford Companion to the Literature of Wales,* would reveal to any interested researcher, Emrys had a French great-grandmother. He knew French and German and taught English at Lausanne before returning to Wales to prepare for ordination with the Welsh Calvinistic Methodists. He vehemently opposed the decision of the Assembly to establish English-language chapels in Welsh-speaking areas, a cause very close to the heart of T. J. Wheldon, and even more importantly, sponsored by Lewis Edwards, the outstanding leader of the denomination, bent on pressing it into a Scots Presbyterian mould. (Lewis Edwards had been educated at Edinburgh.) Emrys challenged the established order. He objected to Welsh funds and Welsh families being used to set up the nuclei of 'English Causes' that would cater for the rising flood of English-speaking immigrants and win their allegiance to a Presbyterian church of Wales that would thus continue to expand and maintain its considerable influence in Welsh life. (As so often in Welsh life, popularity takes precedence before principle.) In any case, Edwards, Wheldon and the bulk of the leadership of *yr Hen Gorff* assumed that Welsh was dying and that English was, in every sense, a better bet. Emrys the European insisted that the language was the soul of Welshness: to conspire in its ruin, however obliquely, was the cultural equivalent of the sin against the Holy Ghost. At a fateful church assembly at Llanidloes in 1881, Emrys was refused ordination ostensibly for a number of heretical views and the Welsh Calvinistic Methodists adopted the Edwards-Wheldon policies which, it could be argued with jaundiced hindsight, led to their present state of polite, well-meaning provincial impotence. It is not entirely frivolous to suggest that churches and broadcasting corporations, if they are to flourish, have at some point to draw a line; and that line is the missionary minimum to which, like Martin Luther, they are obliged to adhere: 'here we stand: we can do no other.'

Emrys saw the Welsh going one better than the children of Israel. They made for themselves two graven images to worship: the Golden Calf and the Calf of Imitating the English. These twin objects of reverence are still very much in evidence. History may not repeat itself but the Welsh condition has a haunting capacity for changing and remaining the same thing. At the end of this turbulent century, *Cofiant T. J. Wheldon* and *Cofiant Emrys ap Iwan* still repay careful study. T. J. Wheldon played his part on the only stage where the Welsh could confront the problem and drama of their precarious national being in the 1880s, that is, the assemblies of denominational religion. They were well aware of this. When Emrys declared at Llanidloes: 'I do not consider fidelity or infidelity to our language a subject for debate. I could not support any move towards Anglicizing our people without going against my political convictions,' it was reported in the Welsh press that he was greeted with derision. At that time the Elders of the Assembly considered it comic that an ordinand should not only possess political opinions but seek to parade them in their common language. Politics, and the decisions of life and death that went with it, belonged exclusively to the English language and the English-speaking imperial parliament. Welsh peasants like Welsh pheasants should keep their heads down and be thankful for the religious undergrowth that all but concealed their plump pietistic existence.

Huw Wheldon's career began to develop in a period where the mass media – above all television – had long replaced organized religion as the chief 'Opium of the People'. Channels of graciousness had replaced channels of grace: but from the onset and particularly in the Welsh context the vexed question of language lay at the heart of the process. It should not be forgotten that radio came to Wales as a BBC extension of a civil service culture where the medium of transmission was middle-class English. Cardiff to begin with was no more than a sub-post office to Bristol and it took many years of campaigning by literary figures such as W. J. Gruffydd and Iorwerth Peate, supported by the more vociferous Welsh religious denominations, to get any Welsh-speakers established on the staff. The 'Welsh Region' of the BBC came into existence as a result of a timely collaboration between the two most gifted (and probably most untypical) Welshmen in public life at that crucial time: the ageing Lloyd George and the still young Saunders Lewis. Lewis made the ammunition and the ex-prime minister fired it to such effect that he dented the armour-plated complacency of Sir John Reith (yet another son of the manse) sufficiently to make a place for a pinch of Welsh in the Reithian messianic vision of middle-class English culture circulating the globe. The Second World War put Welsh broadcasting into cold storage. Indeed the freeze was so deep it could not have been restored to life without the team of exceptional talent whose members were recruited to produce programmes in both Welsh and English (T. Rowland Hughes, P. H. Burton, Aneirin Talfan Davies, Hywel and Lorraine Davies, Elwyn Evans, May Jones, Sam Jones, Ifan O. Williams, Nan Davies, Myfanwy Howell and many others). These producers saw to it that radio played an active and constructive part in Welsh cultural life for a decade or longer. Huw Wheldon was not among them.

On the face of it this may appear surprising. Like his father before him Huw had a distinguished war record. According to Paul Ferris's account, it was through his father's influence ('Sir Wynn Wheldon knew most of those concerned . . .') that Huw became director for Wales of the Arts Council of Great Britain. This was a high-sounding title for the job of dispersing small grants to support 'pockets of culture'. He lasted three years. 'What freed him from Wales', writes Mr Ferris, 'was the Festival of Britain, that noble if eccentric gesture of hope for the future.'

There is a sad sense in which this sentence encapsulates the career pattern of generations of ambitious young Welshmen. In the eyes of the Welsh themselves, Wales passes muster as a nest or a nursery slope, provided the fledgling flies away on a prevailing wind that will land him safely on the rooftops of the heart of the Empire. The Festival of Britain in more prosperous and self-confident times would have been called the Festival of England, a more accurate description. It was the brainchild of the editor of the *News Chronicle* and was intended to echo the Great Exhibition of 1851 at the Crystal Palace in the days when the Empire circled the globe. The original spirit of adventure and jovial savagery which had carved out that profitable enterprise would be replaced by modern design and technology. In a new era of cultural imperialism institutions like the BBC would carry on the divinely directed mission to civilise 'lesser breeds without the Law' and the Labour government at Westminster would lie back and bask in reflected glory. It was a very good thing, from the English point of view, to demonstrate that London was resolved to keep up with Paris and New York; but, as Huw would have been the first to admit, it had very little to do with Wales and its proliferating problems of economic, social and cultural anaemia.

There had been no place for Wheldon in the emerging BBC Welsh Region. The administrative commanding heights in Cardiff were already occupied. Huw was not a poet or an experienced producer. He was a man of action waiting to be stretched. If all that was called for in Park Place was a sedate institution designed to cast a pale hue of native culture over a regional extension of public service, it hardly gave much scope for his talents. He may not have been interested in politics but like his father and his grandfather before him he well understood that cultural power always rested close to where the political decisions were made. He never became alienated or ill-disposed to the Welsh language and its cultural manifestations. What he saw, even in those early uncomfortable years in the BBC publicity department, were the limitations circumscribing Welsh cultural and social institutions. He knew as well as anybody, if only from self-knowledge, that the Welsh were a people lacking that inner conviction that a free nation has of existing for its own sake. Because of this flaw, in either language, the majority were incapable of focusing a view of the world except through English or Anglo-American spectacles. Whatever institutions they managed to create were inevitably weakened by this basic incapacity. To renew themselves from generation to generation they needed a small but steady supply of sacrificial figures, not merely to 'purify the language of the tribe' but to recreate an essential capacity for independent thought. In the Welsh tradition these are poetic functions. There are fewer precedents for men of action, captains of industry, politicians, soldiers, responding to the call. So why should a man with

Wheldon's talent for action tie himself or be tied to the same old scorched stake when there were all those sleek and well-oiled vehicles in the English marshalling yards just waiting for the guiding hand of a thrustful and competent commander?

Huw had courage, confidence and cunning – formidable attributes when found in an intelligent combination, ideal for a military commander and certainly essential for a cultural impresario. Wales could have done with his talents. They were never available because he chose to operate within a 'British' context. He served a 'British' Broadcasting Corporation with the same dedicated loyalty as he had given a 'British' Army. This word so conveniently borrowed from our remote past denotes a nation state that accepts Scots, Welsh and Irish among its most devoted servants. It is their House of Commons which is at present being dragged kicking and screaming into a Community where patient and impatient Europeans marvel at the intransigent nationalism of the English.

I am not sure that Huw ever understood that there is more to culture than taking tea with the Queen Mother. At times he seemed mesmerized by the sound of Sir Kenneth Clark dispensing critical aperçus about the work of often penniless and suicidal artists through (if I may coin an anatomical surrealism) his well-heeled nose.

On the surface our problems always appeared infinitely more intractable. Throughout the last thirty years, in spite of benevolent gestures, the urgent needs of Welsh culture came very low down on the list of priorities of 'British' bodies governing the mass media. It was always necessary to combat ITV, establish BBC2, develop colour television, establish local radio, put the wider interests of the BBC first before even contemplating the application of greater resources and technical expertise to the business of broadcasting in Welsh. While the mass media increased in power and influence daily, we were obliged to watch the language lose ground. New techniques that could have been used to nurture and enlarge an audience and make the work of a Welsh-language channel that much easier and more immediately effective were never developed.

Nevertheless the language remains our chief source of renewal. It makes demands. It insists on a policy based on a thorough understanding of the true nature of culture. Huw Wheldon, in his English context, grasped the fundamental principle that the mass media need to nurture and educate an audience for the simple reason that no art or culture can be renewed in any society without a receptive audience capable of response. Television is an incomparable medium of dissemination. To play a larger role in strengthening a minority culture it needs an audience able to bring to the encounter shared traditions, memories, passions, hopes and mysteries. This does not mean that such an audience must be unusually learned or sophisticated. It is unlikely that the Athenians who went to the play were all philosophers and it is certain that most of the groundlings who kept the Elizabethan theatre going could neither read nor write. Their gift as an audience was to be eager and receptive. They could provide confrontation as well as participation and this must be what the Welsh situation demands.

On a miniature scale, I saw something of the kind occur during the summer of 1964. In establishing Y Gegin at Cricieth, our idea had been a creative centre where audience and artist could confront each other and make something new and stimulating from their shared experience in a shared language. To make a television version of W. S. Jones's *Y Dyn Swllt* (The Shilling Man) we brought an Outside Broadcast Unit from Cardiff to record a performance in which a local audience, who understood all the subtleties of the bitter-sweet vision of the author, could participate 'in vision'. The unforeseen snag was the tongue-tied response of the audience when they saw themselves on the monitors. In that tiny ex-Town Hall (where Lloyd George had made his first public speeches) they were so overawed by the machinery which surrounded them that they failed to respond to the content of the play, neglecting to react in the appropriate places. Their narcissistic passivity looked like being our undoing. Happily, Huw Wheldon turned up. With characteristic brio he took the audience in hand and led the laughter. He turned what could have been an experimental failure into an encouraging success. As we can read in Mr Ferris's book this was a central part of his gift on many such occasions and in many production meetings. But on this occasion, he knew as well as we did, that we were celebrating an aspect of the contemporary life of the home-ground of his ancestor, Robert Jones, Rhoslan.

We were enjoying the privilege of working inside a shared inheritance. Artists like W. S. Jones were equipping themselves with the strength of the old and traditional in order to absorb and overcome and transform the shock of the new. In the end, all art is about survival. To prepare ourselves for an uncertain future we should be armed with a confident knowledge of our medium and with a particular relish for the language which is central to our identity. To be more European, we need first to be more Welsh.

Television and Us

Based on lectures published in *Taliesin* (December 1974) and published in present form in *Miscellany Two* (Bridgend: Poetry Wales Press, 1981), 113–46.

I

We may as well begin this discussion by accepting the given fact that the 'picture' has become the central factor of the process of communication in our time. This in itself is a disturbing challenge to a nation whose continued existence has depended on a tradition which gives pride of place to the 'word', whether spoken or written. Such culture struggles as have troubled the quiet water of Wales up to the modern age were largely conflicts between the oral and the literary: before these had been satisfactorily solved, the new technology has overtaken us and presented us with what appears to be a cultural life and death situation.

II

It might be helpful to begin a definition of the word 'picture' in this context. The most relevant way would be to trace the spiritual pedigree and the material development of the mechanized picture we call a photograph. This common object boasts a very high pedigree indeed: nothing less than the attempts of the great minds of the European Renaissance to plumb the depths of the meaning of existence. We might consider the work of such a versatile genius as Albrecht Dürer. Dürer was the son of a goldsmith of Magyar extraction. He was trained in his father's workshop to engrave pictures on metal surfaces. This was the age of da Vinci, Michelangelo, Bellini, but it was Dürer more than anyone else who perfected the techniques of engraving prepared plates for reproductive printing on paper. This technique was the basis of his fame and his wealth. But Dürer was a product of the Renaissance and he thought of himself not only as an artist and as a practising capitalist, but also as a philosopher and a natural scientist. For him the German word *kunst* meant both the skill to create and produce and a philosophic understanding of these activities so that, throughout his life, whatever developments he made he would be inclined to justify in scientific discourse. Like Leonardo he was always conscious of the significance of any technical development for which he had been responsible. Thus, the development of perspective had more far-reaching consequences than mere alteration in painting style. The development of perspective – 'The technique of representing a solid substance on a smooth surface in order to create an identical impression of relationships, size and distance as that which is given by the object itself when looked at from a given viewpoint' – was nothing less than evidence of the new vision gained by Renaissance Man, a vision which included the meaning of human existence, the relationship between man and society, his environment and the universe. The technique of perspective or some elements of it were not unknown in the classical world. But it was the artists of the Renaissance who saw its possibilities as a new basis for art and as a regular, even scientific method for imitating nature. It is worthwhile bearing in mind that perspective does not play a part of any importance in the art of non-European cultures. Even in Europe it meant nothing in the Middle Ages. We are obliged to accept that perspective, like capitalism, experimental science and industrial development, is a product of an eruption of the human spirit that we find convenient to refer to as the Renaissance and the Reformation. Furthermore it is no accident that Dürer, like Cranach and other German artists, was a staunch follower and admirer of Martin Luther, and that, for such artists, along with their *kunst* went the first sign of a new and more acute national consciousness. For other historical reasons a variety of this consciousness already existed in Wales.

A proper treatment of this theme would need to dwell in detail on the development of artistic and scientific techniques in Europe. As it is one must leap over three centuries to concentrate on the feat of Nicephore Niepce. In the year 1826 he succeeded in producing the first authentic photograph by the reaction of sunlight on a prepared metal surface. Niepce was a scientist, but his more famous collaborator Daguerre was a man of the theatre, a professional stage designer. It was Daguerre who went on to perfect his discovery and turn it into a commercial proposition. But it was the intention of both men to extend the limits of artistic representation and in particular the lithographic and print methods that had formed such an important part of Albrecht Dürer's commercial success three centuries earlier. To their joy, and indeed to everyone else's, the camera lens saw the world from a viewpoint of perfect perspective. In keeping with the spirit of the age the photograph seemed to accentuate the comforting solidity of the material world, and gave to it a new form of immortality on paper. The camera obscura was more than a toy: it was a magical machine for the mass production of votive objects for a new-found materialistic faith. In the early years it was quite an expensive process. Only the rich could afford to possess a Daguerrotype. For a short time they were more fashionable than paintings; but by the middle of the nineteenth century rapid technical developments brought photography within the reach of any family of reasonable means. Its size and reproduction became a recognized symbol of success in every sphere of modern life. W. E. Gladstone, Louis Napoleon, Bismark, glowered down from the wallpaper of the homes of all their loyal subjects in the new nation states that dominated European life. Artists like Charles Dickens and Henrik Ibsen delighted in giving their young female admirers signed photographs of themselves; and even the French Impressionists, when driven by poverty, would use landscape photographs to remind them of the joys of the places they could not afford to visit. It is only in this century that photography was appreciated as something more than an extension of painting and developed from being a social toy into an essential item of equipment in all aspects of scientific research. Such developments inevitably reinforced the strength of its position in the social anthropology of the modern world. Here was the ready-made iconography of a new world religion.

It is pertinent to attempt an enumeration of some of the more obvious characteristics of the photograph. From the economic point of view it has provided the capitalists with a product that can be reproduced to a point of theoretical infinity. We may think for example of taking the perfect colour photograph of Cwm Pennant and then reproducing it on the spot until the valley itself is obliterated and the Drws y Coed mountain gradually sinks out of sight. By the same token the photograph of a parliamentary candidate could be sufficiently reproduced to obliterate the constituency he seeks to represent. These are considerations we shall return to later on in the argument. What needs to be claimed at this point is that the photograph is the most effective and exact record of the surface of life on earth that man has ever invented. If this were only half true then the concept of History as an academic discipline with some claim to scientific method has been utterly changed for ever. It is possible that few documentary accounts of events will stand comparison with the photograph and its terrible offspring the film, in the significance of the factual information that they will provide. A photograph can 'speak volumes' about the nature of a building, a machine, a landscape, a man and the civilization which sustains him in unparalleled material comfort. Furthermore the photograph has revealed aspects of life that were never previously visible. Ultraviolet and infrared have added as much to the power of the human eye as the motor car has extended the power of the human foot: and it is such extensions to the human capacity for communication that have put all language into question. As a lingua franca, as a means of social regulation and instruction, photography and its attendant rituals seem to have progressed well beyond the range of the Latin of the medieval world.

III

Part of the strength of the new language must be its exceptionally simple grammar and syntax. Because it has no words it appears to be un-trammelled by the fiddling details that go with verbs and sentences, not to mention the obsolete sophistication of initial consonant mutation. It is built for speed of execution and instant registration. It is excessively democratic. A photograph is capable of draping the most trivial moment with monumental importance and elevating the least significant object to immortal status. With or without the skill of a photographer there is little to choose between a snapshot of a royal wedding or a well-lit picture of a piece of orange peel in the gutter. Whatever our allegiance, we have to accept that the photograph detaches an object or its subject from its physical place in the order of nature and from our experience of it in the course of animated living. It has a dangerous detachment. The man who pays the cameraman has an infinite variety of pliant picture material available for manipulation.

An individual still picture can have its own alarming intimations of eternity. Because of its apparent removal from the world of space and time, of growth and decay, of birth and life, the frozen moment lasts for ever. Take as example a famous picture of Ypres in 1917. It can be dwelt upon for ever and represent a universe torn apart and extending from the nothing inside itself to a mirror fixed in another galaxy. Or a photograph taken in Biafra or Kampuchea: heaps of skulls in a clearing in a forest, the bodies of starved children. No cruelty is ever to be forgotten or forgiven.

We come now to a paradox in the nature of the photograph. Its surface appears to be excessively and often unbearably real. And yet in its essence it is an illusion designed to create the impression of a presence. An illustrated cookery book presents mouth-watering images of meals that can hardly be equalled in reality. Every successful publisher in this field knows that he must delude the ambitious queen of the kitchen in exactly the same way as Gwydion succeeded in deluding Pryderi. For a portfolio of photographs of thoroughbreds he obtained a herd of genuine pigs. An illusion, of course, can turn to magic not only in the *Mabinogion* but also throughout the entire world from the moment when the technical descendants of Dürer and Daguerre succeeded in creating the impression that the photograph could move. This is not the place to dwell on the development of moving pictures that began in France and America in the 1890s and created a form of industrial culture which fulfilled with scientific precision the leisure needs of the industrial masses throughout the developed world. But it is necessary to note a vital element essential both to the production and the display of films. Every individual frame has to remain still in the light for its appropriate fraction of a second in order to create the impression of movement. That is to say, in the mechanical reality of both the camera and the projector the still moves and the movement is stillness. This is the reality behind the magic, the trick at the heart of the illusion. And it is more than a willing suspension of disbelief. The great cosmos of the cinema, like any other false religion, has been built up on a universally acceptable deception.

IV

It was no accident that the most thriving centre of this new industry of dreams and illusions should be established on the far West shore of the United States of America. There remains an intimate psychological and physiological connection between the Californian El Dorado and the dream factories of Hollywood. Since the Renaissance and the discovery of the New World, the classical dreams of Arcadia and the earthly Paradise were transferred from the Mediterranean to the new continent beyond the ocean that once poured over the edge of the known world. By the end of the nineteenth century the greatest migration in the history of the world had taken place. Millions of workers and peasants from all over Europe poured into the new continent, some fleeing from famine but all in search of a dream. Instead of the distant Paradise they found the back streets of New York, Detroit, Chicago, and entered a spiritual captivity in a concrete Babylon. For children lost in the forest of cities what better diversion than sitting in the dark auditorium to watch the wordless antics of Charlie Chaplin, a brave little man facing obstacles so like the ones they faced but, unlike them, always able to overcome them. Like the illusion itself flickering on the screen he was preserved by magical means and they gained temporary relief from their tribulations by laughing at him. Like the photograph the cinema could speak without words and entertain everyone whatever their language or their circumstances. By 1914 this new art form, the first to grow out of industrial technology, had become firmly rooted in the hearts of the common people throughout the United States and the most remarkable aspect of this conquest was the way in which it reached the innermost parts of their minds and hearts without ever having to knock at the front door of a spoken language. It entered with the stealth of a thief in the night and took possession of a new empire.

While Chaplin was cheering up the spiritual refugees in far-away America, the First World War erupted in Europe to throw mountains of rubble between us and traditional European culture. In less than three years Lenin had journeyed through Germany in his sealed train to lead the Russian Revolution. By the end of that war the pattern of the modern world, our world, had begun to emerge and nothing illustrates our condition more clearly than the development of film both as an art form and as an industry. Whoever controlled this new world would also need to control the machinery of magic and illusion. What was the fate of the cinema to be? Would it continue to feed the fantasies of a deracinated proletariat in order to make great fortunes for sleazy capitalists? Or would it serve the socialist revolution and help to create a new order, an authentic materialist, socialist paradise on earth? Throughout the revolution, the Russian film industry enjoyed the favour, indeed the firm embrace, of the authority of the Bolshevist government. Lenin declared that film was the most important form of culture. It could be moulded as the most effective medium to instruct and control the people in the task of creating a new Communist society. It was the only way to make contact with all nationalities in a revolutionary period, to carry the vital message across the boundaries of language, to lead all the peoples along the peaceful paths of propaganda to the promised land.

For sixty years film production has reflected with great accuracy the polarization of the political world. On the western extremity the capitalist resources of the United States built cardboard castles for the mass production of dreams to respond to the emancipated appetite, to kindle the imagination and tap the pocket of every would-be playboy of the western world. Photographs of desirable individuals in enviable situations were reproduced and distributed in uniform units like packets of chocolate or shredded wheat for regular consumption. Like the star system the basic principle was established early and continues to operate on even more sophisticated levels in the television industry. The picture is the icon of the cult of personality. In the socialist east dreams needed to be more realistic. To be effective propaganda a vision must be expressed in shapes that bear a recognizable relationship to reality. During the early period, entry to the picture halls in Russia was often free of charge. Commercial advantage was never the prime object so that the picture-makers could concentrate on influencing the hearts and minds of the audience. This difference of motivation was respons-ible for notable differences in style and technique. Across the world film-makers were acutely conscious of each other's work. Eisenstein for instance was heavily under the influence of D. W. Griffith, and was very ready to acknowledge this. But before the Stalin dictatorship, he and others were able to develop montage and make film photography a more flexible and subtle language.

The concept of polarization must not allow us to ignore what was happening in the centre, to a Europe whose foundations of bourgeois culture were cracked by the First World War. The most significant contrast lay between the victors and the vanquished. It was in Germany that a brilliant film industry developed and it was the inspiration of this industry that set the pace. On the whole the contribution of victorious England and its British Empire to this new medium was surprisingly weak and ineffective. At least part of the reason must be attributed to the absence of revolution and radical social change. Just as George V was still on his throne, the stars of the West End of London still reigned happily over an entertainment world which was designed to reflect with a minimum of change the life of the English middle class. In contrast with the intelligentsia on the Continent, the English were inclined to keep as closely as they could to their accustomed standards and interests in literature and the arts. The cinema was little better than flicks in the flea-pit, and the working class, whenever it was noticed, was deemed loyal and deserving of alternating pats on the head and the back. When the industrial workers attempted to rouse themselves from their political slumber, in 1926, they were soon driven back to their lairs in the slums by the self-discipline, self-confidence and full bellies of healthy young men from public schools assisted by the classics and rules of the cricket field as well as the army and the police. England in the twenties was no place for experimenting.

V

Nevertheless the English quietly developed a mass medium that appeared to be all their very own. They were too pragmatic a people to ignore all the obvious advantages of so cheap and efficient a medium as the wireless to a central government with a great empire to administer. Quite apart from this, sound radio was without doubt more acceptable than film to the literary culture of a middle class which was intent on running the British Empire as if nothing had changed in the world. Spoken English was the silken chain designed by Providence to bind this far-flung Empire together and the microphone was the natural instrument for its dissemination. With unusual speed and uncharacteristic enthusiasm the governing class built in the heart of London a massive temple to house the small microphone that could keep in touch with the extremities of an Empire on which the sun never set. Through the medium of this miraculous little instrument words of comfort and encouragement could reach the ears of all the faithful citizens of the King-Emperor, from the hills of Kasha to the hills of Ceredigion. Except for the purpose of comedy, these words were always spoken in an Oxford accent of ineffable refinement. (Anyone who doubts this should take a look at a book on spoken English by a former teacher of phonetics and the honorary secretary of the BBC advisory committee in that period, Professor A. Lloyd James – needless to say a Welshman. The title of the book is *The Broadcast Word*.)

It is instructive to take a look at the architecture of Broadcasting House of which photographs are invariably taken from a low angle. What indeed is this but a battleship at anchor? And what is the figurehead but Ariel, Prospero's agent, who can now promise to encircle the world in half a second instead of forty minutes in order to prove that Britannia will go on ruling the waves of the air long after she has been obliged to relinquish her control of the waves of the sea.

The microphone, like the camera, has its own strangely contradictory attributes. By today it is particularly accessible, easy to handle, durable and very cheap to maintain. This was not the case in the early days, and the British Broadcasting Company was anxious to prevent it falling into the hands of the 'wrong people'. In Wales particularly, the Broadcasting

Company was inclined to argue that the dialect of so mountainous a region could never be picked up or transmitted on so delicate an instrument, even if it could be proved that the dialect in question was worthy of such favoured treatment. The story of Welsh broadcasting in the twenties and thirties is a depressing anticipation of the grim story of television in the sixties and seventies. The interesting correlation for the purpose of this thesis lies between the physical nature of the invention, the political social and cultural problems involved in its exploitation and the consistent themes in the excuses provided by the controlling authorities in not allowing the use of the new technology in the service of the native culture.

Consider the microphone again. Even today it does not work all that well unless it is placed at the correct angle to the lips of the speaker or the source of the sound. Worse than this, it has little power to differentiate between various kinds of sounds. This used to mean, and to some extent it still means, that it is almost impossible to create a perfect sound studio. It demands what is virtually a vacuum and to make a perfect recording of a given sound you have also to devise a means of keeping the speaker alive for at least as long as is necessary for him to finish what he has to say. These difficulties were easily elevated to the level of a mystique, and when the BBC possessed a monopoly of sound radio it was not slow to take advantage of the fact.

Acute technical difficulties arose when talking and sound was introduced into the film industry. For a while it brought the development of a promising art form to a literal standstill. The studio floor was renamed the sound stage, the microphone became the temperamental centre of the entire operation. The best directors from Hollywood to Moscow – Chaplin, Pudovkin, Eisenstein and the rest – rebelled in vain against the oppression of this tiny dictator. In film after film the key scene became the moment when the hero and his girl faced each other lovingly across a restaurant table with a convenient bunch of flowers between them concealing the microphone. The golden age of the silent screen had come to an end, and its creative period had been even shorter than the equivalent flowering of the London theatre in Elizabethan England.

VI

So industrialized an art form, whether under capitalism or socialism, would appear to give little scope to the individual talent. It is all the more consoling therefore to observe from the history of the cinema that, in spite of all the restrictions, the most memorable creations bear the hallmark of individuality just as much as a poem, a novel or a play. Here again film reflects with great accuracy the paradox inherent in the human condition in the modern world. It was during the golden age of the silent cinema that one man set about creating, virtually single-handed, the form of cinema which has proved in the end to have been the most influential and to have had the greatest impact on the use of the 'picture', either still or moving, in the business of communication. Robert Flaherty was a wild romantic explorer whose early life was a sequence of prototypical frontier journeys, often in pursuit of an earthly paradise that might also turn out to be an eldorado. Only when the camera was in his hands was he presented with the extraordinary opportunity of translating his dream into a new form of visual reality. With what we might like to call Celtic flare or even Taliesinic inspiration, he seized on the most powerful element inherent in the nature of the photograph, namely its capacity to reproduce the surface of the visible world and the processes of living with phenomenal accuracy and documentary attention to detail. Against the prevailing torrent of Hollywood escapism this Irish American poet and dreamer created the heroic originals of the documentary film: *Nanook of the North, Moana,* and later *Man of Arran.* One need not go as far as to say that only an individualistic Irishman could have achieved this. Nevertheless there are strange historical echoes attached to his career. Like that of St Brendan, his early life was a series of launches into the unknown. Later, when the moguls of Hollywood lost patience with his undisciplined poetic habits, he turned eastwards like an Irish missionary of the Dark Ages, carrying with him the secrets of his new gospel.

The turning point in his career and in the future development of the film industry in Britain occurs in Berlin in the year 1930. Flaherty had gone there in order to make direct contact with the leaders of the film industry in Russia. Pudovkin and Eisenstein were eager to co-operate with the 'Father of the Documentary Film', as Flaherty was already nicknamed, and he himself had a high regard for the work of the Russians. Berlin was still the intellectual capital for European film-makers and a centre of experiment in the arts. Unfortunately for Flaherty and probably for European civilization, Stalin had decided to tighten the reins on film directors just as much as on the Soviet state in general. He was in no mood to allow freedom of experiment. The international possibilities inherent in the nature of the medium and in the genius of the men who were longing to collaborate had to be abandoned.

Flaherty was stranded in Berlin. He had no work and he had no money, and he was in low spirits. It was his wife who picked up the telephone, after seven o'clock in order to take advantage of the cheap rate, to speak to John Grierson in London. (It is as well to bear the cost of the call in mind, when we look at the latest set of figures sent flashing across our Welsh firmament by the Chairman of the Welsh Advisory Council of the BBC.) This turned out to be an epoch-making conversation. Flaherty was invited to London to work in the film department of a new establishment with the imposing name of 'Empire Marketing Board'. This was a crucial step in the history of the development of the New Media in Britain. It was in London, of course, that Flaherty received the necessary support to produce the seminal *Man of Arran*. Other influences were at work. Because of the international respect Flaherty had gained, the English cultural establishment was at last willing to take the documentary film seriously. The sons of well-to-do families came down from Oxford and Cambridge, fired with excitement about a new art form. This also coincided with a period of economic crisis and the spectre of fascism taking shape on the international horizon. These same young men also took to left-wing political views and the romantic English spirit found political expression in a way that it had not done since the heady days of the French Revolution and the Napoleonic Wars. John Grierson was a shrewd Scotsman and he understood how to channel all these energies and create the only tradition of lasting importance in British film-making. Grierson succeeded in gaining government support for the establishment of a Crown Film Unit. A style was established which was in effect an adaptation of Flaherty's method of work. Poetry was infiltrated with propaganda. The results were of great interest, but the more important long-term effect was the foundation of a way of presenting the world which remains the basis of British television style to this day.

VII

The impact of film on Welsh life in the twenties had been curiously limited. Cinemas remained dark and dubious institutions, with their screens more often than not occupied by aliens flourishing long cigarette-holders and lounging on tigerskins. The chapel vestry was still a more congenial centre of entertainment. Creative tensions were still at work between the spoken and the written word, between oral and literary culture, between a profound traditional conservatism and an increasing demand for novelty. Public halls and vestries had to be booked well in advance for a choir practice or a drama rehearsal. Local eisteddfodau north and south seemed to flourish as much as they had ever done even in Mabon's day, and the charabanc and motor-coach greatly expanded the catchment area for competitors. Welsh Wales remained as conservative in its outlook on the nature of entertainment as did the West End of London or the Windsor of King George V. For that matter, there were still pulpit giants in operation. A John Williams, Brynsiencyn, a Lewis, Tumble, or a Philip Jones, Porthcawl, could attract as large an audience as the most sensational film. Welsh public figures who showed any interest in the new art form were few and far between and always very young, and usually ex-service men. Ifan ap Owen Edwards, the founder of Urdd Gobaith Cymru, was an enthusiastic amateur film-maker. Cynan, still to become the impresario of a reformed Gorsedd at the National Eisteddfod, showed a lively interest. Saunders Lewis was among the few literary critics to show an early and intelligent appreciation of the medium.

During the Depression the cinema in the south Wales valley took on a new function. As Gwyn Thomas describes it, it was a refuge and a shelter for the unemployed and their children, helping them to forget their hunger. It was here more than anywhere else that the new medium was able to slip into its predestined social role in modern society. As in the America of the Depression, escapism became more than an escape to a people confronted with an unbearably grim reality. In 1931 the secretary of the Empire Marketing Board managed to rustle up £2,500 to make a film about industrial craftsmanship in England. After many vicissitudes Flaherty shot it with his unique poetic eye and Grierson wrote the smart progressive commentary. This was the landmark that was to open up the whole of industrial Britain as a subject for the documentary film, a development which was to include south Wales and its condition as a very suitable case for treatment.

VIII

The documentary movement reached its zenith of power and influence in London during the war. Under the Ministry of Information talented directors such as Basil Wright and Humphrey Jennings were given an unusual degree of freedom and financial support to create films that would stiffen the morale of the people, lift the hearts of the masses and generally help the war effort. At a time of crisis the power of a new art form was harnessed in order to fulfil the age-old function of the poet – to celebrate the existence of the tribe and stiffen its resolve to triumph over difficulties and resist attack. It was only now that the flicks became respectable and ripe for inclusion as part of the English heritage. But even at the moment of triumph, the promise was never realized. After the war the London-based film industry was struck by a very painful disease – elephantitis. The spirit of Empire still kindled in the hearts of capitalists like J. Arthur Rank. He was too rigidly set in the imperial mould to understand that the world had changed for ever. He could not bear to see the US monopolize the world market for films with English-language soundtracks. This was his language that they were daring to exploit for such mouth-watering profits. In his way he was even more romantic than Robert J. Flaherty, seeing himself like St George riding out to do battle with the American dragon. Unfortunately he had none of Flaherty's talent and, as things were, the dragon was a good deal stronger than the saint. He and his horse were swallowed up in no time. The sacrifice of the documentary film in the interests of the neo-imperial big picture had been all in vain, and its early promise had been blighted for nothing.

The forties were lean years both for the documentary film and for the young men who had been trained in the traditions of Flaherty and John Grierson. They suffered a period of unemployment and homelessness, but this did not last for long. In London even as one door closes another always opens. It was at this time that the BBC decided to reopen and expand its television service. Many of the pioneers of the documentary film found a new home at Alexandra Palace, Finsbury Park. It was a new home with prospects, but in the early years of only limited comforts. To explain why this should be so we must return to the image of Ariel at the mast-head of the headquarters in Portland Place. These geographical situations are important. When the microphone was like the harp of David playing its delectable accompaniment to the verbal culture of the ruling English middle class, Finsbury Park was almost as far outside the Pale as Ferndale or Aberystwyth. The relative importance of public institutions were to be measured by the literal distance between them and the heart of the Empire at Westminster and the Royal Palace. The BBC had been created as a cultural extension to the civil service. Like the Indian civil service on which it was modelled, it was staffed by men trained in the public-school concept of service. The traditional qualities required were a deep respect for the classics, particularly the Romans, Cicero and Julius Caesar; self-discipline and control over the emotions; an unspoken but unswerving adherence to the imperial ideal of exercising benevolent rule over the rest of humanity; an inclination to self-sacrifice or at least self-effacement in the service of a higher cause; and, above all else perhaps, an ability to make decisions and deliver firm and unequivocal orders. The BBC was created to be the last refuge of the imperial mandarin class. This was the pattern laid down by Sir John Reith and to this day heads of department in the BBC are designated by initials in exactly the same way as the civil service. The system that spread out from the headquarters at Portland Place had many virtues; but it was not the most obvious refuge for displaced persons from the documentary film industry; neither was it sufficiently flexible to house and nourish an alternative British culture which still lingered like a forgotten garrison in the mountainous outpost known as Wales.

IX

Here literary culture had survived the Act of Union through the strenuous collaboration of men of the Renaissance and the more enlightened members of the old bardic order. When the natural leaders of society abandoned the native culture it was cherished by the lower classes and maintained in a sufficiently healthy state until the population explosion that accompanied industrialization in the early nineteenth century made possible what was in effect a new nation. Unique among the Celtic communities on the north-west seaboard of Europe, the Welsh enjoyed a relative prosperity. They became a literate people taught by the discipline of religious Nonconformity to value books and education and inspired by indigenous institutions such as the eisteddfod to attempt ambitious cultural projects, to excel in a variety of forms of self-expression and to take delight in such arts as were accessible to them. They also became politically conscious and socially ambitious and it was this last characteristic above all others that made them exceptionally vulnerable to the great changes that were taking place in British society as a whole.

It would not be correct to claim that the 1870 Education Act was a deliberate death sentence passed on the indigenous peasant culture of Wales. In spite of the racist animosity towards the Welsh language so often displayed by *The Times* in the mid-nineteenth century, we are obliged to accept that the most influential leaders of Welsh life at that time, men like Dr Lewis Edwards, Sir Hugh Owen and the Revd John Griffiths, the Eisteddfod reformer, were falling over themselves in their anxiety to obtain an English education for their people. The 'Welsh Not' was not a pleasant ornament to hang around a child's neck on a Friday afternoon, but we have to remember that it was Welsh schoolmasters for the most part that perpetuated the custom. The majority of the people seemed to be eager to acquire the best that both linguistic worlds had to offer, and were quite prepared to see their children suffer in such a good cause. To the faithful, Welsh could well be the language of heaven; but on this earth they only had to look around them to see that English was the language of commerce and worldly success. So long as a proper balance was maintained between the claims of church and state on their allegiance, they could see no reason why the blessings of bilingualism could not continue to shower on their irreproachable heads for ever. Indeed, such was the perfection of philosophical balance on the tight-rope of their condition, that it was possible for them to think of English as a prize awarded to them by providence as a reward for conducting such virtuous lives within the confines of their native language.

Alas, the forces of history rarely operate in such an obliging fashion. From the time of that Education Act, the Welsh people were drawn into the ambit of English popular culture and into a veritable whirlpool of change. And they were tossed into that whirlpool in the most vulnerable condition possible. At a time when they needed it most, they were beginning to lose confidence in the strength of their own language, their own culture and even their own institutions. (At the time when they acquired English the three-volume novel had already passed the peak of its popularity and impact in England.) During the 1890s at least three new media arrived on the scene to compete with each other for the affections of the populace and the right to function as the appropriate channels for mythology and popular storytelling. The cheap novel became a reality and brought the concept of the best-seller within reach of anyone who had learnt to read English in the new system of elementary schools. But more important than these was the advent of the daily newspaper.

The Welsh people had newspapers of their own. About the same year as the *Daily Mail* began its mission of enlightening opinion and giving society a lead, *Trysorfa'r Plant*, the Calvinistic Methodist children's paper, had a circulation of its own of 45,000. Nothing is more remarkable in nineteenth-century Wales than the output of the printing presses. Every denomination had its journals, its newspapers and magazines, and the whole of Wales seemed to be covered by a remarkable distribution system. This was an achievement of the common people themselves and there were moments when the whole country seemed ripe for an un-exampled flowering of literate democracy. What it came to enjoy in reality was an unholy combination of the talents of Lord Northcliffe and David Lloyd George. A newspaper is of course always more than a purveyor of news. Indeed for the most part this is the least of its functions. What it presents day in and day out is a way of looking at the world. It is a 'picture' of the world, a perspective in Dürer's sense of the word which is mythical in its essence and yet persuades the reader that reality is grounded in the comfortable relationship that exists between him as a reader and what is going on in the great wide world. Just as a prosperous burgher could buy a copper engraving of the Emperor's triumphal procession by Albrecht Dürer, the most unobtrusive clerk could buy his picture of the world on the way home or on the way to work and fold it in his coat pocket, and by that very act demonstrate his mastery over his environment. The picture of the world provided by the Harmsworth Press was more glamorous than anything that the denominational papers or even *Y Faner* could manage; and when David Lloyd George got going he needed a team of Dürers to portray his performance as one of the four horsemen of the Apocalypse.

In the same year that the *Daily Mail* was born, Auguste and Louis Lumière opened their first cinema in Paris. From this time forward the common man's picture of the world was liable to movement as if an invisible poltergeist were constantly shifting the furniture of his imagination. In less than a generation D. W. Griffith, who liked to claim descent from 'Griffith King of Wales', had created the film language which was to ensure that the moving picture would finally displace the printed word as the universal means of satisfying the appetite for fiction. Whereas the Welsh had been able to cope very well with the technology of the printing press, the new media arrived at their doorstep at a time of outward turmoil and inner confusion. Nothing illustrates this more clearly than the history of the Rhondda valleys. In 1902, a new Education Act, with the inevitable help of Lloyd George, saw to it that Wales was given a pattern of secondary education which took a new generation further down the road that led them away from their indigenous culture. In 1904 the Rhondda, like the rest of Wales, was boiling over in the heat of a religious revival with a population reaching up frantically for those ropes of salvation which are also the last links with the old Welsh way of life, the old language and the sense of security, self-respect and self-confidence that went with it. In less than ten years the heat of the revival was transformed into an equally ardent enthusiasm in favour of the war against Germany and an unrestrained pride in the new brand of jingoistic imperialism provided for them by the powerful combination of the London press and Mr Lloyd George. In less than ten years after that, in the midst of economic suffering, this warm-hearted community embraced socialism, caught between the calculating caution of the official Labour Party and an impulsive desire to support the idealism of young Marxist leaders.

X

The one thing the Welsh did not have in order to face the New Media and all the challenges it presented was confidence in themselves and in the intrinsic value of their own culture. There are of course many factors which can contribute to the undermining of the will to persist in the face of social changes of seismographic proportions. (This is almost a discipline in itself and it has become a central study for anyone interested in the European condition.) When the melting pot has so much to offer, why not just jump in? If the security and material welfare of western Europe depend so heavily on the American nuclear arsenal, why do we not all follow the example of so many of our nineteenth-century relations and apply directly to Congress for admission as additional states? In this respect it does no harm for us to take a look at what has happened and what is happening to the culture of the remnants of Indian nations in North America. Much work has been done among the Hopi, the Suni, the Pawnee and particularly the Navaho. By some accounts there appear to be tribes among the Navaho who cherish a song or a ritual to heal every ailment, to meet most emergencies and to welcome every day. To these nations language is in fact both a fortress and a fold in which are preserved the hundreds of rituals and songs essential to their existence; even more essential to their well-being, in their view, than their flocks and herds. It is because of the importance that they attach to this system of speech and the way in which it enshrines the meaning of their existence that they are unwilling to attend the schools provided for them by the

Federal Government because English is the medium of instruction. They have come to regard their language as the last line of defence to keep out the elements of an alien industrial culture which threatens a way of life which they believe to be tied in through their culture and language to the true meaning of existence.

Far be it from me to equate the industrious and ambitious Welsh with a bunch of unprogressive Indians. Nevertheless we are obliged to record that in the Welsh Reservations the education system after 1870 was exclusively in English. The tribal Sunday schools continued to be solely responsible for literacy in Welsh. For most people this seemed a satisfactory arrangement. When the chapels were full in a place like Merthyr Tydfil, where the population was still overwhelmingly Welsh-speaking, there were eight Sunday-school teachers to every one professional beavering away in the state schools. But the foundations of the old way of life were already giving way. Loss of religious certainties was of course in no way peculiar to Wales. What the Welsh lost in addition was confidence in their own identity. The badge of all the tribes and the basis of any tenable claim to separate nationality had always been the language. Now all the forces of change, spearheaded by a comprehensive education system from the infant school to the university, seemed to be telling them that their language and for that matter their antiquated religion were no better than chains around their feet. When a character called Ann Evans, in Kate Roberts's brilliant novel *Traed Mewn Cyffion*, whispers in her neighbour's ear at a school prize day, 'Da y gŵyr Duw i bwy i roi BA' (Well doth God know to whom to give the BA), she is not only making a quiet joke at the expense of the row of teachers in their black mortarboards and gowns. She is making a tacit acknowledgement that both providence and progress are on the side of this mighty language which she herself cannot speak.

As a sop to the remnants of their national pride, the leaders of Welsh life made greater use of the word 'national' to designate their public institutions at the very time when the genuine ties of nationality were weakening and falling away. The national university, for example, managed to attract support from colliers and quarrymen with vague though passionate appeal to national sentiment. They even talked of Owain Glyndŵr, but their real inspiration was Owen's College, Manchester, and it was in those echoing green-brick corridors that so many of the brightest children of the *gwerin* first learnt to despise so many of the characteristics cherished by their parents and grandparents. Instead of celebrating the national being, in the manner common to all

national universities from Oslo to Jerusalem and Washington to
Warsaw, the University of Wales flourished on the basis of whatever
provincial contribution it could make to English imperial power. A
political or economic historian might argue that in this respect the
University was doing no more than reflecting accurately the realities of
power. This might well be so, but it cannot be allowed to camouflage the
damage done to the Welsh psyche. A conspicuous feature of the Welsh
condition in the twentieth century has been that sociological phenomenon known as 'culture shame'. It is almost part of the condition that it
should be so little studied. Like a secret vice or an incurable disease, it is
rarely mentioned. But from time to time it breaks out in unexpected
eruptions of 'culture hatred' most frequently directed against the Welsh
language. What used to be an atavistic Anglo-Saxon racial hatred for the
unintelligible lingo of a welshing Taffy now manifests itself in a Welsh
county councillor's abrupt irrational outburst against 'any more of this
Welsh business'.

XI

It will be seen that both radio and cinema arrived in Wales at a
singularly inauspicious time. There were no effective channels open for
them to make any contribution to bolstering up the native culture or
injecting it with exciting new life. There was a direct link between the
absence of technical capability and the nature of existing scholarship
and educational facilities. Well before the First World War the philosophic base of the social application of science had hardened. Practical
capitalists and theoretic socialists were united in their passionate
devotion to the concept of scientific necessity: and in popular terms this
filtered through to the common consciousness in the form of a vague
but potent religion of progress. History was transformed into a machine
driven by this new god. What little chance human beings had of
influencing the direction the vehicle might take was no more than the
degree of trust it was prepared to invest in the god's goodwill. This was
not difficult for a theoretically Calvinist people. But the new version
proved to be far less creative than the original. Instead of stimulating, it
deadened response. The presence of the god of the machine was so
evident, so omnipotent and so lacking in mystery that the only effective
worship appeared to be a condition of helplessness that amounted to
little better than spiritual slavery. Machinery was the church militant on

earth and the machinery of government was only one of its less noisy but more sinister manifestations. The only way really to please this god was to demonstrate complete submission by lining up into endless rows of uniform units for the sacred purpose of listening to the perfection of a self-existent heartbeat. In this new church little Welsh children were never asked to recite verses in public, or to take part in chapel meetings or even contribute to the ministry or the missionary fund. Their only duty was to remain helpless and silent, and among well-brought-up children what could have been easier than that?

XII

Radio came to Wales in the shape of the BBC, as an extension of that middle-class English culture which we described earlier as radiating from its vantage point so close to the heart of the Empire. Cardiff functioned as a colonial sub-post office to Bristol and it took many years of campaigning before anything that could be described as a Welsh region was established. The first big struggle was to get any Welsh-speaking Welshmen established on the staff; and the second was to separate Wales from the West of England and give it some semblance of being a national service. All this took many years to achieve and might never have been achieved but for unlikely collaboration between two of the most talented and probably most untypical Welshmen around at that crucial time. But for a period of wholehearted collaboration between the ageing Lloyd George and the still young Saunders Lewis, it is very unlikely that the Welsh Region would ever have been established. Presumably the minutes of those stormy meetings with the Director-General of the BBC must still lie in the archives of the University Registry. Had the Welsh committee not been led by an ex-prime minister, Sir John Reith with his Messianic vision of English culture circulating the globe would never have given way. And in any case it has to be admitted that the service provided was sketchy and the whole operation remained firmly under central control from London.

There was in fact a curious parallel between the position of the Welsh staff of the BBC and those refugees from the film industry taking refuge in Alexandra Palace in the immediate post-war period. The war had brought no benefit to Welsh broadcasting. Anything to do with Welsh culture was a luxury to be sacrificed along with bananas, silk stockings and soft-centred chocolates. Film had had a much more important role to play. It was only afterwards that the documentary appeared to become as expendable as Welsh and was roughly discarded in the last dash for imperial glory on celluloid.

Inside the BBC the former documentary film-makers found themselves unhappy prisoners of an uncongenial atmosphere. In the first place television was no more than an extension of the broadcasting signal into a sufficient size to accommodate a picture as well as sound. The primitive television studio was no more than a garishly lit expansion of the old sound studio. In a curious echo of what happened in the film industry, the microphone remained firmly on its throne at the centre of the operation, while cumbersome cameras bowed in obeisance from all sides. Along with the microphone went the accent, the impeccable tones of men like Stuart Hibberd, John Snagge and Alvar Liddel. The BBC remained the custodian of English oral culture and this in turn reflected the grim determination of the English middle class to hang on to its essentially aristocratic heritage. Like English Literature, that accent was the product of four and a half centuries' material power, the crowning glory which gave them the right to an outstanding position among the nations of the earth. The microphone, like the accent, was safe in the hands of cultural civil servants, a lay clergy robed to dispense the sacraments and national treasures: custodians and conservers. In contrast, the men from the documentary film world saw themselves as artists. They knew that there was a living relationship between the nature of their medium and a revolutionary approach to the world. Their subject was the life of the masses and the world was their parish. They were the legitimate heirs of the first art form to emerge directly from an industrial civilization. They knew that history was on their side and yet the condition of their employment and the comforts that went with their status depended on their loyalty to a benevolent Corporation which had given them shelter.

During the period of their fretful inactivity in Alexandra Palace, the situation in Wales had taken a turn for the better. Substations were opened in the north and the west. Men and women of exceptional talent were recruited to produce programmes in English and Welsh and for a period of ten years or more it could be claimed that BBC Radio played an active and constructive part in Welsh cultural life, possibly the leading part at a time when very little creative activity could be discerned in other directions. The output did its best to cover the full spectrum of cultural activity from children's programmes and comedy shows, features and drama to the sophisticated poetry of Kitchener

Davies, David Jones, Dylan Thomas and Robert Williams Parry. There could hardly have been a time when Welshness in both languages benefited more from the impact of the new medium of radio technology. Once again, as in the story of the brief heyday of the silent cinema, it could not last. It was not merely a case of the Welsh producers inside the superstructure of a London cultural civil service. (Their time and effort and capabilities were always strictly limited to what they could insert into the vacant slots of an omnipresent and omnipotent London Home Service.) The time-bomb of technical development was ticking away. Television was growing up and getting too big for the confines of Alexandra Palace. In the words of the old Welsh proverb, the year-old frog was now ready to swallow its parent.

A new Television Centre was opened at Lime Grove. (This explains why for many years the majority of television technicians spoke with a Shepherd's Bush accent.) The experience of America had already demonstrated that television was the medium of the future, capable of swallowing both radio and film. Inevitably there were power struggles. The headquarters in the battleship at Portland Place kept a firm hold on the purse strings. It also attempted to control the content and style of television programmes. One of the refugees from documentary film, Andrew Miller-Jones, succeeded with the help of a lively journalist called Malcolm Muggeridge in establishing a programme that was in the Grierson tradition of a window on the world. It was called *Panorama* and it has survived to this day, almost as a living memorial of a compromise that was achieved between the middle-class ethos of the BBC and the freewheeling interest in the human spectacle of the old documentary movement. This compromise could have lasted indefinitely but for a surge of interest in the City of London. By the mid-1950s capitalists had become keenly aware of the potential of television for the exercise of the gentle art of printing money.

The advent of commercial television in 1956 dealt the death blow to the supremacy of the microphone and the concept of cultural civil service which had governed the BBC from its inception. The year 1956 was a watershed, and it is still difficult to disentangle cause and effect among the upheavals of that period. Anthony Eden and a concept of Empire went down the drain at Suez. The cosy notion of a friendly Russian bear met its end on the streets of Budapest. In the London theatre the French windows of Terence Rattigan were blown out by the young men intent on looking back in anger ready to reproach everybody and everything for their own inadequacies and sense of deprivation. But the most far-reaching change was brought about by commercial television. This capitalist's cash register turned out to be Leon Trotsky's secret weapon. It provided the answer to the Marxist dilemma concerning how much bourgeois culture should continue to be nurtured after the revolution and how much proletarian art would be needed to replace the decadent outmoded culture of the centuries of oppression. Commercial television discovered two things which had been largely overlooked by a BBC mesmerized by elegance and refinement: the working class and the north of England. This coincided happily with a fresh surge of creativity among the people of England. Typically a new school of dramatists and actors were given their chance (Osborne, Wesker, Storey, Arden, Pinter, O'Toole, Finney, and so on). It seemed as if, with characteristic stoicism, the English would waste no time or tears lamenting the passing of their Empire before gathering themselves together and preparing for a fresh onslaught to create another one in the new medium offering itself for exploitation. Here at least in a world of dwindling markets they would create a growth industry which they could look on with pride and call the best in the world.

XIII

Needless to say the people of Wales, Welsh- or English-speaking, were not given the opportunity for a parallel revival. When television arrived like Hengist and Horsa it brought with it the Treachery of the Long Masts. Wenvoe and St Hilary were sites outside Cardiff facing the Bristol Channel. The masts were there not in the service of Wales but in the service of the religion of the self-existent machine: the god of progress, whose mysterious ways had never been ours to question. Well-brought-up sons of the manse could declare that they were speaking as servants of the BBC or ITV and not as Welshmen, and this declaration of the purity of their intent could be widely accepted as the hallmark of integrity and dedication. It seemed as if the education system had removed any trace of self-respect along with their self-confidence. It was no longer part of the Welsh character to reason why; only to accept change in the cheerful spirit of a drugged patient on his way to a cultural operating theatre where his individuality would be removed by a painless operation roughly parallel with a frontal lobotomy.

The development of television over the last quarter of a century has been dominated by the extraordinary form of competition between the

BBC and commercial television which Professor Tom Burns in his study of the BBC, *Public Institution and Private World*, has described as 'pacing'. When two runners keep up with each other on an otherwise empty track, what they are engaged in is not a race. It is a perpetual training session conducted in a private world to ensure that both runners are fit enough to defeat any other competitor that might wish to join in a race. In this private world the battles which go on are not those that the public imagines it is witnessing. Dog does not eat dog. All their actions even when they appear to be in conflict are in fact mutually supportive. If, for example, the BBC succeeds in buying a new hair-raising series from the United States, it becomes absolutely essential that the ITV companies do exactly the same as quickly as possible. And if a BBC expert produces impressive findings to prove that there is no relationship whatsoever between violence in television programmes and vandalism among the young, it is always necessary for an authority from the 'independent' side to pop up with his own array of statistics to confirm his learned colleague's findings. On either side, producers and administrators have much more in common with each other than with the public they profess to serve and for whose affections they pretend to compete. The higher up the ladder of command, the easier it is for the dedicated 'professional' to change sides. They are media men living in a media-orientated world and by now operating more closely to the seat of power than was ever the lot of Sir John Reith. He never became viceroy of India and he never achieved the kind of intimacy with prime ministers and members of Cabinet that he would have liked. His faceless successors enjoy far more power. They are in fact viceroys of an electronic empire and the institutions they control have become the most influential in British life. With the passage of time their positions have become more entrenched and any change attempted in the order of fixed and immutable television becomes tantamount to a constitutional change of revolutionary proportions.

During this same period, the story of the New Media in Wales and its impact on Welshness and Welsh culture has not been encouraging. There has been an alarming decline in the percentage of Welsh-speakers among the population, and television may well have accelerated this process. This is a difficult calculation to make and significant figures are not easy to come by. But no one can deny a general sense of unease. The television set has insinuated itself like a sinister visitor from an alien universe and sits in the corner of every household exerting its hypnotic rays and quietly changing the natures of the inmates even as they go about their daily business. Its greatest influence is assumed to be over the children. It has a hold over their imaginations and their thought processes which make the influence of medieval storytellers and Jesuit priests pale into insignificance. That phosphorescent glow, those luminous and beguiling colours, sap the will and undermine the individuality of people, transforming them into worshippers of this latest soporific extension of that self-existent heartbeat, that universal religion that demands nothing more from its adherents than total passivity. All this may sound like a gross exaggeration, and yet our Welsh experience tells us that it must contain more than the grain of truth. This is the new opium of the people that will carry them over from the eternal arms of one religion into the grasp of another, that will tide them across the discomforts and disturbances of the unhappy process of 'culture shift'. It will be television that will transform all those (shifty, shifting, unsure,) hypocritical, welshing, deceitful, untrustworthy, disloyal, unintelligible Taffs into firm cuddly gonks manufactured in the shapes suggested by those popular entertainers who manage to stumble on one way or another of making some sort of Welshness acceptable to the great British-that-is-English public. Again this is an exaggeration, but the truly alarming thought is that such a process would not meet with the disapproval of the satraps of the medium and that they would more than likely go out of their way to encourage it, even demand it, if it improved their ratings, or gained them signs of approval from their masters.

An attempt was made in the early sixties to create something like an independent television service for north and west Wales. It came too late to the feast, and what crumbs it could pick up from the floor were not enough to keep it alive. It was run by starry-eyed educationalists, ministers and trade unionists without sufficient experience or capital. By the 'professionals' in the BBC and ITV their failure was greeted with chuckles of secret delight. It seemed to confirm once and for all that television had no place for amateurs, however enthusiastic or well intentioned. It was a closed shop to be quietly divided up between management, producing staff and unions. This was to be the standard working arrangement: a sandwich with a thin spread of programme output in the middle. No sooner was something called BBC Wales established than BBC Two emerged to demand a lion's share of BBC finances on the grounds that it was going to provide a better class of programmes for a better class of people. The old spirit of Portland Place and English middle-class culture was reasserting itself and regrouping within the confines of the new television empire. Driven on by the process of 'pacing', both the BBC and ITV plunged on into the realm of colour television. This trebled their expenses at a stroke and the development of such a thing as BBC Wales came very low down in the order of priority. A characteristic of the sixties and seventies was the intensification of the struggle between workers and management for their share of the production cake in a Labour-controlled mixed economy. This struggle was very accurately reflected in the private world of television. While the pacing went on, the real conflicts were between rival unions and between management and union members. Discontent was particularly rife in the BBC, whose financial resources were more restricted. The net result on both channels was less finance for programmes and more for profits and wages. In Wales promised developments were again postponed and the quality of programmes often suffered through inadequate finances.

It is perfectly obvious even to the most casual and unconcerned observer that neither the BBC nor the reigning ITV company have any primary concern or commitment to anything that could be described as Welsh culture. The BBC quite rightly claims pride of place among those institutions which exist to defend and propagate the English heritage. In this respect it does more than Parliament or the press, than the universities or the established Church, than the Arts Council and all the celebrated institutions to which this important body gives its financial and moral support. What it has done for Wales has always been minimal and incidental. However anxious it showed itself in the post-war period to recruit a conspicuous number of Welsh-speaking men and women on its producing staff, the total operation was always geared to the requirements of London. There might be well-known Welsh faces in the window of the front office, so to speak, but the factory itself was a branch office fully integrated into the main operation and turning out useful spare parts. Producing staff understood perfectly well that what they did for local consumption was no more than gentle exercise on the nursery slope. The proper ambition and career module was to think of something acceptable for Head Office and suitable contributions for the network. This species of work ethic automatically relegated the Welsh language to the status of a second-class citizen even among professionals who had been recruited on the basis of their creative abilities in that language. The complexity of the situation was compounded by the demands of the non-Welsh-speaking staff for status and budgets commensurate with the increasing percentage of non-Welsh-speakers inside the 'Welsh Region'. In the spirit of the BBC charter they were able to argue their obligation to maintain a service that would inform, educate and entertain this ever increasing majority of the Welsh people. And with every year that passed under this system it was more than likely that the majority would grow rapidly. There was nothing in the BBC charter about defending or propagating the Welsh heritage.

In the late sixties TWW lost its franchise as the company responsible for independent television in Wales and the West of England. Part of the reason given for their dismissal was the inadequate provision and un-satisfactory material they had produced in the Welsh language and in Wales generally. A galaxy of showbusiness talent and Welsh-language establishment figures made common cause with somewhat more hard-headed Bristol-based businessmen to create HTV. They were lavish with their promises to usher in a new era of creative television which would make an unprecedented impact on Welsh life and generally invigorate cultural life in Wales. They did what they could. Their track record was certainly an improvement on their predecessor. They made notable contributions to children's programmes, to Welsh news, to opera, to the less expensive type of discussion programme, to strictly literary matters, to the Eisteddfod, and they made a start with independent drama in both languages. Whatever their intentions there was no way in which they could overcome the growing rigidity of the structure of television in the United Kingdom as a whole. In London the controlling powers of the two giant organizations sat side by side like Gog and Magog, each with a leg raised ready to go out pacing the moment any impatient enquirer should stop to ask them exactly what they were doing. The BBC was welding the entire United Kingdom into one big suburban happy family, and ITV was doing the same, along with the commendable activity of making healthy profits.

When these basic Anglo-Saxon attitudes were transferred to the situation in Wales, it soon became obvious that they were painfully irrelevant to our problem: indeed they actively exacerbated it. Television pacing in Wales meant a peculiarly wasteful exercise in which the further-flung servants of Gog and Magog engaged themselves busily in mirror-image-making, duplicating each other's programmes with comic persistence whenever the tight London schedules allowed them to pop their heads nervously out of the ubiquitous box. The principle of television pacing ruled out what was one of the most immediately obvious solutions to Welsh problems, namely constructive co-operation between BBC Wales and HTV Wales. When the possibilities of bringing to bear dual resources in collaborative efforts or even co-productions were suggested in the early seventies – at a time when the BBC had begun to collaborate with Time-Life and with Communist television organizations beyond the iron curtain – it was pointed out by those in authority and control that a public service corporation like the BBC could never be expected to soil its hands in enterprises that would also involve too close contact with the sullied servants of commerce. It took ten years of strenuous sacrifice, chiefly on the part of Cymdeithas yr Iaith Gymraeg (the Welsh Language Society), to make any noticeable impression on the complacent surface of this attitude.

XIV

It is at this point that we may once more observe the curious and telling coincidence of interest between those restless heirs of the creative documentary film tradition, comfortably trapped inside the metropolitan television structures, and the defenders of the Welsh language under siege, and those producers in Wales most concerned with turning the power of the New Media around and directing it towards the supporting, sustaining and enlarging of the indigenous culture, instead of wiping it out. It is an aspect worth dwelling on if only because it is a heartening feature of what otherwise would be a very sad history indeed. This coincidence of interest in itself suggests that human creativity, at all times and in all places, and even in the impersonal mechanized world of television, is one and indivisible. And more than that, that an element of genuine freedom is an indispensable ingredient of the creative process.

An early-day motion for a debate on the nature of the Fourth Channel was tabled in the House of Commons on 2 December 1971. Before this a group of television and film directors and critics had organized themselves into a campaign to stop the five largest commercial companies from getting their greedy hands on the Fourth Channel. The basis of their protest was a rejection of both existing broadcasting systems. They saw the Fourth Channel as a natural forum for a freer and more enlightened use of the television medium, available to all the people, to independent creative programme-makers and not tied to the monolithic tyranny of either the BBC or the ITV. This was the origin of the movement that ultimately found rational expression in the celebrated Annan Report. By now it looks pretty certain that the Fourth Channel when it eventually appears will be a characteristically pragmatic English compromise based on the philosophy and some of the ideals laid down by the campaign of the creative producers that began in 1971.

In Wales campaigns for cultural values had begun much earlier and on a much wider front, and as usual had proved far more costly, and had gained far less. Cymdeithas yr Iaith Gymraeg (the Welsh Language Society) had come into existence in 1962 mainly as a youthful response to Saunders Lewis's sombre BBC annual radio lecture, *Tynged Yr Iaith* (The Fate of the Language). As if some inexorable wheel had turned full circle, the most acute critical mind at work in the Welsh language was concentrating our attention on the crisis point in the condition of our culture. As far as the New Media were concerned, the control of television now played the role that the control of radio had occupied in the struggles of the early 1930s. But this time the defenders of the language were on much weaker ground. An economic depression, another world war, the triumph of a British Labour Party, popular broadcasting, alien education, a mass retreat from Nonconformity and organized religion, had left the Welsh language and the Welsh identity in what appeared to be an indefensible position. There was no ex-prime minister around to champion the cause in the corridors of power. Some senior Labour politicians were still capable of making their sentimental sentiments known once a year on the National Eisteddfod platform. But in spite of the power and the positions they held, or perhaps because of them, they showed as many signs of active concern and practical determination as a row of sleeping beauties in an opium den. It was as if the corpse of Welsh culture had been measured and all that remained was to make the necessary funeral arrangements. It says much for Mr Lewis's influence that one rare broadcast in his unmistakable voice was sufficient to activate the brightest spirits of the new generation that were still able to understand the language in which he spoke. Like Emrys Wledig in the celebrated speech of his 1936 verse play *Buchedd Garmon*, also written for radio, the broadcast summoned the Welsh people to the defence of their heritage.

The prolonged contemplation of history, ancient or modern, is never without its warnings or its consolations. Even the remote past can sometimes appear astonishingly relevant. From the very origin of the Welsh as a distinct nation, it is possible to discern two contrasting standards of behaviour, often in conflict, sometimes coexisting uncomfortably in the career of some striking personality. Over the centuries they appear to have made themselves indispensable both to the Welsh character and to the vitality of the Welsh tradition. The more successful and aggressive model was rooted in the agreeable fantasy that the whole of the island had once belonged to the Cambro-British (that is, the Welsh) ruling class. Like fantasies it satisfied a frustrated appetite. Generation after generation it encouraged the warrior aristocracy in the painful day-to-day business of defending a Wales and a Welshness that in historic perspective appears to have been under constant attack. Their task was bloody, onerous and painful, but their mythology promised them rich rewards in this world and the next.

Another attitude had a totally religious origin and purpose. Dewi Sant, like all the other Celtic saints, belonged to exactly the same network of aristocratic families as the ambitious warriors: but the solution he offered to the pressing problems of maintaining the integrity of a precarious Welsh civilization were very different. His appeal was to asceticism and altruism. He called upon the people to make sacrifices for the good of their souls and not for any material advantage or for the pursuit of the will-o-the-wisp of neo-imperial glory on the strength of their vaunted Romano-British inheritance. If we were to apply this interpretation of the Welsh tradition to any period in our past it would at least have the merit of relating the marmoreal shapes of academic history to the continuing problem of human behaviour. The long history of a small nation is a convenient receptacle for growing a culture that may enable us to diagnose with greater accuracy notable ailments of the human condition. It is possible to argue that without a stubborn strain of altruism the Welsh people would never have remained loyal to their language through all the storms and stresses of the last four and a half centuries. At any point in time, from the Tudor triumph at the Battle of Bosworth, which the bards hailed as the consummation of all the ancient prophesies about reconquering the Isle of Britain, there were always powerful and influential Welshmen busily enumerating the material benefits that would flow directly from casting off the shackles of the ancient language. Again it could be argued that it was the ascetic and altruistic strain that was responsible for the more creative aspects of Welsh Dissent in the eighteenth century. The remarkable movements among the peasantry and working class in the nineteenth century would never have been possible without the exercise of this most attractive aspect of the Welsh character.

In this perspective, it becomes wholly appropriate that the present-day activists should be conscious of their own descent from this tradition; the children of Dissent in Wales have become responsible for the creation of the first authentic dissident movement in Britain. If one wished to single out the most creative contribution that the advent of television has made to Welsh life, the simple answer would have to be Cymdeithas yr Iaith. Without counting the cost, and in an unbroken sequence of imprisonments and fines, this society of young people has been prepared to challenge the might of the modern state in order to seek justice for this same language that has survived the centuries, in order to give it the opportunity to live and thrive in the modern world.

No doubt the cause was that much more attractive to the young because it was so opposed to the gross materialism and economic determinism of the age. The generosity of youth will always find an appropriate outlet. But I think it is as well for every Welshman now to realize, whether he lives in Abergavenny or Aberystwyth, or even in Liverpool or London, that he owes a special debt to these young people. With their own lives as their only resource they have made themselves the custodians of a very battered Ark of the Covenant. They remind us that the land and the language of Wales are the natural repositories of the memorials of 2000 years of Welsh existence. They contain the shrines of history, the evidence of a people's struggle to preserve the right to live in their own way; what would now be called the fight for freedom and self-determination. In the tradition of the dissidents and of Dewi Sant their protests are rooted in non-violent civil disobedience; and the health of our society and of our civilization may well be measured by our response to their challenge.

Certainly no creative artist, whatever medium he works in, can ignore it. If he does, the work he produces is likely to be immeasurably reduced in stature and significance. What they are telling us is not new. They are saying that our history is worthy of respect and so is our land and so is our language. These are living elements that have always existed for our well-being. We would be less than worthy if we failed them and used indifference to betray the spirit they represent.

Here, as in any other corner of the globe, television is the visual agent of the potential for destruction that must exist in the superstructure of a self-existent Machine that increasingly strives towards a perfection of serving itself and its own purposes, irrespective of any society that makes use of it. History has already shown that the forces of technology can only be kept in check and made to serve creative and socially beneficial ends by societies that still have the will to continue to celebrate their own existence. Welsh culture, the ancient land and language at its core, has as much right as any other to expect the New Media to participate fully in this creative task.

MWT: The publication of *Ghosts and Strangers* (2001) raises the question, 'What kind of fiction do we have here?' Short fiction, obviously, but would you be content with describing the volume as a collection of short stories?

EH: Not entirely. I think these are, in effect, short novels, because they cover quite an extensive range of time. I've never felt that I've made any great mark in the short story as a form, because I've drawn so much on the special characteristics of the short story for use in the novels I've written, particularly from the 1960s onwards. *Outside the House of Baal*, for example, is constructed in episodic form – not vignettes exactly, but each episode has many of the characteristics of the short story. I think it was Kate Roberts who said that it is a flash of light in the gloom of everyday life. A flood of light is thrown on the circumstances of an event, so that you have an understanding of life in the flash of the revelation of this small moment. This is part of the essential form of the short story, and I think I've adopted these features in constructing my later novels episodically, so that in a way I've exhausted my imaginative resources and I have nothing left for the short story as such. The four stories in this volume are therefore better described as novellas, I hope, rather than novelettes!

MWT: That would help explain why, for instance, a short story that is printed in *Mabon* is incorporated later, as an additional episode, in the revised and expanded second edition of *Outside the House of Baal*. It seems to be a clear instance of how very similar in kind – and therefore virtually interchangeable as a form – are the occasional short stories you've written and the episodes from which many of your later novels are constructed.

EH: The episode shares, if only in a certain limited respect, the free-standing characteristics of the short story. The example you mention concerns a minister of religion who is visiting his errant son, and up to a point it stands as an episode on its own, although it is more effective if seen in relation to the sequence of episodes that constitutes the novel as a whole. So in that sense I have absorbed a lot of the techniques of the short story into my novels, but at the cost of therefore being left unable to write short stories in their purest form.

MWT: As the term itself suggests, 'novella' means little novel. And the foreignness of the term is an indication of how relatively rare are examples of this kind of writing in mainstream anglophone fiction. So have you turned to other cultures for your models?

EH: You can see these in Welsh, to begin with, in that the longer short stories of Kate Roberts are examples of this form. But more particularly, you find novellas in French and Italian literature. The genre flourished there, and there could be commercial reasons for this. If you're living in a society where there are many amateur writers, then there may be no great inducement to write at substantial length. After all, one of the great features of English literary culture in the nineteenth century was the pressure on the professional novelist to produce the three-decker novel so beloved by an avid reading public. Contrast that with France, where you had the appearance of Flaubert's *Trois Contes*, or with Russia where the longer short stories of Chekhov are virtually novellas. I seem to recall that it was from them he moved on to writing the three-act play, and so he never embarked on a full-scale novel.

MWT: Is your fondness, then, of a form that you suggest is essentially European in character in itself an expression of your vision of yourself as a European novelist, rather than an anglophone British novelist?

EH: I would like to think that. My material is basically drawn from the Welsh experience, and that experience becomes more intelligible, in my opinion, if it is viewed in a European context. If you're concerned with Welsh-language culture, as in part I am, you're not dealing with a great world language, like English; you're dealing with a language under siege. In the contemporary world that is the situation of French, which is struggling for its world position, and also of Italian. It has a huge literary backlist, so to speak, since it extends back to the Middle Ages, when Italy saw the appearance of the first great vernacular literature, but in the modern era it has been reasonably content to rest on those laurels. So it benefits us in Wales to see ourselves in this context, and not to be swept away by the mighty current of Anglo-American culture. And this current is particularly strong and growing stronger. It is being fed by the extraordinary, brilliant outburst of post-imperial fiction in English from India and Africa and black America. In the last decade the economic power of Anglo-American publishing has created a vogue for what might be called 'cosmopolitan fiction'. This has little room for a cottage industry like mine. On the other hand, it has to contend with the surface glitter of real-life stories of the fashionably wealthy and famous. A lurid biography of a Diana or a Robert Maxwell or a Bill Clinton drives even a 'cosmopolitan' novel clean off the bookshelves. Then at the other extremity, which I am equally unqualified to deal with, is the raw fiction of drugs and poverty on the mean underprivileged streets. English-language fiction at the present time has polarized to these two extremes.

MWT: *Ghosts and Strangers* is obviously concerned with the European dimension – indeed, you send many of your characters to the Continent. Was that a conscious decision reflecting a current interest, across the political spectrum, in the question of how Britain should be related to Europe?

EH: I certainly believe in the benefits of the European Union for Wales and Welshness and the Welsh language. But to provide a European dimension to *Ghosts and Strangers* was no more than instinctive, since the cultural atmosphere that surrounds you, as a writer, impinges on your consciousness in this kind of way. If an idea of the oneness of Europe was already beginning to develop in the sixties, partly as a result of the ever increasing ease of travel to the Continent, then that idea has grown enormously in strength and complexity over the last couple of decades. I would like to think this is a trend that can be developed to our positive advantage.

MWT: But in *Ghosts and Strangers* there is also an element of concern expressed as to the *terms* in which people nowadays are prone to experience Europe. There's a suggestion that they are in danger of travelling light – that they know so little about the distinctive cultural identities of the countries they visit that their sense of Europe is a superficial one.

EH: We are all Europeans and we need to know more about each other's languages and cultures. It's a complex issue. Take the case of Lisa, the young wife in 'Menna', who has to decide whether to become a mother or not, and whether to publish in English or in Welsh. As a creative writer, she has a deep interest in a particular story, but never actually makes anything of it – it is a common experience of writers that they become attached to a story that they never actually write. In her case, it is a story about a Cathar girl in the Middle Ages whom a monk tries to seduce, and this seems to Lisa to reflect a lot of what she understands her own experience to be. In this sense, the characters wander through the European forest discovering things about themselves.

MWT: Indeed; and Lisa is a good example of this. Nevertheless, the novella seems to question how far the parallel she imagines herself drawing between her own present and that incident in the past is a constructive and valid one, and to what extent it might not rather be misleading and destructive. And that would seem to be another aspect of this collection. I find in it a very ambivalent view of how the past exists in and for the present.

EH: I think the past is a dangerous sea in which we swim, and it's important to remain buoyant in it and to breathe the air of the future. We are in some ways more conscious of ourselves, and of ourselves in relation to the past, than were our predecessors. If you consider a nineteenth-century novelist, he's likely to be totally absorbed in the present and in a positive, forward-moving social context which no longer exists, as I see it. We are so self-conscious, and so conscious of the past, that it does inhibit us in some ways. We have to come to terms with it and conquer it in order to continue fruitfully. The battles are different in our time. The planet has shrunk and is more in danger of being blown away. Like an unanchored balloon. And our imaginations are impelled to share the same unstable conditions.

MWT: And if we fail to do that, we're presumably in danger of being 'of no fixed abode', as your character Gwion describes himself in the story 'Ghosts and Strangers'. Because, that's another feature of this collection: we find in it characters who never identify with any particular place, and who therefore roam aimlessly from place to place.

EH: Gwion has been given the ambiguous gift of freedom by his late wife, the ghost who follows him, because she has left him sufficient money to travel wherever he likes. She tells him to go out and educate himself and to see the big wide world, whereas all he's doing, in actual fact, is uprooting himself from the garden where he had enjoyed a reasonably settled existence, and floating about in an ancient motor-car, travelling all around Europe but never knowing where to go next.

MWT: In 'Notes on the Novel', you've written that 'the centrality, often offering itself in some inconvenient form or other, of the love story is evident in the structure of the novel': This would seem to be true of these novellas. All four of them are concerned with some aspect or other of love – some of them positive, others dubious.

EH: My original subtitle for the book was 'Four Love Stories'. It's not included on the title page, but it reflects the way in which I saw the collection, as the novellas represent four different ways in which love is absolutely vital on the one hand, but on the other distorts the lives of the characters in a damaging sense. The power of love is central to the making of the novel as a form, and so the vast majority of novels are an exploration of a love situation of one kind or another. The first of these novellas is more lightweight than the others, because it is in a more satirical, comical style, whereas the others are cast in a more sombre form. Nevertheless, that first story is significant, because it illustrates the madness that is attached to love, and in the end the main character, who is so unkindly described as 'Lady Ramrod', can find comfort of a kind only in the pet dog that has been thrust upon her, after she's suffered several failures in love experiences during her life.

MWT: That reminds me of something else that seems to surface from time to time in your fiction, and that I find again in *Ghosts and Strangers*, namely a sense that, as modern society sees the disintegration of community and therefore the disintegration of a nexus of sustaining relationships that we tend to suppose characterized societies of the past, so love becomes more fatefully central to people's lives. This was, of course, a feeling that found famous voice in the nineteenth century in Matthew Arnold's anguished cry to his companion in 'Dover Beach': 'Ah, love, let us be true / To one another.' That makes the love relationship a very intense one, but it also means it has to take a great deal of weight – more, perhaps, than it can usually bear.

EH: Absolutely. It's carrying a whole host of angels on a pin. And the pin bends under the sheer weight of it. And there's no easy solution to it. We are in the end social beings, and we're having to pay dearly for our freedom. Present society is in many ways much freer and easier than any that has ever existed before. The claims of the family are limited, and not as strict as they used to be. A high percentage of marriages end up in divorce. You have then to build a new kind of society, where an extraordinary amount of weight and responsibility has to be placed on 'being true to one another', that is a personal relationship that has to survive unsustained by wider social structures. There is a kind of pragmatic hypocrisy about our way of life, so that prime ministers can make pious noises about family values that bear very little relationship to the way in which people actually conduct their lives. We live in a strange, and fluid, condition, and it's out of this condition that these stories emerge.

MWT: This is caught in the title of the collection, which suggests that some of these characters are haunted by a past they're scarcely able to understand, while others are little more than ghosts to themselves and strangers to each other, because they seem to lack all substantial being.

EH: All a writer like me can do is try and respond to the world around him on the basis of his own experience, and the older he gets the contrast between what was and what is becomes more and more apparent. It may well be that in my grandparents' day, the marriage bond was so tight that there were problems deriving from that and from the claustrophobia of the wider family situation, and that these problems proved very fruitful for a creative writer. Whereas it is almost the opposite now. Living together is a much freer and easier arrangement, and if people can't get on they say goodbye and move on. But this mobility and fluidity makes it difficult for the writer to create, through fiction, a 'holding environment' in which to explore what's happening. The ways of market forces, so beloved of right-wing politicians, can be just as mysterious and beyond control as those of old-fashioned Providence.

MWT: It's interesting to note that there's been an interval of more than thirty years between the publication of *Ghosts and Strangers* and the appearance in 1968 of *Natives*, the volume which corresponds to it in form. How would you explain that gap?

EH: *Natives* belongs very much to the end of the sixties, just as *Ghosts and Strangers* belongs to the end of the nineties. They reflect their time. And in that, positive, sense of the word they're both 'dated'. For example, the long story in *Natives*, 'Mel's Secret Love', is very much of its period. It wouldn't have been feasible at the end of the nineties, because it is a secret, illicit love and the whole concept of adultery, or extramarital liaisons as they stood at that time, in a city like Cardiff and in the various institutions in which young people worked, couldn't easily be reproduced in the nineties. Whatever the social mores of a given time, the substance of the story must be able to remain valid to the degree that the characters are palpably human, so that the reader – irrespective of period – can feel for them and understand them. In that sense, the reader is allowed a dual entry to the text. He can treat it as a historical document, but he can also view it as a fiction which is outside time, showing how the strife and the strains and the tribulations of individuals are a constant of living.

MWT: One reason why Mel, in the story you've mentioned, embarks on that illicit affair is because she's representative of her generation of Welsh-speakers, a young generation that was experiencing the transition from one kind of world to another. It had been brought up in rural, Nonconformist Wales but had then moved to the new, secular world of the city.

EH: A lot of the stories have a suburban context, apart from *Dinas*, which is about a collapsing farm society, representing a culture that is no longer viable or sustainable on the old terms.

MWT: That story deals with the complementary theme of the impossibility of turning the clock back, and of trying to return to, or to resurrect, a way of life that belongs to the past. The impression given in *Natives* is that of a society that is lost and adrift. I'm reminded of Joyce's *Dubliners*, where the city is felt to be 'the centre of paralysis', as Joyce himself put it. The society in *Natives* comes across as one that is paralysed, because it has lost one form of life and has failed to find another, and so ends up existing as a colonial society, seriously disabled by being alienated from its true sources of indigenous strength.

EH: A writer of stories is infatuated with his material, and is like a lost lover, in the sense that you are constantly being disillusioned by this material for which you nevertheless continue to feel an inexplicable affection. You can't understand why you should go on feeling so concerned. All these stories are explorations of this condition. It's interesting for me to discuss retrospectively the characteristics, as they now seem, of stories published over thirty years ago. But I'm the kind of writer who is not aware at the time of writing of the dominant themes, or characteristics, of the fiction I'm involved in writing. The creation of the story is an exploration of love-hate relationships that the writer has with his material and with this country that infatuates him. It's as if you're not good enough for it, and it's not good enough for you. And in order to resolve this impossible dilemma, you resort to fiction, and this is what gives you the impetus to write. One of the feats, shall we say – rather than the tricks – of fiction-writing is making the unlikely seem inevitable.

MWT: *Natives* was published in 1968, just five years after Saunders Lewis's celebrated radio broadcast, *Tynged yr Iaith*, had roused a whole generation of young people to an awareness of the dire plight of Welsh-language culture, and had moved them to revolutionary political action – a kind of anti-colonial insurrection. They worked for the rejuvenation of their culture and their country. And yet there's no sense whatsoever of this cultural and political reawakening in *Natives*. Rather, the feeling you get is that there can be no substantial movement of meaningful change.

EH: There's a kind of time lag between raw events and a writer's ability to make fiction of them. It's like preparing certain kinds of food: game has to be hung in order to allow it to become properly matured for use; there are also ingredients that have to be marinated before they acquire the necessary flavour. So, too, events frequently need to marin-ate in a writer's conscious – and subconscious – mind for an indefinite period before they can be used. The late sixties was the period of the youth revolution right across Europe, and I myself was involved in some of the events associated with it here in Wales. But you can't write about what is, for you, very much in progress. You have to wait for them to marinate in your subconscious mind before you can put them to conscious use.

MWT: Which is why you engaged with the experiences of this period not in *Natives*, but some twenty years later, in *Bonds of Attachment*.

EH: Yes, and that novel must have long been under preparation, so to speak, in the subconscious mind, because *Bonds of Attachment* belongs to a sequence that began with the writing of *National Winner*, and that was the fiction that appeared directly after *Natives*. I began writing *National*

Winner in 1969, and it is now clear that the concerns I later addressed in *Bonds of Attachment* were already there, in the first novel of the sequence, in embryonic form. But as a writer, you can't – any more than a gardener – keep pulling up the plant and looking at the roots all the time. You have to leave them be, there in the dark, for the growth to take place.

MWT: True, but if I, as a reader, were asked if I could think of any work of English fiction by a Welsh writer that could qualify as an example of what is nowadays called post-colonial fiction, I would immediately nominate *Natives*. The very title suggests as much – 'natives' being so evidently the pejorative term used by the colonizers of the colonized, but also being the term then reclaimed by the colonized to affirm their own aboriginal status.

EH: I seem to remember being asked about the title at the time, and the only way I could think of explaining, and justifying, it was by referring to the root of 'native' in the Latin *natus* – meaning, of course, a person born in that particular place. And these stories were about what was happening to people at that time born and bred in Wales – and living in what you call the post-colonial situation. That situation still exists, of course. A great deal of the post-colonial situation – that is, the consolidation of colonial 'occupation' into a settled state of affairs – depended on the willing subservience of the natives. And this involved breeding in them an admiration of the colonial power. And now that, in Wales, the coercive power of the colonizing nation has been removed, and England is experiencing its own distinctive set of difficulties that are also post-imperial, these are not of much help to the very different post-colonial problems of Wales. That is why I keep emphasizing Wales's need of Europe, which had long been foreseen by writers like Saunders Lewis, Ambrose Bebb and R. T. Jenkins, as early as the 1920s. What was foreshadowed by them in their creative work is now evident to us all as a crucial aspect of our present-day, and every-day, experience. It means going back to your earliest roots – in some way redefining yourself – and thus regaining the confidence to face this new world. That is the only way for us in Wales to work through the trauma of our present lack of confidence.

MWT: What becomes clear in *Natives* is that the deepest – in the sense of the longest-lasting – damage done by colonization is not through the initial subjection of a people to the power of a foreign state, but the way in which that foreign state is translated into the state of mind of colonized people. This is part of that complex state of affairs that Gramsci famously identified as 'hegemony', the 'normalization' of the abnormal so that it comes to seem natural, inevitable and immutable. And the stories in *Natives* seem to me fascinating studies in different aspects of hegemony, exploring the many different forms it can take.

EH: It is an extraordinary situation in which we find ourselves, and it is intimately involved with the bilingual condition. Both of our linguistic cultures are suffering from the same vitamin deficiencies, so to speak, and so their growth is stunted. Our bilingual society is no healthier in this respect than is our monolingual society – which is a very serious problem, because we are all of us so readily recruited to the service of the British media and communications industry which is currently struggling to perpetuate what is left of the English imperial mentality: despising the European Union and grudgingly admiring the United States for commandeering their role and language.

MWT: You provide an example of that in *Natives*. The story 'A List of Good People' turns on the interesting case of the well-intentioned minister Penry Mostyn, who in many ways embodies the best qualities of Welsh Nonconformity, but who is revealed, by the end of the story, to have been seduced and corrupted by the glamour of his film star friend, Peter Zed, and the television commentator, Arnot Gough.

EH: It is endemic in the situation we've inherited, and I don't really know how to change it myself. It is also a European problem – if you're a Sicilian, and you go to northern Italy, the regimes that exist and have existed there (first the Fascist and now the post-Fascist) provide you with two ready paths to integration and success, namely the media and politics. It is equally true in Wales – these are the two channels for self-advancement.

MWT: Another traditional channel, of course, is education, and 'The Rigours of Inspection', another story from *Natives*, is about that, isn't it? There the headmaster manages to turn the tables on the visiting inspector by insinuating that the headmaster has a cousin in high places – an MP – and that gives him the advantage in the power relationship. And yet another means to acceptance by the ruling establishment has, in the past, been the one offered by the Anglican Church, as is illustrated in

'A Mystical Experience', where the archdeacon represents someone who has secured a place within the existing power structure, and it is the poor curate who is made by him to bend the knee to the powers that be.

EH: And given that the colonial mentality is actually being perpetuated, through the media and other 'opinion-forming' institutions, in present-day post-imperial Wales, it is the duty and function of the creative artist to redress the balance, because the relationship between established power and communication is too close. A writer can therefore use the form of fiction to reveal hidden truths – which is, of course, a paradox, since in one sense any work of fiction is necessarily a tissue of lies. In terms of Plato's *Republic*, it's as if the philosopher kings have taken over the communications systems, so it is the despised poet, whom Plato wanted to exile, that has the function of exploring experimentally and existentially the human condition through fiction in order to get closer to the occluded truth – because in fact it is reality as it is represented by the media that is the tissue of half-truths, and not the fictive products of the creative writer.

MWT: That is why you have chosen to publish alongside your novels a series of important essays about the powerful role of the media in modern Welsh life. I'm thinking of your fascinating essay on the life and work of the celebrated media mogul Sir Huw Wheldon, whom you describe as 'The Lost Leader', and your seminal essay on 'Television and Us', which was the product of your own involvement with radio and television, first as a producer for the BBC during the 1950s, and then as a campaigner for a Welsh channel in later decades.

EH: Everybody needs a role, and in our time the artist as creative writer has this distinctive corrective, and perhaps revolutionary, role. Indeed, it is to some extent the role of the modern artist in all the art forms, from the 1880s onwards. And that is why the modern artist had to devise new strategies of communication that aimed to produce both a shock of recognition and the shock of the new. This is certainly evident in the novel – I think immediately of two of my great heroes, Joyce and Lawrence, who almost unconsciously adopted, in spite of themselves, a kind of prophetic role. When Lawrence is at his most raw, he is a Nonconformist preacher pure and simple. You can see more clearly sometimes the fundamental bias of the genius of figures like this when you examine their less perfectly finished or 'achieved' work.

MWT: Another aspect of this concern of yours that modern literature counterbalance the power of the media is your conviction that the creative writer is under an almost solemn obligation to respect the integrity of his language. I know how much you admire realism as a style of writing, and yet if we look at your fiction, whether it be novel or novella, there is no attempt made there at realism – that is at veri-similitude – when, for example, it comes to writing dialogue.

EH: Fiction is fiction. My commitment to what is loosely described as 'realism' is based on the belief that when you are attempting a large-scale work of fiction, too much baroque experimentation and fantastication would be disadvantageous. Hence the deliberate limitation of technical innovation. As for dialogue, I learnt in part from reading Chekhov's plays that it is not necessary to transcribe 'actual' conversational style verbatim in order to produce credibly realistic dialogue. Although I know no Russian, I am reliably informed that Chekhov's dialogues are, in fact, highly 'literary' in register and in style. Yet, such is his penet-ration to the essence of his characters, that their mode of speaking *appears* to be wholly natural, because it is consistent with their mode of being within the play. That also means that the dialogue is valid in whatever cultural setting the play is performed, which is why Chekhov works so well in translation, for example. He is as exciting on New York's 49th Street as he is in Moscow Arts Theatre. In fact, I first came across Chekhov in Welsh translations by Hudson Williams, a professor of Greek who translated all of Chekhov's works. That must have been when I was working in the BBC in the 1950s and 1960s, and was particularly interested in developing a series of programmes on drama in Europe.

MWT: So reading Chekhov helped you evolve a style of writing for your own purposes?

EH: Yes. I had read him, for example, before writing *Outside the House of Baal*, and I was aware that I already had the problem of conveying, through the medium of English, dialogue that had taken place in Welsh. I was absolutely determined to avoid 'Boyo' English – it wouldn't have been appropriate, anyway, for the kind of society I was dealing with. In some ways, my knowledge of the kinds of English spoken by Welsh people was very limited. The kind of English I had heard in north Wales was very much second-language English. It hadn't been acclimatized in the way in which English had been acclimatized in the south Wales valleys. It wasn't a rich sociolect, when I was growing up. So my limited social contacts usually involved me in speaking English to those who had to turn to it as a second language in order to speak to my brother and me. Theirs was a stilted English, apart from that of the rector and his sister, who played a very large part in our lives. He was a Cardiganshire man, but Oxford-educated, and so he spoke Oxford English with a strong Cardiganshire accent! There were certain expletives that they used all the time that nobody else in my part of the world did, like 'Jiw, Jiw' and 'bach, bach'. It was a curious hybrid language that they spoke.

MWT: But that did mean that your attention was concentrated on the peculiarity of language very early.

EH: Very much. And the peculiarities of people, too. I was brought up in what might be described as a very eccentric community – but then, I suppose everybody is!

Bilingual Murmurs

Previously unpublished; revised text of a lecture given at the Association for Welsh Writing in English conference on translation, Gregynog, 2000.

A single language is a version more than a vision of the world.

In any language writers of fiction always have to begin at the beginning. A blank page is the day before the first day, the void without form, the darkness on the face of the depth of experience. Their ink is white and their paper black. Their next problem is the words they use and the language these words belong to.

For creative purposes a language is a collective brain. We are wired up to understand each other. You have to understand before you can misunderstand. Inside the language circuit, the illusion of understanding what others are using words to hide preserves a precarious balance with the abiding discomfort of being unable to understand oneself.

This collective brain functions in order to filter the overall consciousness of existence which might otherwise overwhelm it. By the same token the individual brain inside the language collective is protected from being overwhelmed by experience. Language attempts to impose order and discipline on the chaos which surrounds us. When it is mutually understood it also has the power to bestow particularized significance.

When a new brain is born it requires protection and stimulus from the brain that gave it birth inside the language collective. The need for stimulation increases in direct ratio as the need for protection diminishes. Even so both needs persist to a greater or lesser degree for the entire lifespan of the individual brain.

In a primitive society, if an individual brain aspires to poetry and storytelling, the value of its contribution is measured by the degree of mastery of its craft rather than the originality of its ideas. And since the grammar and accidence of primitive language is extremely complex and sophisticated, it is clear that enormous satisfaction is derived by the practitioner and the collective audience from subtleties of utterance. A new twist on a hallowed idea would be rewarded with at least a collective Ah or Amen. The Amen recognizes the old trick of making the familiar new and bright and somehow strange.

Inside the primitive collective brain there are no crises of identity – or if there are, they are gently resolved by the appropriate riff of the storyteller or the comforting choral chant of the poet. We know from our own experience that it is only when societies become developed and complex and multilingual that crises of identity spring up all over the place.

Technology intensifies this condition. Individual brains are no longer anchored safely in one large, comforting, collective brain. Individuals find themselves let loose as fragments of a powerful process over which they have no control. It is at this point that a nostalgia for a more solid identity gives rise to fresh mythologies about a golden Adamic past.

Our brave new world is dominated by communication and there is movement on such a scale that individual brains find themselves becoming the victims in global clashes of collective languages. This has been going on for a long time, for example, in the clashes between settlers and natives on so many continents of the earth. ('Life, Liberty and the pursuit of Happiness' might well have resonated even better in Iroquois than in eighteenth-century English.)

In the Welsh situation, I would suggest that in the *realpolitik* of the clash between collective brain languages, the processes of translation should be directed towards strengthening the weaker party in order to give it greater prospects of survival. Survival is closely allied to salvation. Through their concern for salvation our Renaissance scholars ensured the survival of our language for another 400 years. Salvation and survival are wrapped up in each other. To be saved you must believe that you are worth saving.

In the name of freedom, equality and justice among collective brains, it would seem that we have an obligation to do all we can to strengthen the weaker collective if we desire to give it a reasonable chance of survival.

The substance of all these foregoing propositions is materially changed when we are confronted, as indeed I am at this moment, with a collective brain that is bilingual. On a social level it seems quite plain that we are able to cope with this condition in surprising comfort. (It comes easily to us Cymry who have always attached so much store to the practice of being agreeable. 'Rydym ni yn bobol glên gynddeiriog'.*)

Difficulties arise in the case of a bilingual brain that has aspirations to becoming a creative writer. Under these conditions the inside of a writer's skull is liable to become a house divided against itself. Not only the writer but every sentence he writes becomes susceptible to a crisis of identity. The strains and stresses of allegiance and loyalty are more intense than any in the political sphere.

* We are a fearsomely friendly people!

Wittgenstein has said somewhere that all philosophy should begin with a confession. This is not philosophy in any disciplined sense and I am not about to make a confession. All I am doing is thinking aloud in an attempt to make myself clear – to myself as much as to anyone. Confession may be good for the soul, but if a writer were to be stripped down to the status of a naked ape all you would find would be a creature shivering with physical cowardice and moral turpitude. A storyteller wraps himself in a coat of many colours and many words in order to conceal his unappetizing nakedness. At the same time, even as a writer of fiction, I am prepared to admit to being driven by a nameless and mysterious force that I have never succeeded in identifying, beyond some obsessive desire to settle accounts with myself.

All I propose to offer is a brief outline of a modus operandi adopted by a twentieth-century practitioner who made a particular effort to acquire a bilingual brain, and has paid the appropriate price ever since.

I have to deal with my own case because it is the only one of which I can speak with any degree of authority. I began to write and to learn Welsh at exactly the same time. Both activities were the products of that new awareness of the world that comes with adolescence. From the top of the hill behind our house there was a spectacular view calculated to inspire and even intoxicate. As Gerard Manley Hopkins wrote : 'When I see Snowdon from Tremeirchion and the mountains in its neighbourhood, with the clouds lifting, it gives me a rise of the heart.' . . . 'Lovely the woods, waters, meadows, combes, vales, / All the air things wear that build this world of Wales.'

Every landscape treasures its secrets. What I felt then I can still feel now. Westwards the white strength of Gwynedd, and the mountains rising like ramparts to touch the setting sun. From every point of the compass this unique landscape hides treasure trove. Even the impassive vastness of the level sea has to conceal sunken cities, with secret histories, myths and legends. To each mystery there must be a key. But the key of keys is the original language which hallows every hill and valley, every farm and every field with its own revered name. I must learn it, and the more difficult it is the better. Hidden treasures like pearls and lost souls need to have their high price.

That was an attempt to recapture the spirit of my youth. The record, alas my record, is far less exalted. I acquired a bilingual brain by dint of effort. I am still reluctant to look too closely into why exactly I made the effort. It leaves me with a multiple burden of guilt – on my own behalf, on behalf of my parents, and on behalf of Welshness and the nation we belong to. It seems more than any other factor in my life to have dominated my faltering creative steps.

To return to a crude outline of my record. The natural ability for literary expression continued to flow far more easily through my first language. Developing as a writer in wartime brought mixed blessings: first, a view of rural societies in Wales that had remained solidly mono-glot; then a taste of, and for, Mediterranean culture and the excitement of the *Italienische Reise* by courtesy of Allied Forces. Subsequently, living in London meant concentrating on the novel, mastering a craft and developing a proficiency in that form along with an ambition to earn a living as a writer. I have to confess that it was only when I returned to Wales to work in the BBC that I was able to resume the missionary ardour of my youth.

There were distinct lines of policy that I was resolved to pursue as senior drama producer in radio. And these came, as it were in traditional pulpit style, under three heads. There had to be an emphasis on writers and fostering new writing in both languages. After that came the need to translate on a substantial scale European drama into Welsh. Last and in many ways least was the duty of making Welsh writing known to a wider world.

I was lucky to catch the last phase of the golden age in radio. For ten years after the war it could be argued that the higher reaches of BBC Radio were dominated by poets and patrons of poetry. This was the age that produced the work of Henry Reed, George Barker, Dylan Thomas, Louis MacNeice, Terence Tiller and W. R. Rodgers, and ended with Martin Esslin and Harold Pinter – an exciting period of English cultural life.

The line of demarcation was made by the arrival of commercial television. Poets were driven out by politicians and profit. Audience research and ratings came to dominate the mass media. This was the time when I began working in television.

To return to my personal priorities. They had to be adapted to the exigencies of television production and distribution in the strictest Marxist terms. The order of my priorities had to be reversed: making Welsh writing known to a wider world became my chief occupation. Willy-nilly the last became first. For example, in order to present Saunders Lewis's *Siwan* through the medium of television, I was obliged to translate it into English. In this case I had a distinct sensation of being a *traduttore* who had turned into a *traditore*.

His plays and those of John Gwilym Jones and W. S. Jones were well received by London critics and occasionally translated and produced in

Europe (*Brad* went down very well among the Germans). The irony
remained that they could not be produced on television in the language
in which they were written. For an extended period I would find myself
producing the original on radio, a translation on television and then,
because of its success, presenting the translation on radio as well.

I have detailed these procedures because they reflect so clearly how
economic and political considerations dominate any public expression
of artistic activity. It is too easy to lose sight of your original priorities. It
seemed to me then, and it still seems to me to be the case, that if you
keep on taking water out of the well without making proper provision
for replenishing the supply, the well will eventually be drained dry. The
need for a steady transfusion of all forms of literature into the Welsh-
language collective brain remains an urgent priority. It is necessary in
the first place to strengthen the idiom. There is always a need to renew,
even to recapture the magic of the great translators of the past. From
Morgan Llwyd and Elis Wynne to Talhaiarn and T. Gwynn Jones and
T. Hudson Williams. This process in itself would enlarge the horizon
and increase our flexibility and resilience in the face of cyclonic technological change. If anybody chooses to call this elitism I would be very
glad to learn of any other method of raising standards.

In order to avoid becoming victims to a linguistic Gresham's Law – that
well-known economic principle which is always summarized as 'bad
money drives out good' – each generation spearheaded by poets must do
more than their bit to purify and modernize the language of the tribe. This
task cannot be sidestepped by playing about with electronic technology.

I think it is worth noting that Welsh has certain fascinating internal
translation problems of its own. There seems to me to be a need for
a thorough and purposeful philosophical examination of this subject.
Our broadcasting channels and our bilingual lives present us with
the problem daily. English as a form of communication has long been
standardized and even parlourized. It has even succeeded in establishing a special relationship with the advance of electronic technology.
With us poor bilinguals we have to cope with *tafodiaith, bratiaith, malu-
awyriaith* of the chat shows (which we are expected to *joio* as well as
mwynhau), *seiatiaith, pulpudiaith,* not to mention *dysgwyr-iaith.** Coping

---

* Editor's note: *iaith* is Welsh for 'language', *tafodiaith* is 'dialect', *bratiaith* is
'debased language'. *Malu awyr* roughly means 'to waffle', *seiatiaith* is a 'pious
language', *pulpud* means 'pulpit' and *dysgwyr* are learners. *Joio* and *mwynhau*
both mean 'to enjoy'.

with this linguistic cornucopia may not add to the gaiety of nations but it certainly gives translators something to think about. In my view, our institutions responsible for education, entertainment and information have a first duty towards the standard literary language. Through this medium more than any other, a steady diet of performance and consumption of European and world classics in Welsh would make up for a serious cultural vitamin deficiency. At the present time actors and writers in particular, and perhaps even more importantly audiences, are being deprived of the opportunity of widening their native horizon. If the language is to survive in a bilingual context it has to be given the maximum capacity to sustain the challenge. A television channel, for example, cannot hope to live for ever on a perpetual diet of masturbatory hysteria and pop and froth. Both the language and people need to discover inside themselves as well as in the world outside the means of creative survival. We have no choice but to equip ourselves to deliver a positive Welsh vision of the world. It is better to aim high and miss than aim at nothing and hit the target with monotonous regularity.

In cultural terms most of the 1960s and all of the 1970s in Wales were taken up by the struggle to secure a Welsh-language television channel. As is so often the case, energies that might otherwise have been directed into creative work – more novels, more plays, and so on – were expended in protest and political activity. Historically this was no more than an extension of the struggle that had gone on since the First World War. And all the time the linguistic abilities of the target audience were deteriorating. The strength of the idiom was being eroded by a process that began in the classrooms of the nineteenth century and is now being continued by mass media that could in many cases be used to revive it if the will existed to support such an effort.

A bilingual nation, like a bilingual brain, is, in the cultural sense, a society of societies. For it to remain bilingual and function creatively on this basis, all the devices of translation should be mobilized to give the older and the weaker partner the strength to persist. It is the older language after all that has access to those primitive powers with which a people struggles to understand the world and celebrate its own precarious existence.

The Third Difficulty

Lecture given at Congrès de la Société des Anglicistes, Brest, May 1986
and first published in *Planet* 61 (Feb./March 1987), 16–25.

Like any politician who has reached the age of retirement and yet clings to office, a novelist who has practised his craft for forty years has an obligation to justify his urge to continue writing. At my age, it is no longer sufficient to say one writes 'to earn a living' or 'to please oneself', although these are perfectly honourable motives in themselves. Age tells us we are fixed as firmly as trees or stars in our time and place. It allows us to mull over the obvious with the naive surprise of second childhood. For example, we did not choose our language, nationality, race, religion: they were presented to us like Greek gifts at our birth and with them a complex of tasks and obligations to torment us for a lifetime and yet give our puny efforts such dignity as they possess.

In my own case, for example, I am a Welsh storyteller because I had no real choice to be anything else. The practice of my craft involves the attempt at reconciling three functions that would otherwise be in open conflict.

The first is to celebrate the culture and society that made me and to do that for the most part in a language that has been historically hostile to both.

The second is to adopt the role of People's Remembrancer at a time when the folk memory is rapidly fading and to activate a past that most would prefer to forget.

The third is to adopt and exploit the analytical and reductive power inherent in the novel form as it has been developed in bourgeois society, at the very time when the new media have usurped the social function of storyteller in a post-bourgeois era, and are remorselessly driving the novel into obsolescence.

These three 'impossible tasks', as they might have been called in *Culhwch ac Olwen*, are intimately related. In reality they cannot be resolved independently of one another. But for the purpose of this discussion and for the sake of civilized brevity, I shall confine myself to the Third Difficulty.

The developed novel, like Impressionist paintings or large-scale orchestral music or realistic theatre, is an expression of pre-1914 bourgeois high culture. It is an important part of the produce of that culture that we still cherish long after the social order that gave it birth had passed away. It is not easy to define what elements in the fiction of Marcel Proust, for example, provide us with some sense of continuity in our values. I doubt whether we would openly admit to 'snobbery' or 'romantic nostalgia'. So much of the charm of the bourgeois novel resides in the way it has preserved ways of life and experience in a verbal garden of Eden before the technological Fall of Man. The women and men of the more heroic narratives of Tolstoy or Stendhal, the bizarre cohorts of Balzac or Dickens, all enjoy a degree of freedom and individuality that seems to have been withheld from us by the brute facts of the history of our own time. The novel is a crippled form of communication because we know it is precisely the advances in the technology of communication that have made the horrors of total war such an indigestible fact of human life on earth in our time. Our grandfathers, or at the very furthest, our great-grandfathers were content to spend, or were obliged to spend, most of their lives on this earth within a radius of thirty miles of the spot where they were born. Our present populations shift about with the intensity of migrating swallows from one continent to another. The tramp of tourist traffic is doing more damage to Venice and Florence than Hitler's armies. Our children can enumerate the swift changes in transport and communication from the horse and trap to space shuttles and call it history. Communication systems of both capitalist and socialist societies have arranged that much of our children's imagining should take place in outer space. Star Wars colonized the nursery long before they reached the agenda of conferences between the superpowers. We are ever more deeply enmeshed in the grip of communication systems. We know in our hearts that nuclear war and the ultimate engulfing of the planet in the final season of freezing desolation would not be possible of translation from fantasy into fact without the intensive development of a great range of technological advances in communication which are accepted by governments, by educational establishments and certainly by newspapers and news media as the most laudable achievements of modern man.

An expertise in communication serves up in our homes, like a packaged breakfast cereal, all the major and minor catastrophes of our time. The expertise is so great that it can provide instant sedation for the terrible conditions it insists on thrusting to our notice. A familiar fanfare summons us to receive our daily dose of facts that have become homogenized into partial fictions. They have been so astutely doctored that the disease and the antidote are simultaneously injected into our minds. The system exists in order to preserve a sufficient degree of sanity to ensure that for the sake of self-preservation we do nothing to disturb such an uneasy equilibrium. In the world of fickle fact there is little room for the individualistic manoeuvres of the protagonists (let alone the heroes) of traditional fiction.

It is commonplace to record that the revolution in communications has uprooted both Heaven and Hell and transported them from their traditional locations. Earth plus wherever the communication systems can reach have been colonized by angels of death and regiments of devils. The characters of the great twentieth-century category known as science fiction have human failings and supernatural equipment. This so far does not offer a recipe for the more subtle forms of character-ization. It is all part of a process which makes it increasingly difficult for us as individual mortals with our own concerns, with our continued longing for the legitimate expression of reasonable autonomy, to maintain a grip on that imaginative understanding of our own experi-ence that is powerful enough to reinforce the meaningful reality of our own existence. Every day there are moments when our consciousness is battered by technological projections which threaten to overwhelm our faculties and reduce us to passive units of reception rather than per-ception: and the attacks are closely analogous to the alarmingly swift procedures of modern warfare.

The most vital element of a cathode ray tube used to be called in English 'a gun'. Certainly, like an Exocet, it is trained in our direction and it fires with relentless heat-seeking accuracy images that overwhelm our sensibilities, capture and lay waste our imagination, occupying our consciousness like a foreign power and ultimately eliminating our existence as independent human entities.

In this environment, which is new in the sense that it never existed during previous human experience as recorded in history, we are permitted to bring up our children. There are important innovative minorities who want to organize upbringing in terms of communes, cellular or state-controlled, of kibbutzim or public schools on the English model, and even of matriarchal units where males have become obsolete and survival is ensured by sperm banks: but in most techno-logical societies, whether capitalist or communist, the family is accepted as the most convenient structure for social and political management. It has comforting features which the self-existent power of industrial technology finds too useful to dismantle. In a disorientating atmosphere of bewildering change, the family can be made to appear a bastion of inherited values and an investment bank of cherishable virtues. But it is precisely this apparent fortress which has been most effectively penetrated by the invisible agents of the superstructure of communications-based technology. By today no family worthy of the name can exist without at least one television set, one motor car, one telephone, one sound-system, one video-recorder, one computer or word-processor. The most flourishing families use the whole range as status symbols: television sets in each bedroom and two or three cars in the garage are conspicuous emblems of success and prosperity.

In the bosom of such families we go through the motions of bringing up our children. We know that once a small child has been fed and clothed and sheltered his next most urgent need will be to be told stories. This is a major appetite, along with hunger and thirst, which prevails as long as the individual survives. This basic need is provided for by the communications network from a very early age. This provision ranks with gas, electricity and water as a development of the machine age to lessen yet another domestic burden. Just as the superstores provide the family with pre-cooked meals, the media provide pre-digested fiction. Attitudes of gratified passivity are inculcated from the very beginning. Consciously the family is cosily secure. It watches endless series about endlessly vigilant police forces out on programmed patrol in the darkening city streets. The most spine-chilling tales are about the enemy within, whether it be spies lurking at the checkpoint for crepuscular exchanges or creatures from Outer Space masquerading as sweetly benevolent parents or immaculately well-behaved children.

An element of infantilism is essential for popular success in any of the new media. The evidence emerges clearly enough from the brief history of their development. Both popular newspapers and the cinema emerged as a technological response to the needs of the urban masses in the great industrial societies of the developed West. The millions who arrived on the shores of the United States at the end of the last century, deprived of their native languages and cultural inheritance, turned to the silent cinema for their storytelling sustenance and as a source of emotional relief from the trials and tribulations of their existence. The figures they took to their hearts were all essentially childlike: Chaplin, Mary Pickford, Laurel and Hardy, Buster Keaton, Harry Langton. This would seem to be much more the case than in the European cinema: an art form reflecting the *naïveté* of a New World.

Perhaps the solitary genius of the cinema to emerge in England was a little fat boy from the grey London suburb of Leytonstone. It hardly needs extensive Freudian analysis to trace the fantasies of a fat boy who never grew up in the technically perfect cinematography of Alfred Hitchcock. His triumph as a technician was to attain such a mastery of one means of communication, one new medium, as to be able to impose subtle transformations of his own childhood fantasies upon the imaginations of millions. The twists and turns of the cinema storyteller are the shadows on the ceiling designed to bring both fright and comfort, threat and rescue, to the lonely child stuffing himself with chocolate in yet another forbidden midnight feast. Exploitation of the camera and the microphone transformed Billy Bunter into a millionaire *Meistersinger* of the modern age. The camera alone provides a record of surface reality which seems to render all previous forms of document-ation inferior and obsolete. Facts in this medium appear to become more tangible than they ever were before. Here before you is an event which is communicated to you directly without passing through the civilizing filter of language. This is the perfect medium with which the sensi-bilities of millions can be manipulated in a way they were never mani-pulated before. In this medium it is possible to merge illusion and reality, so that the assassination of a president or the simulated murder of a naked girl in a motel shower can become equivalent symbols of containable shock.

A film director like Hitchcock can give the sounds and shadows of childhood nightmares or sado-masochistic sexual fantasies a new form of reality, immediate in impact, startling in clarity and immense in profitability. The image of a beautiful young woman being pecked to death by birds is an obvious sexual fantasy. We can turn to many equally frightening transferences in the Grimm brothers' collection of 'House Tales'. But those tales were told free for localized entertainment. The interest of the brothers Grimm was primarily linguistic and antiquarian. What the film-maker can do, often with great financial rewards, is impose his own responses on the story with the un-questionable authority of camera fact and in that very act of technical expertise deprive the spectator, the audience – the receiver – of the essential emotional autonomy he must have in order to recreate for himself within himself both the music and the message that are inherent in the matter of the story itself. The technology has pre-empted the response. The living relationship between the material and the audience has been sequestrated and embalmed for all time in the adolescent grimace of the technician. In the absence of the mediation of language, with its complex syntax, its civilizing memory, and above all its capacity for renewal and rebirth, the splendour of myth has been mummified by manipulation of the medium into the sterile realm of fickle fact.

Our century demonstrates clearly enough the damage – let us hope temporary – that technology has inflicted on the vital relationship between the individual talent and the wide audience for which it inevitably yearns. It could be argued convincingly that in all so-called advanced societies, technology has placed the control of all the new media neatly and completely in the hands of the state. The state apparatus always has more interest in mental law and order than social justice. The price of greater material well-being among its subjects is a form of spiritual obedience that is best controlled by mass media that tell the citizenry what to feel as well as what to think and of course what to vote if that is the accepted version of the source of power. The convenient fiction in a world of fickle fact is that in a free society the individual creative artist has complete freedom to express whatever fancy, however outrageous – and the more outrageous the better – happens to flit through his mind. We are all free to spit against the wind, so long as we do not attempt in any way to change its prevailing direction.

Since Rousseau, of course, every artist has been something of an outsider. We are all aware of the marvellous fruits of Romanticism that flourished in so many fields throughout a nineteenth century that ended in 1914. At some mysterious point in the development of communications technology, the status of 'outsider' was narrowed down drastically and the 'outsider' was, and, I suspect, still is, confronted with a choice that is in reality no choice at all: to be a gladiator or a martyr.

The contrast between the storyteller as gladiator/martyr and the medium manipulator can be seen by comparing the careers of Alfred Hitchcock and Bertolt Brecht. The comparison is not as far-fetched as it might at first appear. Hitchcock learnt his trade in the exciting German cinema of the early twenties when Brecht was a brilliant comet in the German theatrical firmament. It was in Hollywood that Brecht tried to feather the threadbare nest of exile when he fled before the power of the National Socialist house-painter. Hitchcock never lacked for backers. His gift for transforming psychotic fiction and presenting it with the frisson of apparent fact was ideal for capitalist exploitation. Brecht was never so lucky. Had the German public listened to this master of their language with something of the attention they gave to the music of Bach, let us say, or Beethoven, they would hardly have accepted a ranting Austrian house-painter as their one and only Leader. This choice in some measure encapsulates the dilemma of our century: the relation between the mass audience and the poetic vision of the individual singer, *cyfarwydd, bardos,* storyteller. Poor Bertolt Brecht had no luck at all. His final agony was to be elevated to the position of State Laureate of the German Democratic People's Republic. And after his death to take his place alongside the other literary martyrs of the twentieth-century pantheon, like James Joyce, D. H. Lawrence, Dylan Thomas, Saunders Lewis, David Jones and become an object of an academic exploitation curiously parallel in so many of its features to the commercial: canonization, production, publication, distribution and exchange.

From all accounts Brecht was a man endowed with many human failings, but he was a great poet and storyteller. At the zenith of his creative power, when he composed his most challenging work and when he had an urgent message to deliver to a German audience in particular, he was deprived of publisher, of platform, of theatre, of screen or of any of the channels which would have made it possible for him to communicate with an audience large enough to influence the course of events during his lifetime. With Hitchcock the exact opposite was the case. The storyteller without a message could titillate the millions to his profitable heart's content.

Writers, novelists, poets, storytellers, yearn for popularity just as much as film-makers or pop stars. They have to live in a world where the major function of the storyteller has been appropriated by the popular press, by radio, film, television and video. If they are wise, they accept this, and they also accept the technical innovations in the art of storytelling introduced by film-makers of genius like Alfred Hitchcock. The writer of prose fiction in any language has to confront a readership brought up and trained by film and television in new and subtle methods of acute observation. This readership knows that pictures can reveal what words conceal. The technology of the camera and the microphone has given our consciousness an extended dimension of clinical objectivity. There are whole new areas in the spectrum of observed knowledge which can fill us with a cold wonder unknown to our progenitors. We even have to accept as writers and storytellers that language itself in its structure and its function has been altered, perhaps permanently changed, by the massive impact and influence of the new media.

The law of gravity applies in the sphere of imaginative writing as in any other. A superstructure of mass entertainment draws unto itself the fragments of individual talent that are floating about eager for expression and for the rewards that go with it. The first discipline a sober novelist is obliged to accept is that he is not in the business of manipulating masses. There is a minimum freedom that the individual vision requires and this is never provided by the large-scale communications media. They have other more pressing obligations to fulfil. The sober novelist has to accept that his preoccupation with the form of the novel and his obsessive interest in the relationship between fiction and reality confine him to the role of dissident in one form of social and political organization and dissenter in the other. It is within ever narrower confines that he will find the degree of freedom to express himself fully. A minority of one is inexorably drawn to a minority language as if to a blessing in disguise.

Narrower confines can, in fact, lead to larger perspectives, just as the deeper understanding of the particular can cast a completely fresh light on the general. At this juncture in the development of human communication, an artist shrugs off the restrictions of local attachments and concerns at his peril. Electronic technology may justly boast such feats as making the music of J. S. Bach, say, available at the pressing of a button in several billion homes: but any thorough analysis of the historical process must trace that music back to the playing of a single organ in a single church by a *Kapellmeister* composing inside the confines of his salary and tenure of office and the demands and stresses of his family and localized society. History suggests that more often than not the greatness of an artist requires servitude even more than freedom. A squash-player cannot become proficient without a wall. In the European tradition, examined with the wisdom of hindsight which has its obvious uses, minority languages and regional cultures provide solid walls against which generations of artists, great and small, have exercised their abilities and developed their artistic muscle. Today this is more necessary than ever since the strength of his art, even more than the strength of his convictions, is all that the individual practitioner has to resist the gravitational pull of multinational exploitation, at least for long enough to make marks on the stone, the paper, the canvas that are truly worth making.

Of course the novelist hopes for a wider readership. But he must content himself in the first instance with readers who are just as aware of the critical nature of the situation as he is himself. Through the splendours and miseries of a guerrilla war of the spirit and with a language worn and wounded by the processes of the mass media, he must reach out to the happy few prepared to read and listen. Unlike the spy, who is such an archetypical figure of modern popular fiction, the novelist must trust his reader, treat him as a partner worthy of respect and even affection. The writer of sober fiction is not a pusher looking for addicts and half-intoxicated consumers to whom he proffers ever more potent emotional liquor. He accepts that the intelligent reader possesses that 'negative capability' that John Keats attributed to the poet. Stendhal, as ever, has put the matter succinctly: 'Un roman est comme un archet, la caisse du violon qui rend les sons, c'est l'âme du lecteur.' In this act of communication there is a sharing of greater honesty about human experience and the act of sharing is an integral part of the search for more penetrating means of portraying in contemporary mode the rich variety of the human condition.

Certainly one of the aims of the realist novel in the age of the mass media should be to initiate a chain reaction of readership that will in some measure, however small, subvert the stultifying power of communications technology. *Fahrenheit 451* was far from being one of François Truffaut's best films, but before it submerged itself in its own charm, it touched on a raw nerve concerning the secret war between the traditional book and the all-powerful media. The virtues of the printed book as an artefact of Renaissance art and technology are too well known to need listing here. It is as an extension of these virtues that the novel as a form can still boast an armoury of residual strengths. With a sympathetic publisher, the sober novelist can still exercise what they call, in the film industry, 'total creative control' over his output. This is not a licence for self-indulgence. It is a discipline – and the good publisher is well aware of this – and a better discipline than, say, the 'budget' problem of a large-scale film project. The basic needs of a dedicated novelist are time, pencil and paper.

The force of discipline in the tradition of realist writing, which is what I am most concerned with (I am prejudiced against wilful hallucinated forms of fantasy in the novel), extends to cover the balance between imagination, invention and historical reality. This is an area in which the language and conventions of the realist novel still have no rival. No other form can cope so well with the subtle elaboration of complete life-cycles in relation to their historical context. If the new media have established an apparent supremacy in the recording or reflecting of the instant (so that the winning try in a rugby match, for example, can be repeated in action replay beyond the time when all the players are ancient or dead), they have no means of recording the tension and reaction of historical circumstance and individual existence, or of exploring the inter-relationships of human beings over prolonged periods of time or even the strange harmonies evoked by the parallel extrapolation of memory and living moment.

The structure of a novel can have an architectonic relationship to truth. The dramatization of experience can only be sustained over a prolonged period, however realistic the framework, by an ascent (or descent) into metaphor. It has to prove (or even disprove if the author is genuinely so inclined) that there is a magic and that there is poetry in the human experience under almost any condition. The function of the novelist continues to be an attempt to release all these elements and make them available to a responsive reader like written music in the air around us by the rejuvenation of plot and story and by the reconstruction of events in authentic areas of Time and Space.

The last great native English novelist, D. H. Lawrence, claimed that 'the novel is the highest example of subtle inter-relatedness that man has discovered'. He wrote these words in the early 1920s when the new media were already on the march. He died in his own state of tubercular poverty, an English exile in the warmth of Provence. It is instructive to observe the way in which the fruits of his genius have been exploited by the new media and continue to be exploited, because we can discern how their communication processes distort and even falsify the trace elements of truth that were secreted in that extraordinarily individualistic voice. So often the very act of expropriation reduces the vision to a sequence of impotent platitudes and perpetuates in a distressingly mechanical mode the tragic alienation between Lawrence and the country that he loved so much that he could not bear to live in it.

At this point my third difficulty confronts my second and my first. The form of the novel that interests me has driven me to confront the immediate past and the history which gave it its unique character. History does not repeat itself, but the species does. The processes of reproduction are the mainspring of a novel's structure still, and the problems that attend both the historical record and survival are the lifeblood of the art. Whether he likes it or not, the novelist ends up confronted with the first difficulty: how to celebrate and even how to castigate the society that made him and how to do so in an age when traditional language is being subjected to abnormal strain and even the threat of destruction by the sophisticated communications techniques that command all the great agencies of peace and war. Alongside such monolithic structures the production of realistic novels must appear a cottage industry, but there is a good precedent for judging people and production methods by their fruits. The novel remains a crucible for the alchemistic exercise of attempting the apparently impossible: to make time stand still long enough at least to hear its music and even catch a glimpse of its mystery and meaning.

Ghosh !!!

The Empty Space – Creating a Novel

Previously unpublished; text of a lecture given at the American Welsh Conference, Bryn Mawr, USA, 2000.

I have a character who figures in more than one volume of my 'Land of the Living' series, a Wesleyan lay preacher with a club-foot, called Lucas Parry. He has a habit of moralizing pontification that sometimes sounds dangerously like my own. He is the man, as Amy Parry's uncle and guardian, who stands in the way of her receiving the inestimable benefits of an English public-school education, not to mention a second-hand lacrosse stick and tennis racket. Among his several irritating habits he has a way of insisting that the Welsh, especially the Nonconformist Welsh, are 'a pattern-making people'. This diagram I have made for you to look at with a critical eye demonstrates my inclination to agree with him. There are sound historical reasons for this pattern-making habit. A small nation living for so many centuries under a state of siege – whether military, economic or cultural – needs defence in depth. There seems to me to be an intimate relationship between the ditches and ramparts of the Iron Age Celts and the stylized injunctions and commandments of the Methodists' *Cyffes Ffydd* and *Rhodd Mam*. There are specialists at this conference better qualified than I am to comment on the validity of Lucas Parry's thesis. What the diagram illustrates, I suppose, is that in the case of *one* Welsh novelist, pattern-making is a life-long habit. He creates scaffolding structures in the same way as a sculptor assembles a rough mould with the expressed intentions of breaking it. Under ideal circumstances the mould falls apart in lifeless bits in order that the artefact, in my case the novel, can stand in its own space and even stride forth and inherit a life of its own.

This is not a desperate last-gasp attempt to gain some form of academic respectability. It is nothing more than yet another example of a novelist attempting to feather his own nest with bits and pieces of broken twigs of theory. The design is based on subjective intuition and has no scientific basis as far as I am aware. There are no laws here and not even propositions. It is no more than a private attempt to rationalize the irrational. Therefore its application is limited and the language I use in discussing it is only approximate. My pattern is meant to represent what I choose to call the fields of force that condition the creative

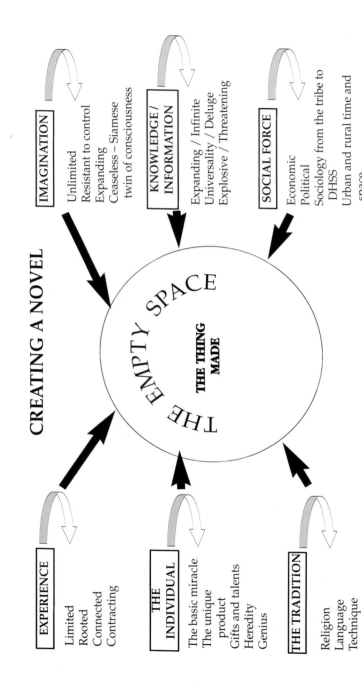

CREATING A NOVEL

IMAGINATION

Unlimited
Resistant to control
Expanding
Ceaseless – Siamese
twin of consciousness

**KNOWLEDGE /
INFORMATION**

Expanding / Infinite
Universality / Deluge
Explosive / Threatening

SOCIAL FORCE

Economic
Political
Sociology from the tribe to
DHSS
Urban and rural time and
space

THE EMPTY SPACE

**THE THING
MADE**

EXPERIENCE

Limited
Rooted
Connected
Contracting

**THE
INDIVIDUAL**

The basic miracle
The unique
product
Gifts and talents
Heredity
Genius

THE TRADITION

Religion
Language
Technique
Material crafts
Education
Systems of retrieval, preservation; from the cromlech to the computer

process. The best that can be said for it is that using it in the past has deepened my understanding of novels and even of works of art in general. If it can become a means to extend the frontiers of appreciation, that could be claimed as some kind of value in itself.

The diagram suggests that at the heart of any artistic endeavour there is an empty space eager to be filled. This is not the same phenomenon as the vacuum that nature is reported to abhor. It seems to be a space in consciousness that our species longs to have filled and to fill. And it exists for everybody. And it goes beyond the primitive sociological truism that humankind is obliged to create rites and rituals in order to make its brief existence more tolerable and meaningful. The continuing desire to create within a given form, be it a building or a novel, a symphony or a play, a film or a sailing ship, is a reliable indicator of the health of a given civilization. And there has to be more to it than the desire of a multinational corporation, or a tourist board, to keep its workforce happy with ten-pin bowling alleys or operatic spectaculars.

Since all forms of creation are organic, this diagram breaks the first law, so to speak, by making positive six separate categories when in reality they are no more than six aspects of the same phenomenon. I have done this in an attempt to gauge the different degrees of pressure each element brings to the creative process: and by the same token the specific contribution an element makes to the finished object that occupies the empty space, whether it be a lyric poem or the Taj Mahal.

The circular centre of the diagram suggests alternative routes: we can begin *inside* the individual and work out towards the society into which that individual finds himself born: or we can begin *outside* with the nature of that society and work inwards in an attempt to explore the mysterious qualities of the individual mind. On this occasion I shall speak for myself: and being Welsh, addressing a conference with a particular interest in Welshness, I begin with three headings which could also be called 'Three Heads' (from the triple-headed goddesses of the Celts to the sermons of our grandfathers we have shown an unswerving allegiance to the mystic significance of the figure three).

In my diagram I have attempted to distinguish between experience, imagination and knowledge.

Experience is:
a) limited (physically you are only born once);
b) rooted (in one place);

c) connected (with one family);

d) contracting (and in your end is your beginning – no doubt there are many other things in between). (' "Issues from the hand of God, the simple soul" ', sang Mr T. S. Eliot, 'To a flat world of changing lights and noise, / To light, dark, day or damp, chilly or warm; / Moving between the legs of tables and of chairs . . . Eager to be reassured, taking pleasure/ . . . Pleasure in the wind, the sunlight and the sea', or, as he also sang, 'Birth, and copulation and death. / That's all, that's all, that's all, that's all.')

As if by direct contrast, *Imagination* is:

a) unlimited (you can be Julius Caesar or a tooth fairy);

b) rootless (you can live on top of Greenland's icy mountains or by India's coral sands);

c) resistant to control (like Arthur, conquer in one day a thousand or ten thousand);

d) expanding and undiminishing, and as long as consciousness lasts, a restless Siamese twin to it. If we really are 'such stuff as dreams are made on', the imagination could rank as the supreme ruler of our existence. We are flotsam in a sea of fiction until solid facts come to our rescue.

But facts too are not without their dangers. In the context of my diagram *Knowledge* has the fearsome capacity of infinite expansion. It is fearsome as a measure of the depth of our ignorance and of our distance from any substantial form of verifiable truth: also in its ability to transform itself into an ether of information in which our sensibilities can be permanently anaesthetized. 'Gwae ini wybod y geiriau heb adnabod y Gair' was written long before we knew how easily the fly of curiosity could be smothered and suffocated in the spider's wider web. There are different forms of nuclear explosion and they can all be as devastating.

When we take the alternative route and approach the individual from the outside according to the crude structure of my diagram, he or she appears if anything more mysterious. The mere fact of individuality borders on the miraculous. It is true that all creatures are sustained by the species to which they belong, but among humans all individuals are also unique creations. Genes from their parents and ancestors nourish their frames, but miraculously, their consciousnesses are all their own and nobody else's. Each individual rules an autonomous republic of rights and responsibilities as well as the machinery of experience, imagination and knowledge. Looked at in this light, a gathering such as ours here is a constellation of consciousness just as awe-inspiring in its way as any given corner of the starry skies above. We are able to assemble because we are wired together by a common language, but the contents of each consciousness is a universe in itself.

Verbal understanding creates aeroplanes and conferences with either amazing ease or amazing effort, but it is out of individuality that inexplicable genius wells up with a capacity to dominate the consciousness of a race. Shakespeare is a good example of the mysterious unaccountability of individual genius and the equally remarkable phenomenon that his poetry can spark off an infinite resonance in an infinite number of consciousnesses. By the same token the music of Bach or Mozart can exercise an even wider influence.

If we move to music – which Schopenhauer considered the purest and therefore the highest art form – we are immediately made aware of the importance of *Tradition* and the vital balance that has to exist between the individual talent and the theory and practice of the art form it attempts to master. Whatever the urges of genius that demand expression there are always techniques and craftsmanship to be mastered. As students of Welsh culture we are perhaps more aware than most of the power of a tradition. In our strict-metre systems it has sustained a flourishing social poetry that has managed to persist in unbroken line for at least fifteen centuries and has thus been a vital element in preserving the identity of a people and a way of life. This tradition dictates that we crown our poets: I suppose for the same reason the supposed effigy of Shakespeare is a ghostly presence on the higher denominations of English banknotes. Perhaps given the benefit of devolution, we can look forward soon to having Williams Pantycelyn staring at us from the face of a postage stamp. Our condition of political subservience suggests that we are more likely to get a Prince William.

Under *Tradition* we list a sequence of factors that both *sustain* and *inhibit* creative effort. In Ireland a hundred years ago, the young James Joyce felt compelled to fly the nets of nationality, language and religion in order to be free to create out of his own untrammelled consciousness. His hero Ibsen had escaped from Norway half a century previously for exactly the same reason. And on a far smaller scale we could say the same for Caradoc Evans. Traditions, we are often told, are things to rebel against when they become ossified and sterile. At the same time, such is the balancing effect of a full historical perspective, we are obliged to remember that culture in all its forms, from the architectural to the literary and musical, could have got nowhere in the Middle Ages without the support and patronage of a rigidly hierarchical Church. Education enlightens us in these matters as well as equipping us to contribute more effectively to the Gross National Product. It is in this prior sense, rather than the latter, that education remains pivotal to the perpetuation of a living civilization.

Civilization in current discourse is an emotive world. Must it depend on more silicon and sliced bread and the minimum of physical effort? I think that in the context of my diagram it would be safer to speak of Social Force. Plainly the form of society, its economic base and political structure is all-powerful in deciding the extent of the artefact, the thing made and the degree of freedom permitted the practitioner. It is self-evident that just as economic, political and social factors decide the nature of a society, they also dictate the resources of time and material and space available for the creation of an artefact. In a capitalist society, where the profit motive is not only the dynamo of economic growth but also controls the machinery of government, creative processes tend to pander to the lowest common denominator. It is not only in Hollywood that the box office rules. And yet, in stark contrast, the chief bene-ficiaries of our system, the billionaires, plunder the grave goods of a more creative past: they spend vast amounts to acquire a Monet or a Cézanne – (how many are there in the Barnes Foundation?) – or a medieval codex or a Palladian mansion or a Monteverdi score. If we are lucky some of these treasures of the past filter down to public systems of retrieval and preservation and the hungry sheep can enjoy a cultural drip feed at stated hours.

The empty space has to be filled by things made in the here and now if our civilization is to flourish. This means, apart from the struggle with the angel, that a creative structure is something plucked out and rescued from the River of Time. There is a sense in which all Art is an attempt to stop the unstoppable: to bend down over the great river and extract a handful at least of the precious fluid and transform it into a petrified gem that is capable of catching the maximum amount of colour from a light that itself is also fleeting. A work of art is made in Time in order not merely to defy the process of Time but also to dare to recycle it. A scene from Tolstoy's *War and Peace* or a passage from a Mozart Piano Concerto returns to a palpable existence whenever it is read or whenever it is played.

My diagram does not indicate the precise point at which young writers rush in where angels fear to tread. To throw a little light on this and kindred problems I must now, with some reluctance, refer to a phase in my own career.

My fourth novel, *Hear and Forgive,* won the Somerset Maugham Award for 1953. It was published here by Putnam and in Paris by Plon and somewhat imprudently I became confident enough of a career as a professional novelist to move to Austria and Italy for a prolonged period and drag my poor family along with me. After a series of crises and misadventures that began to appear as a punishment for hubris I managed to come to grips with my fifth novel. Tucked away in that corner of Europe where German, Slav and Latin meet, in 1954 I imagined I had discovered a magic formula that would show the Welsh condition as a microcosm of the human condition: I could create a fiction that would apply some of the attributes of classical myth to my own perception of the society to which I belonged – or more precisely, that I had insisted on rejoining. Legends and myths and even fairy tales, I told myself, survive the passage of centuries because they contain trace elements of truth about human nature and the human condition. The dramatic method in the novel as much as in any other form that seeks to fill the Empty Space can be used to adapt ancient myth to the contemporary world. It might require an exceptional leap of the imagination to see David Lloyd George on Afonwen Station as an Agamemnon *redivivus* setting out to conquer Troy, but in reality we can claim that the lawyer from Porthmadog had more influence on world history than the kings of Argos. Using an ancient myth in a contemporary setting was an established European literary practice and I was eager to adapt the method to my Welsh novel written in English. The ghost behind my novel *A Man's Estate,* published in 1955, was Orestes, the one who comes back and sees the old dispensation with unpitying objectivity. His story had an importance for me at the time and it was the essential thread to guide me through the dark labyrinth of other people's experience. By now, almost fifty years later, I can see that the ghost was of greater help to the author than to the reader. I doubt whether it adds all that much to the value of the book.

It must have been while we were in Carinthia that the London literary scene was transformed by a phenomenon that came to be known as 'The Angry Young Men'. In novels and plays and films and poetry and on radio there was a resurgence of irritability and undiluted Englishness that delighted press and publishers alike. Some kind of revolution had taken over the stage of the Empty Space, and indignation of one sort or another was the order of the day. The anger seemed to be coming from cohorts of youthful lefties (as Kingsley Amis came to call them in middle age). I have a distant recollection of being told by an older novelist that he and I were already 'has beens'. This was disturbing news. I was still under thirty-five and felt younger. But I could not claim to be angry. Anxious maybe and restless – not angry. And more importantly perhaps, I could not claim to be English and had no desire to make the claim. I came to realize what made the angry young men angry was a decline in the *Importance of being English*: they were cross with the government for being so careless as to lose an empire, and even crosser with providence and historical necessity, left or right, for transferring a hegemony that should have been theirs by divine right into more powerful and wealthier hands across the Atlantic.

Once again the world in which I hoped to earn a living as a novelist was plunged into crisis. It was not just the Cold War or the arrival of commercial television: in terms of my diagram both my methods of working and my raw material were being drawn out of my reach by social forces over which I had no control. What I had considered a calling was being called into question. Very often in the laborious business of composing novels it is easier to give up than to carry on.

As far as storytelling was concerned the new media had the ability to bring popular sagas in an almost medieval mode, with electronic expertise, directly into millions of homes. The serious novel to which I had been prepared to dedicate my energies was in danger of becoming as obsolete as the myths which I had found so inspiring. The novel was bourgeois in origin and had flourished best in a high bourgeois society which no longer existed. The mass media had delivered the art of storytelling into the hands of those best qualified to manipulate the masses. It was one thing to be acutely aware of the crisis: quite another to know what to do about it. I had a distinct impression of ice cracking under my feet and the best thing I could do was to jump, at the very last moment, on a passing raft. I joined the BBC.

This proved to be more than a happy issue out of a threat of many afflictions. BBC Wales in those years was the best possible place for an aspiring chronicler of Welsh life to be. This happy period of eight years experimenting in radio, television and film not only taught me a great deal, and I was always a slow learner: it tied me that much closer to my proper subject. 'Diofryd a roddwyd arnaf' (this was a position to hold on to). My ambition was not merely to be a serious novelist: I had to be a serious Welsh novelist. I had a proper task to perform and I could confront it with the heady optimism of Culhwch confronted with the impossible tasks imposed by Ysbaddaden Pencawr: 'Hawdd yw gennyf gaffael hynny, hyd tybychych na bo hawdd' (I can easily get that done, even though you think it's well and truly beyond me).

I need to refer to that word *serious* again: and this time in strictly Welsh *o ddifrif*. In the context of this diagram it means being aware of the multitude of forces that are at work in the world and their effect both on the society of which you are a part and on the parallel forces that are swirling about in your own subconscious. The practice of a *serious* craft is the discipline necessary to shape all the competing and conflicting elements into a convincing and relevant fiction: a work that can lay claim at least to be a competent artefact, a thing made, a thing finished if not necessarily a work of art.

Of course a serious novelist is not obliged to be totally devoid of a sense of humour. In those far-off days I was close enough to the entertainment industry to realize that on the printed page just as on the stage or the screen nothing succeeds better than a prolonged giggle. I did not and I do not underrate the sheer sweat and sustained effort involved in comic writing: indeed I made one or two attempts at it myself. But the habit of seriousness kept breaking in and I attribute this failing to a lifelong obsession with the Welsh condition as a reflection of the human condition. Nothing very original about that, you might say: it's been going on since Gildas. At least since his time our people have been inclined to find a curiously significant relationship between the theological concept of the Fall of Man and the historical quasi-myth of the Loss of Britain and Fall of a Nation. Our Empty Space has more often than not been concerned with the Paradise we were turned out of and to which in one way or another we aspire, conspire and yearn to return.

This is a new century and I would like to apply my diagram to the prospects of an unknown new novelist who aspires to be both serious and Welsh. On a superficial level the omens are not good. It sometimes seems that Anglo-American publishers have much more interest in the sexual antics of Outer Mongolia than the splendours and miseries of life in our little land of the living. More seriously she or he will have to cope with the dangerous imbalance that is at work in the section of the diagram I have called Social Force. The nuclear threat is like the sleeping giant in the fairy story. He lies across the gateway to the Garden of the Hesperides and the politicians of the great powers tiptoe around him armed with drugged cakes in case he should suddenly wake up. By the same token, the golden apples of economic stability and equable distribution lie just out of reach, guarded by the jealous dragons of the financial markets. All the communication channels – newspapers, the internet, television companies, publishing, the universities – are ultimately controlled by the same financial powers. It is with this monstrous conglomerate of social forces that our new novelist will have to contend. It is not enough to have something unique and vital to say and to perfect a means of saying it. The novelist has to operate in a climate that is fundamentally hostile to the independent form that has to be mastered and by extension to what it is the author feels compelled to say. Writing novels is an obsessional occupation. An author needs more than a single transferable democratic vote; a sympathetic audience is also required. Somehow or other this precious and indispensable element has to be mined from the stubborn and resistant rock quarry of *vox populi*. Pop groups may appeal to the spontaneous warmth of as yet unmuzzled youth. It is only when large profits loom that singers and audience are open to the power of financial manipulation. The serious novelist, however young, has to seek out a more patient audience. Sufficiently patient to wait over a period of years to allow time to complete protracted labours. There may be some bitter little pills to swallow en route. I have a vivid recollection of being invited to the Annual Conference of Merched y Wawr (sometime in the 1980s) to talk about 'Y Nofel Heddiw' (The Novel Today) or some such topic. I arrived early and wandered into W. H. Smith's (still called a bookshop). I overheard a conversation between two prosperous-looking members of Merched y Wawr. They both held copies of the works of Jeffrey Archer in their jewelled hands and were struggling to remember whether or not they were volumes that their husbands might not have read. A novelist will have to realize that readers do not lurk in the local W. H. Smith's more than on every tree.

A novelist also needs to be aware of the dangerous gap that is opening between global communication systems and the stability of community life. There is a need to develop techniques of building bridges across this widening abyss. It will not be enough to e-mail the next chapter in a thrilling cosmopolitan novel to a devoted admirer in Beijing if one's next-door neighbour in Pontyberem believes one to be a dubious merchant selling dope or junk bonds.

In my diagram, *Tradition* lies waiting patiently to come to one's aid. The first on the list, religion, may not be as weak and ineffectual as it looks to the sharp eyes of ferreting journalists and intellectual spin-doctors. It has the initial advantage of having been around a long time. Bryn Celli Ddu, a circular religious enclosure and burial ground four miles from my home, has been standing there for at least four thousand years. Since the Renaissance, our national language has been preserved mainly for religious purposes, and up to as late as the middle of the twentieth century our best poetry has been intensely religious in content, for example the work of Gwenallt, Waldo Williams and Saunders Lewis in Welsh, Dylan Thomas and R. S. Thomas in English.

A duality of language is also a problem that our new Welsh novelist will have to face. His only choice in the twenty-first century is to be monoglot English or bilingual. Neither course offers plain sailing. If he is monoglot the centralizing tendency of the media will press him to look to what the television managers call the network. Publishers, small and big, yearn for a metropolitan market which means London and/or, *mirabile dictu*, New York. Devolution is a phenomenon still to occur in the minds of cultural managers. Welsh media facilities are still no more than depots to be used at the convenience of the central authority. The mind of the serf is haunted by a God whose temple is in a distant city. The habits of centuries die hard.

Looking at the diagram again, I would suggest that the ace that the bilingual novelist has in his hand is his ancestral language. I have spoken elsewhere of the difficulties that can arise in the case of a bilingual brain of a person who aspires to become a creative writer. The inside of the writer's skull under these conditions is liable to become a house divided against itself; not only the writer but every sentence he writes becomes susceptible to a crisis of identity. The strains and stresses of allegiance and loyalty can be more intense than any in the political sphere.

In the bilingual condition there will be continuing crises of honour and courage to be encountered. These could destroy or be turned to good advantage. Writers usually live dangerously. In any event they will increase the emotional temperature. My diagram should have affirmed more clearly, perhaps, the primary importance of emotion in the creative process. The trick for the bilingual novelist is to use these language conflicts to intensify cerebral activity. Cultivated inside their separate traditions they could intertwine as separate threads to strengthen the flexible net with which the writer trawls the darker depths of his subconscious. Two languages should make a writer more aware of the complexities of a multilingual world. It is possible that being bilingual will reinforce the ability both to feel deeply and to cast a cold eye – both essential attributes to the aspiring novelist.

It is perfectly feasible that our new novelist will decide to write exclusively in Welsh since this would at least provide the nucleus of a sympathetic audience without which no serious novelist can survive on any long-term basis. (I venture to say this in spite of the bitter pill I swallowed in W. H. Smith's.) Writing in Welsh would also protect from the dangers of self-conscious provincialism. A world language has a sneaky habit of flashing its own distorting mirror in order to amuse a hostile public and show nothing more than windbags or no-good-boyos. For the young writer there are riches and resources in twentieth-century Welsh still to be exploited. The writer could immerse him or herself in the intellectual vision of Saunders Lewis, the zeal and eloquence of Ambrose Bebb, the analytical honesty of Kate Roberts, the idiomatic strength of W. J. Gruffydd, the urbane sophisticated narrative of R. T. Jenkins, the moral integrity of Lewis Valentine.

Whichever language our young writer uses, it seems to me there will be a need to exercise three skills to fulfil three functions (three 'heads' again!): something of the authority of a people's remembrancer; the remorseless persistence of a researcher of what Richard Hughes called 'the Human Predicament'; and, of course, a talent to entertain.

Looking at my diagram for the last time I am obliged to admit that the novel of the future has no automatic right to occupy that empty space or demand pride of place among things made. In the nineteenth century it was, of course, powerful social forces that secured the novel a place among the pre-eminent artistic forms. We need only to glance at the status of Balzac and Dickens and Dostoevsky and Tolstoy to see how well their careers – triumphs and disasters – fitted into the social structures of their day. The extent of their achievement can be intimidating until we call to mind our obligation to demonstrate the cultural vitality of our own time by creating things to furnish our own empty space. We need to believe that we have a past of our own to celebrate – our piece of the manifest destiny of humanity to inhabit and cultivate. In Wales the wrong sort of ambition has too often tempted the talented young to sell their own country short or down the river. I recall the title of a sycophantic biography of the 1920s: *The Early Life of the Right Honourable David Lloyd George together with a Short History of the Welsh People*. It sometimes seems as though our will to live comes in historical fits and starts.

That word 'will' brings me back to Schopenhauer. About artistic creation, he writes:

> in regard to the inner significance of what appears, it is quite immaterial whether the objects on which the action hinges are trifling or important, farmhouses or kingdoms. Just as a circle of one inch in diameter and one

of forty million miles in diameter have absolutely the same geometrical properties, so the events and the history of a village and of a kingdom are essentially the same: and we can study and learn to know mankind just as well in the one as in the other.

As you can see, my empty space is also a circle.

Notes on the Novel

First published in *The New Welsh Review* 35 (Winter 1996/7), 9–10.

When a human child has been cleaned and housed and fed its next need is to be placated with stories.

* * *

Stories come in all shapes and sizes. They can be sung or spoken by one or by several voices. When a human being has been sufficiently educated and is capable of being solitary and thoughtful, she/he can read novels.

* * *

Novels are spun out by storytellers. Like insatiable spiders they seek to capture readers in their web. These spiders can be poets, preachers, would-be politicians, conscientious historians. They can also be fantasists and liars. Whatever they are, they always need an audience to entertain, surprise, inform, even educate. In our day and age they need the patience and obsessional will to challenge with a sling and a stone high-technology entertainment controlled worldwide by an unholy alliance of commercial and political power.

* * *

The best environment for creating durable fiction comes into being when a dedicated author shares a language and a culture and a range of concerns and aspirations with an educated reading public. These conditions obtained when bourgeois culture reached its nineteenth-century zenith and produced a great age of the novel in most European languages.

* * *

Not that it was ever easy. Before Time's winnowing processes allowed them to settle like stars in the literary firmament, most of the great practitioners were obliged to battle with their own set of peculiar problems. The career of Dostoevsky, for example, veered vertiginously from early success to abject failure, imprisonment, rehabilitation, and the ultimate acclaim of a state funeral. Stendhal was not acclaimed in his lifetime. Even at the age of fifty-three he maintained that his true vocation was to write a novel in a garret. He was always more inclined to please himself than set out to please others. He described his writing as a ticket in a lottery in which the prize was to be read a hundred years hence.

* * *

D. H. Lawrence claimed that the novel was 'the highest example of subtle interrelatedness that man has discovered'. Certainly in his time it was the ideal form through which to explore the splendours and miseries of twentieth-century existence. Nothing gives us a more vivid understanding of that vanished England than *Sons and Lovers*, *The Rainbow* and *Women in Love*. Here is a poet and a prophet exploring the potential of the novel and the short story. At the same time an Irish exile was extending the range of the novel in an exercise of genius that was a paean of praise to the past of his native city. And while they were writing, the film and the radio and the mass-circulation newspapers were rapidly extending their grip on the imagination of a public swollen by the new literacy introduced through universal education.

* * *

In the course of our century, language – which is after all the novelist's only tool – has been altered in both structure and function by the impact of mass politics and mass communication. We all know that communications technology is coveted by politicians for power and by capitalists for profit. These ghostly figures are not obliged to bear in mind the inclination of all forms of technology to pre-empt the response of the people who use it. For them it is an academic question as to whether the ghosts control the machine or the machine controls the ghosts. For the novelist, however, it is a question to which one must devote a lifetime in search of an answer.

* * *

You can write novels to please others or to please yourself. These are not necessarily incompatible extremes. They can exist to counterbalance each other: given time and place they can create a field of force sufficiently powerful to magnetize a viable number of readers. To write merely to please yourself can degenerate into self-indulgence. To concentrate solely on winning the widest circulation with the lowest common denominator can become as banal as painting by numbers.

* * *

The novel was born of a misalliance between an angel and an ape. The angel provides the aspiration but also the meddling intellect that is prepared to murder to dissect. The ape radiates a brutal innocence and an overwhelming instinct for survival. The shape of a myth demands the power to aspire combined with the strength to reproduce and perpetuate. This accounts for the centrality, often in some inconvenient form or other, of the love story in the structure of the novel.

* * *

There was always the penny-dreadful but now it comes clothed in all the glittering splendour electronic technology can provide.

* * *

This is our day and age. This is where we are now. So what is to be done? The novelist can retreat into the philosopher's cave armed with no more than paper and pencil. He or she stares at the flames on the wall and waits like a latter-day Celtic saint or last century's scholar gypsy for the spark from heaven to fall. In isolation one can wait a long time.

* * *

Why not begin at the beginning? The only reason for beginning at the beginning is that it is the best place to start.

* * *

All Welsh poetry in any language should begin with Yr Hengerdd. All Welsh storytelling in any language should begin with the *Mabinogi*.

Just as a poet born today needs a mother to resent and recoil against, the new novelist needs a society to embrace with love and criticism.

* * *

Parallel with the dichotomy between the individual talent and the mass media lies the tension between the metropolitan and the regional. Without a regular injection of individual talent the mass media become sclerotic. Without the immediacy and the freshness of the parochial the metropolitan suffocates and chokes on its own mannerisms.

* * *

There are other consolations. Like a megalomaniac film producer the humble novelist enjoys total creative control over his or her own work. The only restraint is to persuade a sufficient number to read it.

* * *

The infinite flexibility of written language compared with all other mechanized forms of communication. A sentence has no time limit and an infinite range of correspondences. Elusive truths are more easily caught in a small syntactical net.

* * *

Individuals, and therefore the individual talent, whether they like it or not, are products of a given society. They are fortunate if that society is small enough to be cherished and at the same time large enough to allow the individual a full and satisfying life. This is a sufficient foundation for Welshness and should provide all the necessary raw material for the full range of fiction from the documentary to the magical.

* * *

The main function of the novelist remains to celebrate: and by one means or another to perpetuate the language of the tribe.

A Selected Bibliography

The Little Kingdom, London, 1946.

The Voice of a Stranger, London, 1949.

A Change of Heart, London, 1951.

Hear and Forgive, London, 1952.

A Man's Estate, London, 1955.

The Italian Wife, London, 1957.

Y Tri Llais, Llandybïe, 1958.

A Toy Epic, London, 1958.

The Gift, London, 1963.

Outside the House of Baal, London, 1965.

Natives (stories), London, 1968.

Ancestor Worship (poems), Denbigh, 1970.

Dinas (a play with W. S. Jones), Llandybïe, 1970.

* *National Winner*, London, 1971.

* *Flesh and Blood*, London, 1974.

Diwylliant Cymru a'r Cyfryngau Torfol, Aberystwyth, 1977.

* *The Best of Friends*, London, 1978.

The Kingdom of Brân (poetry), Beckenham, 1979.

Landscapes (poems), Beckenham, 1979.

Theatr Saunders Lewis, Bangor, 1979.

The Anchor Tree, London, 1980.

The Taliesin Tradition, London, 1983.

Jones, London, 1983.

* *Salt of the Earth*, London, 1985.

* *An Absolute Hero*, London, 1986.

* *Open Secrets*, London, 1988.

The Triple Net (Kate Roberts and her friends), London, 1988.

* *Bonds of Attachment*, London, 1991.

Outside Time (Y Pedair Cainc), London, 1991.
Unconditional Surrender, Bridgend, 1996.
The Gift of a Daughter, Bridgend, 1998.
Dal Pen Rheswm, Cardiff, 1999.
Collected Poems, Cardiff, 1999.
Ghosts and Strangers, Bridgend, 2001.

* This sequence of novels was reissued as seven volumes in the 'Land of the Living' sequence, by the University of Wales Press, Cardiff, 1999–2001.